MW01007879

OTHER SCARECROW TITLES BY ISABEL SCHON

Basic Collection of Children's Books in Spanish
The Best of the Latino Heritage
A Bicultural Heritage
Books in Spanish for Children and Young Adults
Books in Spanish for Children and Young Adults, Series II
Books in Spanish for Children and Young Adults, Series III
Books in Spanish for Children and Young Adults, Series IV
Books in Spanish for Children and Young Adults, Series V
Books in Spanish for Children and Young Adults, Series VI
A Hispanic Heritage
A Hispanic Heritage, Series II
A Hispanic Heritage, Series III
A Hispanic Heritage, Series IV
The Latino Heritage, Series V
Recommended Books in Spanish for Children and Young Adults,
    1991-1995
Recommended Books in Spanish for Children and Young Adults,
    1996 through 1999

The Best of Latino Heritage 1996-2002

A Guide to the Best Juvenile Books About Latino People and Cultures

Isabel Schon

The Scarecrow Press, Inc.
Lanham, Maryland, and Oxford
2003

SCARECROW PRESS, INC.

Published in the United States of America
by Scarecrow Press, Inc.
A Member of the Rowman & Littlefield Publishing Group
4501 Forbes Boulevard, Suite 200, Lanham, Maryland 20706
www.scarecrowpress.com

PO Box 317
Oxford
OX2 9RU, UK

British Library Cataloguing in Publication Information Available

Library of Congress Cataloging-in-Publication Data

Schon, Isabel.
  The best of Latino heritage 1996-2002 : a guide to the best juvenile
books about Latino people and cultures / Isabel Schon.
     p. cm.
  Includes index.
  ISBN 0-8108-4669-1 (pbk. : alk. paper)
  1. Latin America--Juvenile literature--Bibliography. 2.
Spain--Juvenile literature--Bibliography. 3. United States--Imprints.
I. Title.
Z1609.C5 S34 2003
[F1408]
016.98--dc21

                                                    2002154088

To

Dick

Vera, Joe, Eric, Alex

My mother, Anita

Yoya, Lili, Enrique, Patricia

Contents

Introduction   ix

Argentina   1

Central America   4

Chile   5

Colombia   6

Costa Rica   7

Cuba   9

The Dominican Republic   16

Ecuador   19

El Salvador   21

Guatemala   23

Latin America   25

Mexico   37

Panama   59

Peru   62

Puerto Rico   66

South America   70

Spain   71

United States   77

Uruguay   122

Venezuela   123

Series Roundup   125

Author Index   145

Contents

Title Index	151
Subject Index	167
Suggested Grade Level Index	249
About the Author	269

Introduction

The Best of the Latino Heritage: A Guide to the Best Juvenile Books about Latino People and Cultures 1996 through 2002 is designed as an aid for librarians and teachers who are interested in exposing students to the cultures of Latino people through noteworthy books for children and adolescents.

It is intended to provide students in kindergarten through high school with an understanding of, and an appreciation for, the people, history, art, and political, social, and economic problems of Argentina, Central America, Chile, Colombia, Costa Rica, Cuba, the Dominican Republic, Ecuador, El Salvador, Guatemala, Latin America, Mexico, Panama, Peru, Puerto Rico, South America, Spain, Uruguay, Venezuela, and the Latino-heritage people in the United States.

It is arranged into chapters that explore specific countries and cultures, as well as one each on Central America and Latin America as a whole. The chapters are followed by a series roundup that lists series books for students who want basic information about a particular topic or country for school assignments or for personal use. The books are listed in alphabetical order by author surname. These countries are representative of Latino/Hispanic cultures and should assist librarians, teachers, and students in their efforts to better know and comprehend the marvelous richness and diversity of the cultures of Latino people.

Although I have attempted to include the best in-print books in English published since 1996 in the United States that relate to the countries and people listed above, as well as general books on Latin America, I undoubtedly have missed some important books. Their omission is due to unavailability, nonexistence at the time of compilation, or my own lack of awareness of them. The books listed have been selected as the best on the basis of their quality of art and writing, presentation of material, and appeal to the intended audience. They contain recent information, are entertaining, and possess high potential for interest and involvement of the reader. As opposed to many books that contain obsolete information or that expose a very limited or one-sided view of Latino/Hispanic people, customs, or countries, these books are refreshing, imaginative, or illuminating and present new insights into Latino people and cultures.

As any librarian or teacher knows, it is very difficult to assign a grade level to a book. And even though I have done so for the convenience of some teachers or students, please use the grade level only as a tentative guideline. The individual student's reading ability, interest, taste, and purpose should be the main criteria for determining the true level of each book and should never stop a student from reading or viewing a book in which he or she expresses interest. In addition, I have provided a price for each book. It is important to note, however, that prices of books will vary with dealer and time of purchase.

In the annotations I have expressed my personal opinions of the books, emphasizing what I believe are the strengths or weaknesses of each. I have summarized and highlighted specific ideas explored in the books about Hispanic countries and people.

In anticipation of user needs, I have provided four indexes: an author index; a title index; a subject index, including references and cross-references; and a suggested grade level index.

It is my hope that this guide will encourage readers, librarians, teachers, and even publishers to expand their interests into the fascinating cultures of Latino/Hispanic people both in the United States and abroad.

I wish to express my appreciation to the students and volunteers of the Barahona Center for the Study of Books in Spanish for Children and Adolescents, California State University San Marcos, for their invaluable assistance; and to Ms. JanetLynn Mosemak, Ms. Karen Pulver, Mrs. Natalie Diamond, Ms. Sheree Li, Ms. Magnolia Martinez, Mr. Greg Park, and Ms. Carolina Plata for their marvelous cooperation.

Isabel Schon, Ph.D.
Founding Faculty and Director
Barahona Center for the Study of Books
    in Spanish for Children and Adolescents
Centro Barahona para el Estudio de
    Libros Infantiles y Juveniles en Español
California State University San Marcos
June 2002

Argentina

Aira, César. *Argentina: The Great Estancias.* Photos by Tomás de Elia.
New York: Rizzoli International Publishers, 1995. 220p. ISBN: 0-
8478-1905-1. $60.00. Gr. 9-adult.

Exquisite color photographs and a brief text present an
enchanting view of twenty-two magnificent Argentine *estancias*—
country estates and working ranches—located throughout the
country. Beginning with the *vaquerías* of the seventeenth century
and including the days of splendor in the late 1880s when cattle
ranching and farming were Argentina's main sources of material
and intellectual wealth, this lavish volume is a joyous depiction of
rural life in Argentina.

Borges, Jorge Luis. *This Craft of Verse.* Edited by Calin-Andrei
Mihailescu. Cambridge, MA: Harvard University Press, 2000.
154p. ISBN: 0-674-00290-3. $22.95. Gr. 9-adult.

In the fall of 1967, Borges delivered these six lectures in English at Harvard in which he spoke candidly about the metaphor,
word-music, the difficulties of verse translation, epic poetry, and
his own writing as well as his favorite authors. With informative
notes and an afterword by the editor, Borges's admirers will be
able to relive such special Borgesian convictions as poetry is not a
task, it is "a passion and a joy"; "I know for a fact that we *feel* the
beauty of a poem before we even begin to think of a meaning"
(p.84); and "Words are symbols for shared meanings." Because of
his failing eyesight, Borges had to deliver these lectures extempo-
raneously. It is up to us now, his devoted fans, to continue to
marvel at his humility, literary insights, and joy of poetry.

Dujovne Ortiz, Alicia. *Eva Perón.* Translated by Shawn Fields. New
York: St. Martin's, 1996. 325p. ISBN: 0-312-14599-3. $24.95. Gr.
10-adult.

The life of the controversial and enigmatic wife of the Argentine dictator Juan Perón is presented here with minute details from her birth as the illegitimate daughter of poor Argentine farmers to her portrayal after death as an adored martyr/saint as well as a despicable social climber thirsting for power. Sophisticated readers will appreciate the numerous anecdotes, comprehensive analyses, and informed interpretations about the many personal and political issues that surround Eva Perón. Recognized in Argentina as an authoritative biography, this well-done English rendition offers a most complete view of one of the most intriguing women of the twentieth century.

Nickles, Greg. *Argentina: The Culture.* ISBN: 0-86505-246-8; pap. ISBN: 0-86505-326-X.

———. *Argentina: The Land.* ISBN: 0-86505-244-1; pap. ISBN: 0-86505-324-3.

———. *Argentina: The People.* ISBN: 0-86505-245-X; pap. ISBN: 0-86505-325-1.

Ea. vol.: 32p. (The Lands, Peoples, and Cultures Series) New York: Crabtree Publishing, 2001. $20.60; pap. $7.95. Gr. 3-5.

The culture, land, and people of Argentina are introduced to young readers through numerous color photographs and a simple text. With much verve and gusto, the books highlight such unique aspects of Argentina as gaucho culture, tango music and dance, the Pampa plains, and other features of this South American country.

Sinclair, Andrew. *Che Guevara.* Gloucestershire, UK: Sutton Publishing, 1998. 119p. ISBN: 0-7509-1847-0. pap. $9.95. Gr. 9-adult.

Highlighting Che Guevara's intelligence, courage, originality, and asceticism, this brief, accessible biography introduces readers to Che's life and numerous contradictions. From his cold ruthlessness when "Spilling blood was necessary for the cause" (p.27), to his brilliant guerrilla warfare strategies, to his "utopian anarchism and primitive communism," to his "love for humanity" and his concern for the ultimate good of mankind, Sinclair provides an engrossing view of one of the most admired and beloved revolutionaries of his time. A chronology, notes, and bibliography are also included.

Symmes, Patrick. *Chasing Che: A Motorcycle Journey in Search of the Guevara Legend.* New York: Vintage/Random, 2000. 302p. ISBN: 0-375-70265-2. pap. $13.00. Gr. 9-adult.

Eager to retrace Che Guevara's 1952 journey across South America, Symmes, a freelance magazine journalist, sets off nearly fifty years later on his BMW motorcycle to discover the man before he became a worldwide myth. With the keen eye of a serious observer and the bravado of an adventurer, Symmes depicts the sights, sounds, and people as seen by a young Guevara. Excerpts of Guevara's and his companion's personal diaries are intermingled with the author's comments on the current political and economic conditions in Argentina, Chile, Peru, Bolivia, and Cuba. Especially appealing to adolescents are the author's misadventures with his motorcycle as he runs out of gas in an Argentine desert and impresses the local residents with the "fantastic" speed of his BMW. Serious Che Guevara's admirers will rejoice in this literary-political-commentary travelogue that offers an interesting perspective of what the Che Guevara legend has now become.

Central America

Patent, Dorothy Hinshaw. *Quetzal: Sacred Bird of the Cloud Forest.*
Illus.: Neil Waldman. New York: Morrow, 1996. 40p. ISBN: 0-
688-12662-6. $16.00. Gr. 5-8.
See review p. 52.

Viesti, Joe, and Diane Hall. *Celebrate! in Central America.* Photos by
Joe Viesti. New York: Lothrop, Lee & Shepard Books, 1997. 32p.
ISBN: 0-688-15161-2. $16.00; lib. ed. ISBN: 0-688-15162-0.
$15.93. Gr. 3-5.
    The color, flair, and traditions of the seven Central American
countries—Guatemala, Belize, El Salvador, Honduras, Nicaragua,
Costa Rica, and Panama—as they celebrate their holidays with
song and dance, food and fun, parades, and prayer are joyfully
depicted through sharp, full-page color photographs and an informative text. This is not an encyclopedic overview of Central
American holidays; rather, it is a most captivating introduction that
beautifully captures the integration of Spanish and indigenous
traditions highlighting the uniqueness of each fiesta or celebration.
A large, clear map, and brief, chatty captions add further to the
informational/recreational value of this invitation to celebrate in
Central America.

Chile

Pitcher, Caroline. *Mariana and the Merchild: A Folk Tale from Chile.* Illus.: Jackie Morris. Grand Rapids, MI: Eerdmans, 2000. 26p. ISBN: 0-8028-5204-1. $17.00. Gr. 1-4.

The sea is a plentiful provider in this retelling of a traditional Chilean folk tale. Old Mariana, who lives alone on the beach gathering food and fuel from the ocean, feels sad and lonely. One day a storm brings an infant mermaid inside a crab shell and Mariana promises the Sea Spirit that she will care for the baby until the seas lie calm again. Despite a sometimes stiff and affected narrative, the luminous double-page watercolors definitely capture the ambiance and tone of the Chilean countryside by highlighting the folk arts, people, and mythical characters of Chile.

Colombia

Jenkins, Lyll Becerra de. *So Loud a Silence.* New York: Lodestar Books/ Dutton, 1996. 154p. ISBN: 0-525-67538-8. $16.99. Gr. 6-10.

Set in Colombia amid terrorism and poverty, this fast-paced, coming-of-age novel tells about seventeen-year-old Juan Guillermo, who is caught up in the fighting between the guerrillas and the army. When he visits his grandmother, a landowner in rural Colombia, he eventually realizes the importance of family ties and the special role that each member of his family plays in his life and happiness. Perhaps the relationship between Juan and Chía, a twenty-one-year-old girl, and her death as a victim of Colombia's terrorists groups is a bit too contrived. Nevertheless, this novel is a realistic portrayal of contemporary life in many Latin American countries.

Rawlins, Carol B. *The Orinoco River.* (Watts Library) New York: Franklin Watts, 1999. 63p. ISBN: 0-531-11740-5. $24.00. Gr. 4-7. *See review p. 123.*

Costa Rica

Collard, Sneed B. *Monteverde: Science and Scientists in a Costa Rican Cloud Forest.* New York: Franklin Watts, 1997. 128p. ISBN: 0-531-11369-8. $22.50. Gr. 6-9.

Through the eyes of the scientists who live and work in Monteverde, a cloud forest preserve in Costa Rica, readers are introduced to the ecology of tropical forests. From ruthless "strangler fig" trees to resplendent quetzals to close encounters with numerous species of bats, the author presents a lively, dramatic account of this unique ecosystem. He concludes with a sensitive report of the threats to the cloud forest such as illegal hunting, or poaching of animals and plants, and the serious human population explosion in Costa Rica. Numerous black-and-white and stunning color photographs, suggestions for further reading, a glossary, and an index complement this exciting view of the natural beauties of Monteverde.

Strauss, Susan. *When Woman Became the Sea: A Costa Rican Creation Myth.* Illus.: Cristina Acosta. Hillsboro, OR: Beyond Words Publishing, 1998. 32p. ISBN: 1-885223-85-4. $14.95. Gr. K-3.

Adding a contemporary feminist tone to this creation story of the Cabecar and Bribri people from the rain forests of Costa Rica, Strauss, a professional storyteller, vividly recounts the origin of land, sea, trees, and water. Despite the Creator Sibu's orders, Thunder's pregnant wife asserts her independence, which results in a series of magical transformations: A magnificent tree, birds of every color, distant shores, and that body of water we call Sea. Yet we can still see Thunder and Sea together when "the lightning and clouds dance together among the Cloud Forest trees." Acosta's bold, tropical forest scenes magically transport viewers to a long-ago Costa Rican rain forest. Instead of a source note, the introduction explains "the science in the myth," relating ancient myths to simple scientific observations on the cycle of water.

Cuba

Ancona, George. *Cuban Kids.* New York: Marshall Cavendish, 2000. 40p. ISBN: 0-7614-5077-7. $15.95. Gr. 3-5.

Through stunning candid color photographs and a well-written text, photojournalist George Ancona presents an up-to-date portrait of Cuban children and their families, and reports a most positive account of the Cuban Revolution. Even though the photographs depict the joy of the people amid the lack of material comforts and equipment and the prevalence of makeshift toys, the text emphasizes "the hunger, sickness and illiteracy," "the misery of the poor," and the lack of opportunities before the Revolution. Ancona concludes that, "Despite the hardships, the shortages, and the embargo, Cuban kids are growing up with a love of their country, traditions, and culture" (p.39). A beautiful, albeit utopian, panorama of Cuba, the country, and its people as viewed by a return traveler.

Ephron, Amy. *White Rose/Una rosa blanca.* New York: Morrow, 1999. 259p. ISBN: 0-688-16314-9. $23.00. Gr. 9-adult.

Set in Cuba during the struggle to oust the Spanish during the 1890s, this suspenseful novel intermingles romance with intrigue amid the special interests of William Randolph Hearst and Cuban patriots. Caught in the turbulence of the times are beautiful nineteen-year-old Evangelina Cisneros and Karl Decker, a Hearst newspaper reporter sent to rescue her from a Havana prison. Whether enjoyed as an engaging morality tale where the hero does what is right regarding his wife and children, or as a delicately written exposure of "the avarice of the Americans' Manifest Destiny draped in a flag called democracy and freedom for all" (p.66), readers will applaud the efforts of the Cuban people and their pleas as they proclaim, "*Viva Cuba Libre.*"

Fernandez Barrios, Flor. *Blessed by Thunder: Memoir of a Cuban Girlhood.* Seattle, WA: Seal Press/Distributed by Publishers Group West, 1999. 244p. ISBN: 1-58005-021-2. $22.95. Gr. 9-adult.

With passion and nostalgia, this engrossing memoir recalls the author's childhood under Fidel Castro in which "'Innocent people are getting killed by the *milicianos.* . . . They're killing all those who don't like Castro, anybody under suspicion for counterrevolutionary activities,'" (p.19). She describes the effects of Castro's Agrarian Reform on her family; her love for Carmen, her Afro-Cuban nanny; her feelings for her paternal grandmother, Patricia, who mentored her "in the ways of the spirits and the world of healing"; the pressures at school where children "were reminded that to be good citizens, we must be dedicated Communists, always obedient and loyal to the Revolution, ready to sacrifice everything for the cause and the country" (p.87); and finally, her family's exile and life in California. Some adolescents will be touched by Fernandez Barrios's strong family bonds and cultural attachments; others will enjoy the humorous reminiscences (such as the gossip about Castro: "'Fidel has a big *pinga* '") as they consider the effects of loss and immigration.

Foss, Clive. *Fidel Castro.* Gloucestershire, UK: Sutton Publishing, 2000. 112p. ISBN: 0-7509-2384-9. pap. $9.95. Gr. 9-adult.

In this short and most accessible introduction to Fidel Castro, Foss, a professor of history at the University of Massachusetts, provides a lively overview of "one of the best-known and most enduring of world leaders" (p.xi). From Castro's rustic origins, through his studies and political activities in Havana, to his revolutionary leadership and the "triumph that allowed him to make fundamental changes, moving Cuba in a new direction, replacing American dominance with Communism," (p.xii) to his handling of the serious economic catastrophes of the 1990s, Foss describes Castro both as a "revolutionary hero" and an "ossified despot." Also included are references to his personal life, including his marriage, lovers, and children. A chronology, notes, and bibliography add further to this brief pocket biography of one of the world's most engaging and controversial political leaders.

García, Cristina. *The Agüero Sisters.* New York: Knopf, 1997. 300p. ISBN: 0-679-45090-4. $24.00. Gr. 9-adult.

Forty-eight-year-old Reina Agüero and her half-sister Constancia are as different as any two sisters can be. Yet they share their Cuban background as well as numerous family lies and myths that continue to affect their relationships with husbands, lovers, and children. By juxtaposing Reina's life in Cuba as a master electrician with Constancia's life in New York as a cosmetics saleswoman who has a successful husband, García presents an engrossing novel about life's important and not-so-important entanglements. Mature readers, as well as fans of Isabel Allende and Julia Alvarez, will enjoy the romantic predicaments and family jealousies both in Cuba and in the United States.

Gibb, Tom. *Fidel Castro: Leader of Cuba's Revolution.* (Famous Lives) Austin, TX: Raintree Steck-Vaughn Publishers, 2001. 48p. ISBN: 0-8172-5718-7. $18.98. Gr. 4-6.

In a lively and engaging narrative, Gibb tells about the life and times of Fidel Castro. Highlighting important aspects of his life, such as the Moncada Assault, the Granma Invasion, the Bay of Pigs, and the wide disagreements between his critics and admirers, the author provides a balanced perspective of this most controversial leader. Numerous candid black-and-white and color photos (a few overexposed) on every page, as well as informative sidebars, a brief text, a glossary, a date chart, and an index add to the usefulness of this book.

Harvey, David Alan, and Elizabeth Newhouse. *Cuba.* Washington, DC: National Geographic Society, 1999. 215p. ISBN: 0-7922-7501-2. $50.00. Gr. 9-adult.

With stunningly evocative color photographs by David Alan Harvey as well as insightful and most informative essays by Elizabeth Newhouse, this exquisite album provides an honest, human depiction of Cuba today. From splendid street scenes, to music and festivals, to schools, science labs, churches, and homes, viewers will experience life in Cuba amid the struggles and frustrations of Castro's regime. Readers interested in the history, politics, economy, and current issues of life in Cuba will appreciate the well-written essays, liberally sprinkled with popular jokes and hard facts.

Hoff, Rhoda, and Margaret Regler. *Uneasy Neighbors: Cuba and the United States.* New York: Franklin Watts, 1997. 191p. ISBN: 0-531-11326-4. $22.00. Gr. 9-12.

From the diary of Christopher Columbus describing the beauty of what he believed was China but is now Cuba to present-day conflicts between the United States and Cuba, this compilation of primary source material highlights important incidents in the relations between the two countries. Students will find numerous documents, personal accounts, and official reports that attempt to explain the different points of view between neighbors such as Winston Churchill's impressions of Cuba upon joining the army, Fidel Castro's well-known speech, "History Will Absolve Me," "Che" Guevara's farewell letter to Fidel Castro, and many others. This compilation will add depth to students' reports on Cuba vs. the United States.

Kohli, Eddy. *Cuba.* New York: Rizzoli International Publishers, 1997. 120p. ISBN: 0-8478-2065-3. $60.00. Gr. 8-adult.

This "voyage in images" by a well-known international photographer captures numerous impressionistic views of rural Cuba. From everyday images, to the foods and national drinks, to the finest tobacco leaves, to young communists celebrating the Revolution, this large-format album provides provocative insights into Cuba. Some readers/viewers might object to some of the obviously pro-Castro captions, others to photographs of a nude woman, scantily dressed nightclub dancers, or the birth of a pig. Nevertheless, these at times sharp, at times tender, photographs with numerous quotes from such authors as Reinaldo Arenas, Graham Greene, and Federico García Lorca are not just pretty; rather, they are intense and stimulating.

Lamazares, Ivonne. *The Sugar Island.* Boston: Houghton Mifflin, 2000. 205p. ISBN: 0-395-86040-7. $23.00. Gr. 9-adult.

Born and raised in Cuba, Lamazares candidly depicts Cuba in the 1960s where in "The world's biggest sugar grower . . . there isn't a spoonful to go around. . . . They give it to the Russians, *niña.* Everything good goes to the Russians" (p.110). Tanya, the wonderfully convincing narrator, describes her mixed feelings about her mother, who is always eager to start life, even if it means running off to the mountains to become a rebel *guerrillera* when Tanya was only six. Always romantic and unreliable, Tanya's mother manages to complicate life for her two children and Tanya's generous great-aunt. Alone and worried, Tanya experiences the abuses of power and the hardships caused by extreme deprivation. Tanya's mother finally succeeds in getting them to Miami, where they face a new life with the same mother-daughter conflicts and misunderstandings. Yet, Tanya's love for her mother shines through despite the friction and disagreements. Mature readers will be touched by Lamazares's unaffected style and terribly human characters as they confront reality in Revolutionary Cuba and in a new country.

Leiner, Katherine. *Mama Does the Mambo.* Illus.: Edel Rodriguez. New York: Hyperion Books for Children, 2001. 32p. ISBN: 0-7868-0646-X. $15.99. Gr. K-3.

Set in Havana, Cuba, this endearing story describes Sofia's feelings following her papa's death. She is especially worried that her mama will never dance again. The sensitive text, peppered with Spanish words and phrases, is enhanced with Rodriguez's graceful ink linework with touches of pastel, gouache, and spray paint. These result in a joyous realistic tone that conveys the importance of music, dance, love, and sorrow that affectionately unite mama and daughter. A glossary assists non-Spanish speakers.

Leonard, Elmore. *Cuba Libre.* New York: Delacorte Press, 1998. 343p. ISBN: 0-385-32383-2. $23.95. Gr. 9-adult.

Set in Cuba during the period just before the Spanish-American War when Cubans were struggling for independence, this easy-to-read, fast-paced novel intermingles adventure with a tender love story amid the sinking of the *U.S.S. Maine*, American interests in Cuba, the infamous prison in El Morro Castle, villainous General Weyler, and the contemptible Guardia Civil officers. This is not a serious historical narrative; rather, it is an action-packed love story with kind, courageous, and handsome protagonists who overcome nefarious characters in their search for each other. They also get to keep a bundle of the evil man's cash as the hero gets used to living in Cuba with his beloved Amelia, a New Orleans-born beauty. This is just right for reluctant readers of history—Cuban or otherwise.

Martí, José. *Versos sencillos/Simple Verses.* Translated into English by Manuel A. Tellechea. Houston, TX: Arte Público Press, 1997. 123p. ISBN: 1-55885-204-2. pap. $12.95. Gr. 9-adult.

Revered by many as the national hero and cultural icon of Cuba, José Martí's bilingual collection includes excellent English renditions in facing pages of what is described as Martí's spiritual autobiography. A well-done introduction by the translator explains that each "poem captures an experience, a sensation, or a moment which shaped the poet and the man" (p.8). From Martí's patriotic verses, to his famous love poems, to his poems about friendship and death, this collection is a wonderful testament to his literary genius and political leadership.

Missen, François. *Memories of Cuba.* Photos by Olivier Beytout. New York: Thunder's Mouth Press, 1998. 143p. ISBN: 1-56025-182-4. pap. $22.95. Gr. 8-adult.

Through brief, touching interviews of Cuban men and women in their golden years and 123 stunning full-page color photos, the author and photographer present a panoramic view of Cuban people, cities, and countryside. This is not an in-depth, sociological study of Cuba; rather, it is an artistic photo essay of life in Cuba with a few pages of poignant memories. Especially engrossing are interviews with Fernando Campoamor, who tells about his experiences with Hemingway in Havana, and Ramón Collazo Truabijo, a proud *tabaquero* (cigar maker), who made cigars for Churchill and Stalin.

Salas, Osvaldo, and Roberto Salas. *Fidel's Cuba: A Revolution in Pictures.* New York: Thunder's Mouth Press/Distributed by Publishers Group West, 1998. 175p. ISBN: 1-56025-192-1. $34.95. Gr. 9-adult.

From Fidel's handpicked photographers, Osvaldo and Roberto Salas, and with photo captions by Roberto Salas, who lives in Havana, this is a dramatic, intimate view of Cuba just before the Revolution. As an insider's view of major Cuban events in recent history—from Castro in Central Park in 1955, to the triumph of the Revolution, to Castro with Hemingway and Che Guevara, to the fiasco of the Bay of Pigs and the Missile Crisis—this collection of award-winning photos provides viewers with a flattering, invariably positive foreword and text highlighting Fidel Castro's and Che Guevara's successes. This is indeed an artistic portrait "firmly based on the importance of community and of art as a motivator for social change" (p.20). Castro's (and Che's) admirers will treasure; others will view it as artistic political propaganda.

Sinclair, Andrew. *Che Guevara.* Gloucestershire, UK: Sutton Publishing, 1998. 119p. ISBN: 0-7509-1847-0. pap. $9.95. Gr. 9-adult.
See review p. 2.

Staub, Frank J. *Children of Cuba*. (The World's Children) Minneapolis, MN: Carolrhoda Books, 1996. 48p. ISBN: 0-87614-989-1. $14.96. Gr. 3-6.

This is a joyous, enticing overview of the people of Cuba through spectacular color photos and an informative text. From Cuba in the mid-1500s to Cuba in the 1990s, readers/viewers are exposed to the culture, economy, and lifestyle of the country. Despite the food and oil shortages, the long lines of patient Cuban shoppers, and the decline in the price of sugar, Cuba's biggest crop, the author/photographer presents an optimistic view of Cuban children beautifully depicted by the numerous smiling faces throughout the book.

Wolf, Bernard. *Cuba: After the Revolution*. Photos by the author. New York: Dutton, 1999. 64p. ISBN: 0-525-46058-6. $16.99. Gr. 4-6.

Through striking, candid color photos and a simple text, photojournalist Wolf presents an engrossing view of Cuba in the late 1990s. Especially affecting are the wonderful photos of Cubans as they go about their lives—chatting with friends, waiting in long lines, going to school, and visiting family members. Despite an optimistic tone, Wolf tries to present a balanced view: "While there is no starvation in Cuba, few people can boast of having full stomachs. Finding ways to get more food is a common preoccupation" (unpaged). Later, he states: "The quality of medical care in Cuba is outstanding. The only major problem is the lack of critical medication and advanced technical medical equipment needed to diagnose and treat serious illnesses." The second part of the book focuses on the daily lives of two artists and their daughter, Ana, an aspiring ballet dancer. Readers/viewers interested in Cuba today will find much to ponder, to criticize, and to behold.

The Dominican Republic

Alvarez, Julia. *The Secret Footprints*. Illus.: Fabian Negrin. New York: Knopf, 2000. 32p. ISBN: 0-679-89309-1. $16.95; lib. ed. ISBN: 0-679-89309-6. $18.99. Gr. 1-4.

Based on Dominican legends, Alvarez re-creates a magical tale about *ciguapas*, beautiful creatures with golden skin and long black hair. Because they are so smart, their feet are attached backward so their toes face where they come from. In this version, Guapa, a brave, bold, and beautiful *ciguapa*, threatens the safety of all the *ciguapas* by carelessly venturing into the human world. Negrin's luminescent double-page spreads beautifully capture the fauna and flora of the Dominican countryside and project a touch of magical realism as Guapa is saved by the mysterious *ciguapas*. From delicious *pastelitos* to Alvarez's personal note in the appendix, this story is sure to bring forth sweet memories, especially from former Caribbean residents.

Appelbaum, Diana. *Cocoa Ice*. Illus.: Holly Meade. New York: Orchard Books, 1997. 50p. ISBN: 0-531-30040-4. $16.95; lib. ed. ISBN: 0-531-33040-0. $17.99. Gr. 2-5.

In a wonderfully imaginative way, the author links the island of Santo Domingo, where the sun bakes "the earth until it is hot and steamy like a roasted plantain," with Maine, where, in winter, "the days are short, bright, and so cold that sometimes nothing moves, not the wind, not the birds, not even the river." The story is told through fresh, first-person narratives of two girls: The first, from the Caribbean island, describing everyday life, including growing, harvesting, and trading cocoa beans for ice and, the second, from Maine, whose Papa and uncle work for an ice company. Readers will be able to experience life in two completely different geographical settings. The delightful smell and taste of chocolate provide the perfect ambiance to this informative story about harvesting cocoa and collecting ice in the late 1800s. The colorful cut paper and gouache illustrations and an author's note on the cocoa/ice trade add further to the enjoyment and informational value of this story.

Christopher, Matt. *At the Plate with . . . Sammy Sosa.* Boston: Little, Brown, 1999. 108p. ISBN: 0-316-13477-5. pap. $4.95. Gr. 4-7.
   From Sammy Sosa's poor childhood in the Dominican Republic to his home run record-breaking 1998 season, this biography depicts the personality, triumphs, and difficulties of this much-admired baseball player. Baseball fans will especially enjoy the drama and statistics of the game, which culminated in the National League's MVP award to Sosa. Others will find enough personal information amid the baseball jargon and milieu.

Joseph, Lynn. *The Color of My Words.* New York: Joanna Cotler/ HarperCollins, 2000. 138p. ISBN: 0-06-028232-0. $14.95. Gr. 5-8.
   In a heart-rending, first-person narrative, Ana Rosa, a twelve-year-old girl from the Dominican Republic tells about the beauty of her island contrasted with her family's travails and government abuses. Despite the lack of freedom of the press, Ana Rosa's greatest wish is to write. Fortunately, an understanding mother and a most generous brother encourage her dream. Amid the allure of the music, food, and beaches of the Dominican Republic, Ana Rosa's poignant coming-of-age story chronicles her father's constant drinking and her brother's tragic death by government soldiers. Also available in Spanish.

Preller, James. *McGwire & Sosa: A Season to Remember.* New York: Aladdin Paperbacks/Simon & Schuster, 1998. 32p. ISBN: 0-689-82871-3. pap. $5.99. Gr. 4-7.
   With gusto, admiration, and numerous action-filled photographs on every page, this oversize paperback depicts the excitement of the 1998 Sosa/McGwire season. Concentrating on the highlights, and briefly recounting episodes about the lives of these two baseball players, this is an enthusiastic recounting of the unforgettable summer when they broke the record of home runs in one season. Fans of these two great athletes will rejoice while reliving the 1998 baseball season. Sosa's and McGwire's batting statistics are also included.

Savage, Jeff. *Sammy Sosa: Home Run Hero.* Minneapolis, MN: Lerner
    Publications, 2000. 64p. ISBN: 0-8225-3678-1. $21.27; pap.
    ISBN: 0-8225-9858-2. $5.95. Gr. 4-7.
    Emphasizing Sosa's talent as a home run hitter as well as his
pleasing personality, this biography of the Chicago Cubs out-
fielder, originally from the Dominican Republic, will certainly
appeal to his numerous fans. A glossary of baseball terms, candid
color photos, and major and minor league statistics are also
included. A Spanish version is available.

Ecuador

Blum, Mark. *Galápagos in 3-D*. San Francisco: Chronicle Books, 2001. 54p. ISBN: 0-8118-3132-9. $18.95. Gr. 5-8.

The fauna and flora of the Galápagos Islands are beautifully depicted through three-dimensional color photographs and an easy-to-understand text that highlights their uniqueness, preservation efforts, and challenges. Scientists-to-be and wildlife enthusiasts also will appreciate the glossary and the inclusion of the scientific and local Spanish names for each creature.

Heller, Ruth. *Galápagos Means "Tortoises."* Illus.: the author. San Francisco: Sierra Club, 2000. 42p. ISBN: 0-87156-917-5. $14.95. Gr. 3-5.

Through joyous rhymes and most appealing double-page spreads that realistically depict twelve of the Galápagos Islands' unusual animals, readers are introduced to the fauna of these "Islands of Enchantment." With humor and whimsy, Heller tells about giant tortoises that "wallow in puddles made by the rain," blue-footed boobies that "spread their wings as they romance," massive thick-necked sea lions, and graceful flamingos that "float like swans when the water is deep." An author's note adds further to the reader's appreciation of the Galápagos.

Lewin, Ted. *Nilo and the Tortoise*. Illus.: the author. New York: Scholastic, 1999. 40p. ISBN: 0-590-96004-0. $16.95. Gr. 4-6.

Nilo, who is about eight, is waiting overnight on an island in the Galápagos while his father repairs their fishing boat. As he explores the shore, he encounters an angry sea lion, a happy chattering tiny red and black bird, a hawk, and a giant thick-legged tortoise with whom Nilo spends the night. In the morning, he follows the hawk to the beach, where his father is waiting. Nilo's story seems contrived as he explores, alone and unconcerned, a deserted island. Yet the beauty and remoteness of the Galápagos Islands are definitely conveyed in the double-page pastel watercolors that show beautiful scenes of Nilo and the exotic landscape and wildlife. Informative notes, a map, and an explanatory afterword provide further information on the Galápagos.

Lourie, Peter. *Lost Treasure of the Inca.* Honesdale, PA: Boyds Mills Press, 1999. 48p. ISBN: 1-56397-743-5. $18.95. Gr. 5-8.

With the gusto and excitement of a modern-day treasure hunter, this chronicle recounts the author's expedition into the Llanganati Mountains of Ecuador in search of 750 tons of gold treasures, which the Incas hid from the Spanish *conquistadores* after Pizarro executed the Sun King, Atahualpa. Emphasizing that by feeding the gold fever the "Inca people are getting their revenge on the Europeans who murdered their king and conquered their empire" (p.9) and by describing key historical facts, such as the death of Atahualpa and Valverde's expedition in the sixteenth century, this stirring account of the author's own search for gold will entice readers into the still-enigmatical realm of the Inca. Color and black-and-white photos on every page make the readable text even more alluring.

Tagliaferro, Linda. *Galápagos Islands: Nature's Delicate Balance at Risk.* Minneapolis, MN: Lerner Publications, 2001. 88p. ISBN: 0-8225-0648-3. $25.26. Gr. 5-8.

From its geological origins, to its amazing fauna, to its fragile ecosystem, readers are introduced to the Galápagos Islands through an easy-to-understand text and numerous clear color photographs. Tagliaferro includes such high-interest topics as the male frigate bird's efforts to attract the attention of the flying females during mating season, and the male marine iguanas' competitions to stake out their territories. The author presents most convincing arguments to ensure that the Galápagos will remain a "living laboratory of evolution." A glossary, bibliography, list of resources, and an index complement this informative overview.

El Salvador

Alphin, Elaine Marie. *A Bear for Miguel.* Illus.: Joan Sandin. (I Can Read Book) New York: HarperCollins Publishers, 1996. 64p. ISBN: 0-06-024521-2. $14.95; lib. ed. ISBN: 0-06-024522-0. $14.89. Gr. 1-4.

In a compelling and engrossing manner, this sensitive, easy-to-read story tells about María, a young girl, and her family from El Salvador who are caught in the guerrilla warfare and internal political struggles of their country. Told from a child's perspective and set during market day, young readers will empathize with María, who finds the courage to trade her beloved teddy bear, Paco, for the milk, cheese, butter, and eggs that are very much needed at home. The simple watercolors and an effective use of words and phrases in Spanish add to the emotional impact of this beginning reader. An author's note, a map, and a glossary with a pronunciation guide make *A Bear for Miguel* even more useful. Unfortunately, numerous Spanish words are missing the Spanish diacritical mark—both in the glossary and in the text.

Benítez, Sandra. *Bitter Grounds.* New York: Hyperion, 1997. 445p. ISBN: 0-7868-6157-6. $22.95. Gr. 9-adult.

The tragedy of life in El Salvador from 1932 to 1977 is chronicled through the lives of three generations of Salvadoran women who experience marriage, childbirth, and death in a country torn apart by politics and anarchy. Based partly on her own experiences, Benítez recounts the horrible abuses committed against poor coffee pickers and the luxurious lifestyle of wealthy landowners where women in both extremes suffer constant heartbreak and betrayal. This is not an upbeat novel set in this lush Central American country; rather it is a powerful, engrossing novel with vivid characters who portray the intrigue of the human drama that many Salvadorans have known all too well.

Gorkin, Michael, and others. *From Grandmother to Granddaughter: Salvadoran Women's Stories.* Berkeley: University of California Press, 2000. 256p. ISBN: 0-520-22240-7. pap. $20.00. Gr. 9-adult.

Gorkin, an American psychologist and former Fulbright scholar, collaborated with two Salvadoran women psychologists to interview and write about three generations of women in El Salvador. From a wealthy upper class family, to a middle class family, to a very poor *campesino* family, these nine women describe the *machismo* in Salvadoran society; their intimate experiences and thoughts about virginity, rape, and marriage; and the effects of El Salvador's recent civil war on their lives. Especially touching are the descriptions of several of the women of being raped and abused by their partners and misunderstood by society. Some adolescents may object to the somewhat lengthy and academic text, but this is a realistic overview of the lives of women in El Salvador today.

Nickles, Greg. *El Salvador: The Land.* ISBN: 0-7787-9367-0.
———. *El Salvador: The People and Culture.* ISBN: 0-7787-9368-0.
Ea. vol.: 32p. (The Lands, Peoples, and Cultures Series) New York: Crabtree Publishing, 2002. $20.60. Gr. 3-5.

The land, people, and culture of El Salvador are introduced to young readers through simple text and numerous full-page color photos on every page. Readers are exposed to such aspects as Mayan beliefs, the arts, as well as the civil war and the 2001 earthquake, in which more than 1,100 people died.

Guatemala

Amado, Elisa. *Barrilete: A Kite for the Day of the Dead.* Photos by Joya Hairs. Toronto: Groundwood Books/Distributed by Publishers Group West, 1999. 32p. ISBN: 0-88899-366-8. $15.95. Gr. 2-3.

Through young Juan, a resident of Santiago Sacatepéquez, a small village in Guatemala, readers/viewers are exposed to a unique Day of the Dead celebration, when on November 2, the people fly some of the biggest handmade kites in the world. Juan's excitement about his village's traditions is further enhanced by the simple narrative and the candid black-and-white and color photographs. It is important to note that the photographs were taken in the 1970s; hence, they vary in quality and interest. Nonetheless, this is a joyous, if dated, celebration of a different Day of the Dead tradition. Spanish speakers will be especially interested in the conclusion, which includes a brief explanation of the ten different words used for kite in the Spanish-speaking world.

Brill, Marlene Targ. *Journey for Peace: The Story of Rigoberta Menchú.* Illus.: Rubén De Anda. New York: Lodestar Books/ Dutton, 1996. 56p. ISBN: 0-525-67524-8. $14.99. Gr. 3-5.

In a powerful and affecting narrative, the author simply relates the suffering and difficult life of Rigoberta Menchú, the winner of the 1992 Nobel Peace Prize. Emphasizing the deprivations and struggles of the Mayan Indians of Guatemala, Brill exposes the numerous abuses and lack of justice that are prevalent in Guatemala. Menchú's childhood as a field laborer as well as her family's personal hardships that culminated in her father's imprisonment, torture, and murder are followed by the massacre of her mother, brothers, and sisters. The black-and-white photos and illustrations add a sense of immediacy to the life of a courageous woman who has "broken the silence around Guatemala." Also included are a map, endnotes, a glossary, a bibliography, and an index.

Gage, Amy Glaser. *Pascual's Magic Pictures*. Illus.: Karen Dugan. Minneapolis, MN: Carolrhoda Books, 1996. 32p. ISBN: 0-87614-877-1. $19.95. Gr. K-3.

Young Pascual, who sells colorful weavings at the market in Tikal, wishes he could photograph the baby howler monkeys as they jump from branch to branch in the rain forest near his home in Guatemala. When an American tourist suggests using a disposable camera, he knows that's his answer. As an engaging story with colorful illustrations about rural Guatemala, this tale may serve a purpose. Unfortunately, it's the female American tourist who has the answers—like many other books about Latin America.

Gerson, Mary-Joan. *People of Corn: A Mayan Story*. Illus.: Carla Golembe. Boston: Little, Brown, 1995. 32p. ISBN: 0-316-30854-4. $15.95. Gr. 2-4.
See review p. 45.

Hoepker, Thomas. *Return of the Maya: Guatemala—a Tale of Survival*. New York: Henry Holt, 1998. 146p. ISBN: 0-8050-6007-3. $40.00. Gr. 9-adult.

This is not a beautiful depiction of Guatemala today; rather, it is a most powerful portrayal of the misery, hunger, poverty, terror, and abuses that the Mayas have endured during the last forty years. From the horror of women who were present when their husbands were shot to death, to the remains of torture victims, to women and children who wait for their drunken husbands and fathers, to men, women, and children who carry heavy loads on their backs, these compelling full-color photographs present a vivid testimony to the life of the Maya in Guatemala. Stunning photographs of festivals and archaeological sites are also included, but the brief text and most of the photographs describe the effects of the brutal civil war upon the Maya, who now must learn to deal with the "lures of capitalism and pop culture." Artistic photography at its best.

Latin America

Ada, Alma Flor. *Gathering the Sun: An Alphabet in Spanish and English.* Illus.: Simón Silva. Translated by Rosa Zubizarreta. New York: Lothrop, Lee & Shepard Books, 1997. 40p. ISBN: 0-688-13903-5. $16.00; lib. ed. ISBN: 0-688-13904-3. $15.93. Gr. 2-4.

Alma Flor Ada's bilingual poetic celebration of the bounty of the harvest and the Mexican heritage of the farmworkers and their families is further enhanced by Silva's robust sun-drenched gouache paintings reminiscent of the great Mexican painters: Rivera, Orozco, and Siqueiros. Using the Spanish alphabet as a template, these twenty-seven poems tell about the joys of nature as well as the pride of family, language, and culture. It is important to note that Zubizarreta's English renditions are as joyful as Ada's original Spanish poems.

Chin-Lee, Cynthia, and Terri de la Peña. *A Is for the Americas.* Illus.: Enrique O. Sánchez. New York: Orchard Books, 1999. 32p. ISBN: 0-531-30194-X. $15.95. Gr. 3-5.

Using the letters of the alphabet as an introduction, this easy-to-read and heavily illustrated book presents colorful aspects of the culture, history, and geography of the Americas—North, Central, and South. This is not a systematic study of the Americas; rather, it is a brightly colored overview of some of its most appealing facets—from the pyramids of Yucatán to the mystery and splendor of Niagara Falls—with a focus on Latino and Native American people. This book is also available in Spanish—*A es para decir Américas.*

Delacre, Lulu. *Golden Tales: Myths, Legends and Folktales from Latin America.* Illus.: the author. New York: Scholastic, 1996. 74p. ISBN: 0-590-48186-X. $18.95. Gr. 4-8.

Twelve well-known myths, legends, and tales from Puerto Rico, the Dominican Republic, Cuba, Mexico, Colombia, Peru, and Bolivia are included in this attractive large-format publication. This collection is especially valuable as an introduction or as supplementary reading in the study of pre-Hispanic cultures of the Americas. Well-written source notes and numerous full-page oil paintings convey the drama of these ancient civilizations. Perhaps some "concerned" adults will object to some of the themes discussed in these legends, such as parental abuse and extramarital affairs. The prose is at times difficult to read, but its time-tested authenticity is unquestionable.

Dent, David W. *The Legacy of the Monroe Doctrine: A Reference Guide to U.S. Involvement in Latin America and the Caribbean.* Westport, CT: Greenwood, 1999. 418p. ISBN: 0-313-30109-3. $59.95. Gr. 9-adult.

In a well-organized and most readable manner, this reference guide provides a synthesis of the major themes in the history of United States involvement in Latin America and the Caribbean since the independence of the Latin American nations. Through timelines, editorial cartoons, and 24 country-chapters, the author, a professor of political science, describes the role of the United States in Latin America since the Monroe Doctrine and critically analyzes its faulty assumptions and destructive rationalizations. Readers interested in understanding United States intervention, military occupation, policy blunders, and other important effects of the Monroe Doctrine on hemispheric relations will find this an invaluable reference work. Selected readings at the end of each chapter, a glossary, and an index will further assist serious researchers.

Ehlert, Lois. *Market Day: A Story Told with Folk Art.* Illus.: the author. San Diego, CA: Harcourt Brace, 2000. 36p. ISBN: 0-15-202158-2. $16.00. Gr. Pre-2.

Brimming with the color and exquisite simplicity of mainly Latin American folk art, Ehlert takes readers/viewers to and from a farmers market. In easy, snappy rhymes she invites children to: "Get out of bed. The chickens need corn. Pull up some carrots. Shake off the dirt." At the market, people buy and sell, and work and play, until they return home, ready to eat. Especially alluring are the vibrant, double-spread tableaux filled with toys, baskets, textiles, and other images from Mexico, Guatemala, Colombia,

Panama, Bolivia, and other countries. A two-page pictorial key, explaining the origin and composition of each piece, completes this joyous folk art fiesta.

Encyclopedia of Contemporary Latin American and Caribbean Cultures. 3 vol. Edited by Daniel Balderston and others. New York: Routledge, 2000. 1754p. ISBN: 0-415-13188-X. $399. Gr. 9-adult.

   In approximately 4,000 entries, this accessible encyclopedia presents "all the forms of contemporary cultural expression" in Latin America and the Caribbean through "different forms, genres, movements, spaces, and institutions." Hence, it includes such literary masters as Borges, Paz, and Fuentes as well as popular heroes and customs like salsa, Maradona, and Cantinflas. Arranged alphabetically, it also provides a thematic entry list as well as two- to three-page introductory articles that review the decades of the 1920s to the 1990s, and an index. Despite an uneven coverage and the lack of maps and photographs, this is a starting point for students in search of basic information about this area.

Encyclopedia of Latin American and Caribbean Art. Edited by Jane Turner. New York: Grove's Dictionaries, 2000. 782p. ISBN: 1-884446-04-3. $250.00. Gr. 9-adult.

   The arts and culture of every country in the Western Hemisphere except Canada and the United States, from the European conquest to the present day, are included in this well-researched encyclopedia. Serious students of Latin American art will find introductory articles on the arts of indigenous peoples, essays on the melding of European and native art forms, and biographies ranging from Eduardo Abela (Cuba) to Mateo de Zúñiga (Guatemala). Well-organized and easy-to-use, this updated encyclopedia will be of great interest to lovers of the arts—from architecture to interior design to fine and decorative arts. Despite the inclusion of 84 color plates in the center of the volume, readers will be disappointed to note that most illustrations are in black and white, which certainly detract from the original beauty of the works. Notwithstanding this caveat, this is a most useful and informative encyclopedia about Latin American art.

Encyclopedia of Latin American History and Culture. 5 vol. Edited by Barbara A. Tenenbaum and others. New York: Scribner, 1996. ISBN: 0-684-19253-5. $449.00. Gr. 9-adult.

Serious students of Latin America will find much valuable, up-to-date information on the political, economic, social, anthropological, literary, academic, and artistic culture as well as its effects on the history of the region. More than 5,000 alphabetical entries, which range from short biographies and definitions to lengthy essays on such topics as imperialism, income distribution, and environmental movements, are included. In contrast to other reference works, it is important to note that Brazil, the largest and most populous nation in Latin America and the Portuguese Empire, is accorded appropriate treatment in all entries concerned with the region as a whole. Users will appreciate the "see also" references at the end of most entries that call attention to articles of more general relevance and the most complete index in volume 5, which includes full cross-referencing.

Encyclopedia of Latin American Literature. Edited by Verity Smith. London: Fitzroy Dearborn Publishers, 1997. 926p. ISBN: 1-884964-18-4. $125.00. Gr. 9-adult.

In addition to entries on writers, works, and topics relating to the literature of Latin America, this large, one-volume encyclopedia includes brief, but comprehensive, articles on the continent's individual countries. This is not a specialized source for experts; rather, it is a most useful starting point for students who need a perspective in the literature of the continent's past as well as an overview of contemporary authors and their works.

Gold, John C. *Environments of the Western Hemisphere.* ISBN: 0-8050-5601-7.

Gold, Susan Dudley. *Governments of the Western Hemisphere.* ISBN: 0-8050-5602-5.

Ea. vol.: 96p. (Comparing Continents Series) New York: Twenty-First Century Books/Henry Holt, 1997. $17.98. Gr. 6-9.

In well-organized, easy-to-understand narratives, the authors provide straightforward introductions to the environments and governments of the Western Hemisphere. Numerous maps, color photographs, glossaries, and informative inserts add to their value. *Environments of the Western Hemisphere* describes the lands, temperatures, and climates from the permanently frozen tundra of the Canadian territories to the hot, damp jungles of the South American rain forest. Especially significant are the serious discussions of Latin America's environmental problems such as the destruction of rain forests, water and air pollution, and the negative effects of erosion and soil damage. *Governments of the Western Hemisphere* provides interesting comparisons between the various forms of government of the nations of North and South America. It examines sophisticated pre-Columbian civilizations in Mexico, Guatemala, and Belize as well as the repressive regimes and military coups in several Latin American countries. It also contrasts the stable governments of the United States and Canada with the lack of experience in self-government of Latin American nations. Also included in this series is *Religions of the Western Hemisphere.*

González, Lucía M. *Señor Cat's Romance and Other Favorite Stories from Latin America.* Illus.: Lulu Delacre. New York: Scholastic, 1997. 48p. ISBN: 0-590-48537-7. $17.95. Gr. 1-3.

Six delightful stories from Latin America are retold here with the flair and gusto of the originals. The long popularity of these stories in the Spanish-speaking world attests to their time-tested appeal. From the little half-chick who had only one wing and one leg, to Juan Bobo's ingenuity, to Martina's many suitors, to Billy Goat's rudeness, to Uncle Rabbit's tricks, to Señor Cat's romance, these stories will be enjoyed by all readers or listeners. Delacre's playful watercolor and gouache artwork and the brief notes about each story add to the joy of these *cuentos favoritos.*

Henderson, James D., and others. *A Reference Guide to Latin American History.* Armonk, NY: Sharpe, 2000. 615p. ISBN: 1-56324-744-5. $165.00. Gr. 9-adult.

Well-organized and comprehensive, this guide presents significant events of Latin American history through the year 1999. Serious students of Latin America will appreciate the chronological information, from the arrival of the first humans in the Americas through July 1999. Others will be interested in the regional geographical divisions; the topical chronology with such general themes as society, economic developments, and popular culture; and the brief biographical sketches of three hundred Latin Americans, from José de Acosta to Juan de Zumárraga.

Jade and Iron: Latin American Tales from Two Cultures. Edited by Patricia Aldana. Translated by Hugh Hazelton. Toronto: Groundwood Books/Distributed by Publishers Group West, 1996. 64p. ISBN: 0-88899-256-4. $18.95. Gr. 3-6.

From pre-Columbian and colonial times, this collection of twelve well-known tales from Latin America tells about great warriors, beautiful maidens, poor women, outrageous thieves, courageous prisoners, and their relationships with the natural world. The brevity of these tales—from two to five pages each—and the full-page colorful illustrations with a strong, albeit stiff, Latino flavor make them ideal for use in conjunction with units on Latin America. Since a glossary is not included, some readers will require further explanations, especially about certain foods specific to the region. The slight introduction isn't much help either.

Johnson, Sylvia. *Tomatoes, Potatoes, Corn, and Beans: How the Foods of the Americas Changed Eating around the World.* New York: Atheneum BFYR/Simon & Schuster, 1997. 138p. ISBN: 0-689-80141-6. $16.00. Gr. 7-10.

In a readable and enticing narrative, Johnson describes the early use, preparation, transportation, and worldwide consumption of maize, beans, peppers, peanuts, potatoes, tomatoes, and chocolate as well as other food plants native to the Americas such as squash, pineapple, vanilla, and avocado. In addition to a basic introduction to each food, the author provides interesting historical information. She states, for instance, that for centuries, "many people in England and in other northern European countries believed that the tomato, like the potato, was an aphrodisiac. . . . Whatever the reason, upright and moral people would not have anything to do with this dangerous food" (p.89). Numerous black-and-white reproductions of sixteenth-century life, codices, archival prints, botanical diagrams, and photographs add interest to this overview of foods from the Americas. This is indeed a most appetizing introduction of the contributions of pre-Columbian people to the peoples of the world—just right for reluctant readers of history.

Latin American Art in the Twentieth Century. Edited by Edward J. Sullivan. London: Phaidon Press/Distributed by Chronicle, 1996. 352p. ISBN: 0-7148-3210-3. $69.96. Gr. 9-adult.

Written from a uniquely Latin American perspective by art historians, this handsomely illustrated volume presents the history of modern Latin American art in sixteen scholarly essays beginning with Mexico up to Chicano Art. Serious students of Latin American art, especially the arts of painting and, to a lesser extent, sculpture, and the graphic and decorative arts, will enjoy the diversity of approach in each of these essays as well as the exquisite color reproductions.

Latin American Folktales: Stories from Hispanic and Indian Traditions. Edited by John Bierhorst. New York: Pantheon Books, 2002. 386p. ISBN: 0-375-42066-5. $26.00. Gr. 9-adult.

Selected and translated by Bierhorst, a recognized authority in pre-Columbian language and literature, this collection of Latin American folktales includes early colonial legends featuring Aztec and Inca rulers—Montezuma and Mayta Capac—twentieth-century stories which are "told at wakes in order to pass the time, or, more to the point, to prevent people from falling asleep" (p.45); and twentieth-century myths that describe the war between nature and culture. Stories range from the ever-popular Latino trickster, Pedro de Urdemalas, to "Don Dinero and Doña Fortuna," to Charcoal Peddler, who chooses to share his humble meal with Death rather than Luck because death treats everyone equally. They provide a joyous display of the wit and wisdom of Hispano-American people. Serious folklorists-to-be will appreciate the author's notes, register of tales and motifs, glossary, and bibliography.

The Latino Encyclopedia. 6 vols. Edited by Richard Chabrán and Rafael Chabrán. New York: Marshall Cavendish, 1996. ISBN: 0-7614-0125-3. $459.95. Gr. 9-adult.

Latino life, culture, and history are explored in this six-volume set, which focuses on the Latino experience in the United States. More than 1,900 entries are listed, ranging from 28 signed articles with annotated bibliographies and cross-references to unsigned paragraphs without bibliographies. One thousand black-and-white photographs highlight the diversity of backgrounds and interests within Latino society. One of the most valuable aspects of this encyclopedia is that it provides arguments for and against important topics such as affirmative action and bilingual education. Conspicuously absent is information on the literature for children and adolescents, completely disregarding noteworthy Latino authors and illustrators for young readers.

Marley, David F. *Wars of the Americas: A Chronology of Armed Conflict in the New World, 1492 to the Present.* Santa Barbara, CA: ABC-CLIO, 1998. 722p. ISBN: 0-8736-837-5. $99.00. Gr. 9-adult.

Beginning with the discovery and conquest of Latin America, including the occupation of Puerto Rico in 1508, the conquest of Cuba in 1511, the Cholula Massacre in 1519, and going to the Panama campaign (1989) and Haitian operation (1994), as well as Chilean General Pinochet's retirement in 1998, this annotated chronology provides a quick overview to past conflicts in the New World. Numerous black-and-white engravings, paintings, drawings, and maps provide additional information about the wars, battles, and hostilities in the Americas. Key historical events such as the Alhóndiga de Granaditas, Mexico (1810); the Alamo (1836); "Cinco de Mayo" (1862); and others are succinctly described providing readers with enough basic information about the military conflicts since the arrival of Columbus. The only caveat in this well-designed chronology is the insufficient index that basically includes names of individuals but lacks names of countries, battles, and others.

Orozco, José-Luis. *Diez deditos/Ten Little Fingers and Other Play Rhymes and Action Songs from Latin America.* Illus.: Elisa Kleven. New York: Dutton, 1997. 56p. ISBN: 0-525-45736-4. $16.99. Gr. Pre-3.

Like the author's previous *De colores*, this bilingual collection of thirty-four finger rhymes and songs from the Spanish-speaking world is sure to please the young as they sing, chant, clap, dance, or listen. Each selection includes the lyrics in both Spanish and English, musical arrangements, visual prompts to cue children to appropriate body movements, as well as author's notes and a most useful subject index. What makes this volume so very special are Kleven's vivacious collage illustrations that overflow with the color, tempo, and style of Latino people and culture. From "Diez deditos" to "Adios, amigos," this volume is for children and adults alike.

The Oxford Book of Latin American Short Stories. Edited by Roberto González Echevarría. New York: Oxford University Press, 1997. 481p. ISBN: 0-19-509590-1. $30.00. Gr. 8-adult.

Just by reading the preface and introduction of this superb volume, serious readers of Latin American literature will be motivated to further explore the wealth of the Latin American short story in well-rendered English versions. Beginning with texts from the colonial period up to Rosario Ferré (Puerto Rico), this anthology includes fifty-three selections of the best Latin American

writers such as Borges, Machado de Assis, Quiroga, Cortázar, and
García Márquez, as well as selections by younger writers such as
Cristina Peri Rossi, Nélida Piñón, and Reinaldo Arenas. In addition
to the excellent selections, students will appreciate the brief and
informative headnotes for each story that highlight the author's
central themes, influences, and major works. What a tantalizing
selection for English-speaking readers.

*The Oxford Encyclopedia of Mesoamerican Cultures: The Civilizations
of Mexico and Central America.* 3 vol. Edited by David Carrasco.
New York: Oxford University Press, 2001. 1385p. ISBN: 0-19-
510815-9. $466.50. Gr. 9-adult.

As a major reference work that "organizes and interprets new
knowledge concerning Mesoamerican cultures," this comprehensive encyclopedia presents a consensus of the issues that have
affected the pre-Hispanic, Colonial, and contemporary periods of
Mexico, Guatemala, Belize, El Salvador, and parts of Honduras,
Nicaragua, and Costa Rica. Arranged alphabetically, more than
600 articles written by some of the world's best scholars of
Mesoamerica discuss such broad topics as "Acculturation,"
"Economic organization and development," and "Writing
systems," as well as more specific topics such as "Motecuhzoma
(a.k.a. Montezuma) Xocoyotl," "Nutrition," and "Sin." Black-and-
white drawings and maps, bibliographies, a synoptic outline of
contents, and an index complement this valuable compendium of
Mesoamerican history, geography, economy, social organizations,
arts, and people.

Pomerantz, Charlotte. *Mangaboom.* Illus.: Anita Lobel. New York:
Greenwillow Books, 1997. 40p. ISBN: 0-688-12956-0. $16.00. Gr.
K-3.

Set somewhere in a tropical fairyland, this original story with
a fairy-tale flavor tells about Daniel, a young boy who knows a
few words in Spanish, and his new friend Mangaboom, a lady
giant who speaks Spanish and English, likes to skinny-dip, and to
turn cartwheels on the beach. In addition, she is very picky about
men. The large, voluptuous watercolor-and-gouache paintings provide the right texture and tone to this entertaining tale about a
determined, strong female who wears a flowery dress with a
ruffled hem and high-heeled pink slippers with satin bows. The
fast-paced text is sprinkled with well-known Spanish words and
phrases.

Shirey, Lynn. *Latin American Writers*. New York: Facts on File, 1997. 134p. ISBN: 0-8160-3202-5. $17.95. Gr. 8-12.

Brief biographical profiles of eight great Latin American writers—Jorge Luis Borges, Gabriel García Márquez, Jorge Amado, Carlos Fuentes, Julio Cortázar, Rosario Castellanos, Mario Vargas Llosa, and Isabel Allende—are included in this volume. In an engaging prose, Shirey relates the lives and achievements of these authors along with the political events and literary influences that shaped their styles and techniques. The brevity of each entry and the simple introductory criticisms of their major works make this book an ideal, readable introduction to these writers for adolescents. A well-done introduction, black-and-white photos, individual chronologies, and bibliographies complement this volume.

Skármeta, Antonio. *The Composition*. Illus.: Alfonso Ruano. Translated by Elisa Amado. Toronto: Douglas & McIntyre/Groundwood Books, 2000. 34p. ISBN: 0-88899-390-0. $16.95. Gr. 3-5.

Through Pedro, a nine-year-old boy whose main interest is playing soccer, readers are exposed to life under an unidentified dictatorship, where people are arrested simply because they disagree with the government, where children are encouraged to report on their own parents, and where the police are the undisputed masters. Pedro's warm relationships with his family and friends are contrasted with the power and intrusion of the ever-present military. Ruano's realistic illustrations complement the intense Latin American ambience in which people are subjected and controlled. An afterword explains life under a dictatorship. Written by the well-known Chilean author Antonio Skármeta and first published in Spanish in 1980, Pedro's story will especially touch many adults from Latin America who, to a greater or lesser degree, have shared his fears.

Torres, Leyla. *Liliana's Grandmothers*. Illus.: the author. New York: Farrar, Straus & Giroux, 1998. 32p. ISBN: 0-374-35105-8. $16.00. Gr. Pre-2.
See review p. 116.

Twentieth-Century Latin American Poetry: A Bilingual Anthology. Edited by Stephen Tapscott. Austin, TX: University of Texas Press, 1996. 418p. ISBN: 0-292-78138-5. $55.00; pap. ISBN: 0-292-78140-7. $24.95. Gr. 9-adult.

This bilingual anthology attempts to include the major twentieth-century Latin American poets and their major works, which appear both in the original language (Spanish or Portuguese) and in English translations. The editor explains that he regrets not having included more works by what he calls the "Hispanic diaspora" (Chicano poems, etc.) and that limitations resulted in a preference for lyric forms. Yet serious poetry students will find the comprehensive introduction as well as the criticisms that precede the eighty-five poets selected most informative. First-time readers, as suggested by the editor, might want to bypass the criticism and head straight for the poems. This is indeed a joyous encounter with some of the world's best poetry of the twentieth century, from Nobel laureates Gabriela Mistral, Pablo Neruda, and Octavio Paz to the more experimental younger poets, Raúl Zurita and Marjorie Agosín.

Vargo, Sharon Hawkins. *Señor Felipe's Alphabet Adventure: El alfabeto español.* Illus.: the author. Translated by Ann Kelly Beale. Brookfield, CT: Millbrook Press, 2001. 32p. ISBN: 0-7613-1860-7. $21.90. Gr. K-2.

Señor Felipe, a parrot photographer, is given an assignment to photograph objects that begin with each letter of the Spanish alphabet. As Señor Felipe and Paco begin their picture-taking adventure, they walk past a 'tree' "*A el árbol*," step into a small 'boat' "*B la barca*," . . . and so on until they zoom past the 'shoes' "*Z los zapatos*." This is indeed a lighthearted way to introduce the Spanish alphabet to English speakers, who will appreciate the simple Spanish pronunciation guides and definite articles. Spanish learners should note that even though "ch" is, as correctly noted in this book, the fourth letter of the Spanish alphabet, current Spanish dictionaries use international alphabetizing rules; hence, "ch" is considered as the combination of two letters, "c" and "h," and is alphabetized accordingly, not as shown in the afterword.

Winther, Barbara. *Plays from Hispanic Tales: One-Act, Royalty-Free Dramatizations for Young People, from Hispanic Stories and Folktales.* Boston: Plays, 1998. 149p. ISBN: 0-8238-0307-4. pap. $13.95. Gr. 4-8.

Lively and fun, these eleven plays based on traditional folktales and legends from Latin America and Spain feature familiar Hispanic characters and themes. From well-known trickster tales like Pedro de Urdemalas, Hormiga and Cucaracha, to traditional

Posada celebrations, to popular pre-Columbian legends, these royalty-free, brief dramatizations should appeal to young actors and audiences alike. Useful production notes with suggestions for staging, costumes, and settings follow each play, and a glossary of Spanish words is also included. A few of the plays can be faulted for stressing Latino stereotypes (e.g., *tortillas, frijoles, sombrero*), including a ridiculous sombrero on the cover, but despite this caveat, and with a little sensitivity on the part of the teachers, these plays provide a humorous view of Hispanic culture.

Mexico

Alarcón, Francisco X. *From the Bellybutton of the Moon and Other Summer Poems/Del ombligo de la luna y otros poemas de verano.* Illus.: Maya Christina Gonzalez. San Francisco: Children's Book Press, 1998. 32p. ISBN: 0-89239-153-7. $15.95. Gr. K-4.

With gusto and without restraint in two languages, Alarcón celebrates his childhood memories of summers in Mexico in this bilingual (English-Spanish) collection of twenty-two poems. From the "tender breath of mountains" to the smell of his grandma's gardenias, to his grandpa's makeshift blackboard, young readers/listeners, especially those from Mexico, will be touched by the poet's whimsical panorama of rural Mexico. Gonzalez's bold and fanciful double-page spreads perfectly complement this enchanting tribute to family and a simple life.

Anaya, Rudolfo. *Maya's Children: The Story of La Llorona.* Illus.: María Baca. New York: Hyperion Books for Children, 1997. 32p. ISBN: 0-7868-0152-2. $14.95; lib. ed. ISBN: 0-7868-2124-8. $14.89. Gr. 2-5.

La Llorona, the legendary tale from Latin America about the crying woman who haunts rivers, lakes, and lonely roads, is retold by Anaya in a simple, evocative style. Deleting the most frightening aspects of *La Llorona*, Anaya has re-created a tale set in ancient Mexico where the beautiful and magical grandchildren of the Sun God are endangered by the threat of *Señor Tiempo,* who is jealous of their immortality, destroys them, and breaks their mother's heart. Baca's rich, gouache artwork with enticing borders provides an exquisite surreal tone to this well-known tale that Latino children have heard in at least one of its many versions.

Ancona, George. *Charro: The Mexican Cowboy.* San Diego, CA: Harcourt Brace, 1999. 48p. ISBN: 0-15-201047-5. $18.00; pap. ISBN: 0-15-201046-7. $9.00. Gr. 4-7.

The life of the charro, a Mexican horseman, is explored in this handsome photo-essay with Ancona's stunning color photographs that capture the excitement, joviality, and tradition of *las charreadas.* From charros wrestling the bulls to the intricacies of the participants' exquisite garments, readers/viewers will delight in this unique Mexican festivity. In contrast to the sometimes-awkward Spanish version, this English rendition, liberally sprinkled with Spanish words, resonates with the enthusiasm of *"El día del charro."*

Ancona, George. *Fiesta Fireworks.* New York: Lothrop, Lee & Shepard Books, 1998. 32p. ISBN: 0-688-14817-4. $16.00. Gr. K-3.

From the preparation to the actual burning of the *castillos* (fireworks), this exquisite photo-essay describes the "fiesta" that honors San Juan de Dios, the patron saint of Tultepec, Mexico, a small town near Mexico City. Sharp, full-color photographs and a brief text show Carmen and her family preparing for the fiesta by making *toritos* (papier-mâché bulls), decorating the church, attending a procession and, finally, enjoying the fiesta that includes balloons, clowns, food, and lighting the *castillos.* An author's note, a map, and a glossary provide further information about this Mexican fiesta. For those who have never experienced a Mexican fiesta, this book offers a wonderful, close-up panorama of a real festival.

Ancona, George. *Harvest.* Photos by the author. New York: Marshall Cavendish, 2001. 48p. ISBN: 0-7614-5086-6. $15.95. Gr. 4-7.
See review pp. 80-81.

Ancona, George. *Mayeros: A Yucatec Maya Family.* New York: Lothrop, Lee & Shepard Books, 1997. 40p. ISBN: 0-688-13465-3. $16.00; lib. ed. ISBN: 0-688-13466-1. $15.93. Gr. 4-6.

The Mayan people of Yucatán, Mexico, flourish in this contemporary view that describes their lives and customs. Through an engaging text and full-color photographs, Ancona takes readers to the land of his ancestors where they share their daily activities, food, fiestas, and special interests. Also included is an author's note that provides an overview of Mayan history and a glossary.

Berendes, Mary. *Mexico*. (Faces and Places) New York: Child's World, 1998. 32p. ISBN: 1-56766-372-9. $22.79. Gr. 1-3.

From Mexico's pre-Columbian pyramids and palaces to its many foods, to its colorful holidays, to its variety of plants and animals, this is a simple introduction to the geography, history, people, and customs of our southern neighbor. Numerous full- and half-page color photos and a brief, easy-to-understand text with appealing sidebars highlight important facts that the very young can comprehend. A glossary, index, and country facts section add to this inviting overview of Mexico.

Bunting, Eve. *Going Home*. Illus.: David Diaz. New York: HarperCollins Publishers, 1996. 32p. ISBN: 0-06-026296-6. $14.95; lib. ed. ISBN: 0-06-026297-4. $14.89. Gr. K-3.

Carlos and his family are going home for Christmas. Home to the parents is their village, La Perla, across the border in Mexico. But Carlos and his sisters are not so sure even though they were born there. The parents' excitement about going home where they can speak in Spanish, visit Grandfather, Aunt Ana, and many friends, as well as dance barefoot in the street, is joyfully portrayed despite the children's apprehensions about being able to return to the United States. In spite of the cluttered effect of using color photographs of Mexican folk art objects as borders for Diaz's powerful paintings, this is a tender story about a hardworking Mexican family who left their home, like many of us, for "the opportunities" the United States offers.

Burr, Claudia, and others. *Broken Shields*. Toronto: Groundwood Books/Distributed by Publishers Group West, 1997. 32p. ISBN: 0-88899-303-X. $15.95. Gr. 3-6.

Based on the *Historia general de las cosas de Nueva España* by the Spanish missionary Bernardino de Sahagún, who came to Mexico shortly after the conquest, this first-person account narrates the tragic downfall of the Aztecs. In a moving, simple English text, it laments the Aztecs' grief, suffering, and subjugation upon the arrival of the Spaniards in the 1500s. The images taken from *Historia de las Indias* by Diego Durán beautifully complement this vivid rendition of the most important incidents that led to the conquest of Mexico.

Burr, Claudia, and others. *When the Viceroy Came.* Toronto: Groundwood Books/Distributed by Publishers Group West, 1999. 32p. ISBN: 0-88899-354-4. $15.95. Gr. 2-4.

Based on a celebratory screen portraying the Mexican people honoring the arrival and accession of the Viceroy Albuquerque in 1702, this lighthearted English rendition depicts life in Mexico City during the colonial period. This is not a serious study of the colonial era; rather, it is a joyous portrait of the fashions, gossip, and amusements of the times through period illustrations.

¡Cámara! Ciudad de México: Monumentos de una nueva generación/Picture Mexico City: Landmarks of a New Generation. Los Angeles: Paul Getty Museum, 1997. 126p. ISBN: 0-89236-490-4. pap. $19.95. Gr. 6-12.

Fourth in a five-part series of Landmark projects, this revealing bilingual publication presents the personal views of ten students—ages nine to eighteen—who photographed personal landmarks as well as designated heritage sites of Mexico City. The result is a stunning, kaleidoscopic collection of seventy-five black-and-white photographs with personal comments about Mexico City as seen and experienced by young people. From an eleven-year-old drug addict who lives in one of Mexico City's worst slums to adolescents who live in Mexico's most exclusive neighborhoods, these photographs and comments present the reality of Mexico City in the 1990s. Reluctant Spanish-speaking readers will especially appreciate the brief text reflecting the vernacular of Mexico City youth; others will find the introduction and self-portraits most informative.

Castillo, Ana. *My Daughter, My Son, the Eagle, the Dove: An Aztec Chant.* Illus.: Susan Guevara. New York: Dutton, 2000. 48p. ISBN: 0-525-45856-5. $12.99. Gr. 7-adult.

With a few adaptations by Ana Castillo, this English rendition of a *huehuehtlatolli*—Mexica (Aztec) teachings that were meant to instruct young people about life—is a sample of the intellectual creations of the people of ancient Mexico. Maintaining the earnest and deeply felt tone of the original that parents and other adults will especially appreciate, it tells about pain and sadness, laughter, honor, duty, and concludes with a parent's universal wish: "May the gods give you a long and happy life. . . . " Guevara's illustrations which combine elements taken directly from the *Codex Mendoza*, a post-Hispanic account of early sixteenth-century Aztec life, with contemporary views of young people's lives painted on *amate* (Mexican bark) paper, are a most appropriate visual response to this time-honored Aztec creation.

Climo, Shirley. *The Little Red Ant and the Great Big Crumb: A Mexican Fable.* Illus.: Francisco X. Mora. New York: Clarion Books, 1995. 40p. ISBN: 0-395-70732-3. $14.95. Gr. K-3.

A little red ant finds a big crumb, but she's not strong enough to carry it all the way to the anthill. She asks *El Hombre, El Coyote, El Gallo, El Sol,* and *El Largato* to help her, until she discovers that she is the strongest of all. Bold, lively watercolors add a special flair to this buoyant rendition of a Spanish/Mexican tale with the underlying theme "You can do it if you think you can." An appropriate glossary of Spanish words with pronunciations will assist non-Spanish speakers.

Coburn, Jewell Reinhart, adapter. *Domitila: A Cinderella Tale from the Mexican Tradition.* Illus.: Connie McLennan. Auburn, CA: Shen's Books, 2000. 32p. ISBN: 1-885008-13-9. $16.95. Gr. 3-5.

Domitila, a poor young Mexican girl, is a talented cook and leather artist. Her mother's teachings incessantly encourage her to "do every task with care, and always add a generous dash of love." So even though the family is suffering terrible hardships, she makes a lasting impression on Timoteo, an arrogant politician's son, who ultimately is transformed into a compassionate governor and loving husband. McLennan's colorful oil-on-canvas illustrations depict traditional rural Mexican scenes with a dash of nostalgia in this variation of the Cinderella theme. Especially touching to Latino young readers (and their parents) are the well-translated popular Mexican proverbs (rendered in both Spanish and English) that border the text.

Cowan, Catherine, adapter. *My Life with the Wave.* Based on the story by Octavio Paz. Illus.: Mark Buehner. Translated by Catherine Cowan. New York: Lothrop, Lee & Shepard Books, 1997. 30p. ISBN: 0-688-12660X-X. $16.00; lib. ed. ISBN: 0-688-12661-8. $15.93. Gr. K-4.

This imaginative rendition of Octavio Paz's short story by the same title maintains the excitement and flavor of the original in a flowing language that young readers can understand. Buehner's powerful, humorous acrylic and oil paintings beautifully capture a young boy's special friendship with the wave as it progresses from a friendly, loving wave to a moody, monstrous wave that has to be carried back to the sea. To be sure, this is a wonderful introduction in the English language to the work of Mexico's Nobel Prize laureate, Octavio Paz.

Crawford, Mark. *Encyclopedia of the Mexican-American War.* Santa Barbara, CA: ABC-CLIO, 1999. 349p. ISBN: 1-57607-059-X. $75.00. Gr. 9-adult.

The purpose of this encyclopedia is "to increase the reader's awareness of the Mexican-American War by exploring people and events—some big, some small, but all of them important" (p.xiii). Arranged alphabetically in 458 brief entries—from two paragraphs to four pages—taken from primary and secondary sources, the author provides a well-balanced view of the grievances, misunderstandings, and reactionary responses that resulted in "one of the least-understood conflicts in United States history. . . . Yet it had one of the highest United States mortality rates of any United States war, gave the United States California and the Southwest, and devastated the struggling new Republic of Mexico . . . " (p.xiii). Students of the Mexican-American War will appreciate the author's concise introduction that summarizes the causes of this conflict, the chronology, and numerous references.

Day, Nancy. *Your Travel Guide to Ancient Mayan Civilization.* (Passport to History) Minneapolis, MN: Runestone Press/Lerner Publications, 2001. 96p. ISBN: 0-8225-3077-5. $26.60. Gr. 4-7.

Presented as a travel guide, this "passport to history" takes readers on an exciting journey back in time to experience life during the ancient Mayan civilization—600 to 800 A.D. Highlighting aspects of the culture that young readers can understand, such as cities to visit, sports and recreation, side trip trivia, and foods to try, it explains why the Mayan culture was one of the most brilliant and powerful cultures in ancient America. The only caveat in this otherwise lively introduction to the ancient Maya are the color photographs—several are too dark and unclear, detracting from the appeal of the sites.

Eboch, Chris. *The Well of Sacrifice.* Illus.: Bryn Barnard. New York: Clarion Books, 1999. 236p. ISBN: 0-395-90374-2. $16.00. Gr. 5-8.

Through Eveningstar Macaw, a courageous teenage girl, readers are exposed to life in a Mayan city in the ninth century, when the Mayan civilization was at its height. Some readers may be overwhelmed by the gory emphasis on the Mayan practices of human sacrifice and ritual bloodletting; others will be enthralled by the adventures of the strong-willed protagonist, who, despite the odds, succeeds in avenging her brother's death and saving herself from an ambitious and contemptible high priest. As an exciting, fast-paced thriller that brings to life how a great Mayan city may have been abandoned, as well as other accouterments of Mayan civilization such as sumptuous markets and other details, this narrative can be appealing, if somewhat controversial. Unfortunately, the less-than-inspiring, black-and-white illustrations are intrusive and unsavory.

Ehlert, Lois. *Cuckoo/Cucú.* Translated by Gloria de Aragón Andújar. San Diego, CA: Harcourt Brace, 1997. 40p. ISBN: 0-15-200274-X. $16.00. Gr. Pre-2.

This exhilarating bilingual (Spanish-English) adaptation of the well-known Mayan tale about Cucú, a colorful bird who sings her sweet song all day tiring the other animals, but ends up earning their respect and gratitude, is simply told in both languages. Especially noteworthy are the bright paper-collage pictures that definitely convey the joyous Mexican crafts and folk art that inspired them.

Elya, Susan Middleton. *Eight Animals on the Town.* Illus.: Lee Chapman. New York: Putnam, 2000. 30p. ISBN: 0-399-23437-3. $15.99. Gr. 1-3.

In a carefree, rhyming text, liberally sprinkled with Spanish words, this jovial counting book depicts eight *animales* as they travel to the market to find their supper and dance all night long. Notably beguiling are Chapman's colorful oil paints on canvas-framed illustrations that joyously capture the cheerful spirit of Latino (more specifically Mexican) folk art and customs. From exquisite Mexican village scenes, to authentic market sites, to lively party and surreal rural settings, these illustrations are pure fun. The only caveat in what could have been a most engaging selection for bilingual readers or Spanish-language learners is the lack of the Spanish definite articles, which must agree in number and gender with the noun they accompany and are used very frequently in Spanish. Unfortunately, these are missing in the glossary and in the borders. How are children going to learn that it is *el baile, la leche,* etc.?

Encyclopedia of Mexico: History, Society & Culture. Edited by Michael S. Werner. Chicago: Fitzroy Dearborn Publishers, 1997. Vol. I, 764p.; Vol. II, 984p. ISBN: 1-884964-31-1. $250.00. Gr. 9-adult.

Designed to be a useful component for courses on Mexico in the social sciences and humanities, this comprehensive encyclopedia, primarily historical in scope, provides, in a straight alphabetical format, longer articles as well as basic information on specific historical events, figures, and institutions of the history of Mexico. Articles vary in length—from one page on such topics as "Superbarrio" to fifteen pages on "Education." Serious students interested in acquiring a broad overview of Mexico, as well as a deeper understanding of contemporary Mexico, will not be disappointed.

Fine, Edith Hope. *Under the Lemon Moon.* Illus.: René King Moreno. New York: Lee & Low Books, 1999. 32p. ISBN: 1-880000-69-5. $15.95. Gr. 2-4.

Set in rural Mexico, this story features Rosalinda, a young Mexican girl, who is awakened one night to find the Night Man stealing the lemons from her beloved tree. With the help of *La Anciana* and others in her community, Rosalinda finds a way to help both her sick tree and the poor man and his family "with their worn clothes and hungry faces." Despite an empty cart, Rosalinda's heart "was as full as a lemon moon." The soft watercolor and pastel illustrations depict romanticized views of Mexican people and village scenes. Numerous words and phrases in Spanish, interspersed throughout, can be understood in context. Notwithstanding the not-so-subtle moralistic intent, this is a nostalgic view of Mexico and its people. (A glossary of Spanish words is also included.)

Fisher, Leonard Everett. *Gods and Goddesses of the Ancient Maya.* New York: Holiday House, 1999. 32p. ISBN: 0-8234-1427-2. $16.95. Gr. 4-7.

Twelve of the most important Mayan gods are introduced through bold, brightly colored illustrations on one page and a few informative paragraphs on the facing page. A succinct three-page introduction highlights Mayan achievements in mathematics, and a pronunciation guide, bibliography, and explanation of the Mayan numbering system conclude this colorful, understandable guide to Mayan mythology.

Geeslin, Campbell. *How Nanita Learned to Make Flan.* Illus.: Petra
Mathers. New York: Atheneum BFYR/Simon & Schuster, 1999.
26p. ISBN: 0-689-81546-8. $16.00. Gr. K-3.

Set in a Mexican town where Nanita's father is the only shoe-
maker but is too busy to make shoes for his daughter, the young
protagonist's hard work and perseverance prevail. Especially when
Nanita makes her own shoes, which take her far away to a mean
ranchero's house. After *Señor* Parrot teaches her to make the best
flan and helps her to go back home to papa, Nanita is able to celebrate her First Communion. Of course, at the fiesta, everyone
enjoys Nanita's delicious flan. Lighthearted folk-art-style
watercolors depicting whimsical scenes of rural Mexico add a
tinge of Mexican fantasy to this original fairy tale. A not-so-simple
recipe of Nanita's flan is included.

Gerson, Mary-Joan. *Fiesta Femenina: Celebrating Women in Mexican
Folktale.* Illus.: Maya Christina Gonzalez. New York: Barefoot
Books, 2001. 64p. ISBN: 1-84148-365-6. $19.99. Gr. 4-8.

To celebrate the special talents and extraordinary aspects of
Mexican women, Gerson relates eight popular Mexican tales that
feature powerful women. Especially appealing for younger
children is "Why the Moon Is Free," which shows the Moon gig-
gling with pleasure as she outwits the Sun. Older children, particularly from Mexico, will recognize two old-time favorites: "The
Virgin of Guadalupe," which re-creates the appearance of Our
Lady of Guadalupe to Juan Diego, and "Malintzin of the
Mountain," which recounts the importance of this Aztec princess
in the conquest of Mexico. Gonzalez's lavish acrylic paintings and
Gerson's spirited retellings combine to make this a joyous fiesta of
Mexican folklore. A well-done introduction, source notes,
glossary, and pronunciation guide add to its usefulness.

Gerson, Mary-Joan. *People of Corn: A Mayan Story.* Illus.: Carla
Golembe. Boston: Little, Brown, 1995. 32p. ISBN: 0-316-30854-4.
$15.95. Gr. 2-4.

Based on the *Popol Vuh*, the Mayan sacred book, this book
tells the Mayan creation story, recounting the gods' several unsuccessful attempts to create grateful people who would thank and
praise their creators. Even though this is an accessible rendition of
the Mayan creation tale, youngsters will not enjoy reading it by
themselves. Nonetheless, this is an excellent book to enrich the
study of Mayan culture. A brief and well-written author's note as

well as a closing source note make this myth more appealing. In addition, Golembe's bold and colorful gouache paintings certainly depict the majesty of the Mayan landscape and people.

Goldstein, Ernest. *The Journey of Diego Rivera.* Minneapolis, MN: Lerner Publications, 1996. 104p. ISBN: 0-8225-2066-4. $17.21. Gr. 7-12.

This journey focuses on Diego Rivera's murals, which portray the history of Mexico as well as his depictions of capitalists as the exploiters of downtrodden workers. Goldstein's enthusiastic analysis of Rivera's art and creative development is rendered in an almost scholarly, yet easy-to-understand, text. In addition, readers/ viewers will obtain glimpses of the artist's vivacity: "For the rest of his life his reputation would suffer from his erratic behavior" (p.19). This attractive volume is only marred by numerous spelling errors as well as a few blurred illustrations.

Gollub, Matthew. *Uncle Snake.* Illus.: Leovigildo Martinez. New York: Tambourine Books/Morrow, 1996. 32p. ISBN: 0-688-13944-2. $16.00. Gr. 3-5.

Inspired by an ancient belief from Oaxaca, Mexico, and maintaining Mexican storytelling techniques and characters, Gollub tells what happens when a fearless boy ventures into the forbidden cave: His face is changed into that of a snake and no *curandero* can change him back to what he was. Only the *nahual*, a magic worker who lives on top of a faraway mountain, knows that the answer is in the clouds. Martinez's watercolor spreads provide the perfect ambiance and authentic Mexican setting to this original story. The author's note will further assist readers in understanding pre-Hispanic folklore and motifs.

Gonzalez, Ralfka. *My First Book of Proverbs/Mi primer libro de dichos.* Illus.: Ana Ruiz. Emeryville, CA: Children's Book Press, 1995. 32p. ISBN: 0-89239-134-0. $15.95. Gr. 3-7.

Twenty-seven proverbs collected by the authors in Mexico and the United States are included in this bilingual book. Vivid, watercolor illustrations in bright Mexican colors depict Mexican themes framed by geometric Mexican-type designs. These are sure to catch the eye of all listeners/readers.

Helly, Mathilde, and Rémi Courgeon. *Montezuma and the Aztecs*. (W5
Series/Henry Holt Reference Book) New York: Henry Holt, 1996.
96p. ISBN: 0-8050-5060-4. $19.95. Gr. 7-12.

As a zestful introduction to the Aztecs, this cleverly designed
large-format edition may be just right for students tired of traditional historical narratives. Each two-page spread is highlighted
by flashy magazine-style graphics, reworked paintings and
photographs, collages, numerous fonts, maps, and timelines, as
well as catchy chapter headings, such as "After Three Months of
Siege, Fat Rats Look Tasty," "Eat Your Heart Out," and "How
Cortés Tore Up His Return Ticket." Unfortunately, gory depictions
and emphasis of human sacrifice add to the sensationalistic style of
this book. Despite the minimal index and at times shocking-for-
effect content, this is an intriguing introduction to the Aztecs, their
leaders, lifestyle, and conquerors.

Johnston, Tony. *The Magic Maguey*. Illus.: Elisa Kleven. San Diego,
CA: Harcourt Brace, 1996. 32p. ISBN: 0-15-250988-7. $15.00. Gr.
K-3.

The people of a small pueblo in Mexico love their huge
maguey that grows on Don César's land. But Miguel is especially
fond of his maguey as it provides shade in which to do his lessons
and to play with his friends. So when Don César threatens to cut
the plant after Christmas, Miguel comes up with a plan that saves
the maguey and makes everyone happy. Kleven's festive mixed-
media collage with watercolors, pastels, and cut paper, which
glitters with the colors and folk arts of rural Mexico, provides a
buoyant tone to this rather predictable yet appealing story. The
sprinkling of Spanish words intermingled in the text add to the
Mexican ambiance. Some Latino readers/viewers may be bothered
by the curio-type portrayal of Mexico, but this joyous story,
balanced with other books on contemporary Mexico, will provide
fun reading/viewing, especially at Christmastime.

Joose, Barbara M. *Ghost Wings*. Illus.: Giselle Potter. San Francisco:
Chronicle Books, 2001. 34p. ISBN: 0-8118-2164-1. $15.95. Gr.
K-3.

Set at the Magic Circle, a place in the Mexican forest where
monarch butterflies begin their journey north, a young Mexican
girl fondly remembers the day her grandmother died. With warmth
and affection, she tells about their special relationship and activities they enjoyed. Especially touching are the Day of the Dead

celebrations when the family sets up the *ofrenda*, cleans the grave, sings Grandmother's favorite songs, and reminisces together. It is unfortunate that the soft ink, watercolor, and colored pencil illustrations, which beautifully depict the setting and ambience of the Mexican countryside, fail to convey the family's closeness and heartfelt emotions. The informative appendixes on the Day of the Dead and monarch butterflies will be appreciated by fans of Mexico.

Kimmel, Eric A. *Montezuma and the Fall of the Aztecs*. Illus.: Daniel San Souci. New York: Holiday House, 2000. 32p. ISBN: 0-8234-1452-3. $16.95. Gr. 3-5.

The fall of the Aztec Empire and the Spanish conquest of Mexico are recounted in a lively narrative that highlights Montezuma's role as a powerful yet indecisive ruler. The author must be commended for including the most important people (Cortés, Malinche), and events in an account that even the young can understand. San Souci's double-page watercolors add immensely to young people's understanding of this dramatic encounter. Some historians may object to this somewhat oversimplified, almost sensationalistic, chronicle; yet, the basic facts are here. The author's note and glossary will be useful to the young, but not the bibliography, which includes mainly scholarly adult works.

Krauze, Enrique. *Mexico, Biography of Power: A History of Modern Mexico, 1810-1996*. Translated by Hank Heifetz. New York: HarperCollins Publishers, 1997. 872p. ISBN: 0-06-016325-9. $35.00. Gr. 9-adult.

Threading the lives of the most important leaders of Mexico during the last two centuries into a single biography of power, Krauze, a renowned Mexican historian, presents a most readable political history of his country from 1810 until 1996. Despite its length, serious students of Mexico will be fascinated to read many seldom spoken truths about its leaders. For example, about Father Miguel Hidalgo, he states: "He attended banquets, dances, ceremonies, plays, parades, gala functions where he accepted the homage of politicians, military men, and priests in the midst of banners, flags, exquisite refreshments, bursts of music, and peals of bells. . . . That priest-king could be munificent to some and terrible to others" (p.99). About Antonio López de Santa Anna: "The truth is that up until 1847 everybody thought of him as the savior of the nation. The vices and virtues that so marked him were not his alone but those of the Mexican people who incessantly sought him out and welcomed him, cheered and cursed him" (p.151). And about recent presidents he states: "Stories of the corruption current under [Miguel] Alemán would fill a long series of volumes" (p.555). About Adolfo López Mateos: "Within the country, a joke spread far and wide: 'When they take orders from López Mateos on the day's agenda, they ask, 'What do we do today, a trip or a woman? (. . . viaje o vieja?)'" (p.663). Either as an insightful interpretation of the making of modern Mexico or as a source for high-school report writers, this well-translated narrative with black-and-white photographs, chronology, and notes will be treasured by readers in search of a fresh perspective.

Kroll, Virginia. *Butterfly Boy*. Illus.: Gerardo Suzán. Honesdale, PA: Caroline House/Boyds Mills Press, 1997. 32p. ISBN: 1-56397-371-5. $15.95. Gr. K-4.
    Set in Mexico, this story depicts the love between Emilio and *Abuelo*, his grandfather who can no longer speak, but who loves to watch the butterflies as they flutter around the garage wall. When Emilio's father paints the garage blue, *Abuelo* becomes agitated and Emilio convinces his father to re-paint the garage white to continue to attract the butterflies. Suzán's surrealistic double-page illustrations done in watercolors, acrylics, and salt provide the right tone to this tender story about a happy Latino family and their love of nature and beauty.

Levitt, Helen. *Mexico City*. New York: Norton/Doubletake, 1997. 141p. ISBN: 0-393-04549-8. $35.00. Gr. 9-adult.
    Helen Levitt's stunning photographs of Mexico City in 1941 are depicted here with a most informative introduction by James Oles, translated also into Spanish. Levitt's sensitive and poignant photographs provide an uncensored view of the people who lived and worked in the working class districts of Mexico City. As a testament to the tragic lives of many residents of Mexican cities— the poor, the downtrodden, and the crippled—this admirable volume presents a prophetic vision that still resonates in Mexico today.

Lourie, Peter. *The Mystery of the Maya: Uncovering the Lost City of Palenque*. Honesdale, PA: Boyds Mills Press, 2001. 48p. ISBN: 1-56397-839-3. $19.95. Gr. 4-7.

Lourie relates his experiences in the Mexican jungle as he explores Palenque and the mystery of Maya history. From his encounter the first day with a fer-de-lance, one of the most poisonous snakes in Central America that can grow to eight feet long, to his visit to "one of the most sophisticated aqueduct systems anywhere in the world," to knowledgeable *curanderos*, this is an inviting view of the temples, fauna, flora, and people that contribute to the excitement of this pre-Columbian site. Numerous clear color photos, maps, glossary, and suggested readings are also included.

Lourie, Peter. *Rio Grande: From the Rocky Mountains to the Gulf of Mexico*. Honesdale, PA: Boyds Mill Press, 1999. 48p. ISBN: 1-56397-706-0. $17.95. Gr. 4-6.
See review pp. 98-99.

Macdonald, Fiona. *The Ancient Aztecs: Secrets of a Lost Civilization to Unlock and Discover*. Philadelphia: Running Press, 1996. 32p. ISBN: 1-56138-619-7. pap. $19.95. Gr. 4-7.
After unlocking a treasure chest, readers will find a fact-filled paperback publication that describes basic facts about the Aztec civilization from its origins up to the Spanish conquest. Also included is *Patolli*, an Aztec game, an Aztec flute, feathers for a headdress, a pendant, and beads for a necklace. Unfortunately, the small size of the book limits its appeal, but this is a comprehensive introduction to the Aztecs.

Marzollo, Jean. *Soccer Cousins*. Illus.: Irene Trivas. New York: Scholastic, 1997. 48p. ISBN: 0-590-74254-X. pap. $3.99. Gr. 2-4.
The excitement of soccer and the special emotions of the Day of the Dead celebration in Mexico are beautifully combined in this fast-moving story about David, a Mexican American boy, who visits his cousin Miguel in Mexico. David's initial experiences playing soccer leave him depressed and frustrated. But practicing soccer with Miguel is fun and *Abuelito*'s kind spirit certainly helped during the big game. The colorful illustrations and a few Spanish words interspersed in the narrative add a most authentic "Mexican" feeling to this story that all children will enjoy.

McDermott, Gerald. *Musicians of the Sun*. New York: Simon & Schuster, 1997. 40p. ISBN: 0-689-80706-6. $17.00. Gr. K-4.
McDermott's dignified retelling of the Aztec myth features the principal Aztec deity, Tezcatlipoca, and the wind god, Ecehatl, as

they battle Tonatiuh, the sun god, to bring music and color to earth. The double-page spreads, rendered in acrylic fabric paint, opaque ink, and oil pastel on paper handmade in Mexico are vintage McDermott with a strong Aztec flavor. This is indeed a wonderful introduction to Aztec traditions and beliefs that the young can understand.

Mora, Pat. *Uno, dos, tres, One, Two, Three.* Illus.: Barbara Lavallee. New York: Clarion Books, 1996. 43p. ISBN: 0-395-67294-5. $14.95. Gr. Pre-2.

The numbers 1 to 10 in English and Spanish provide the background for a wonderful rhyming text about two sisters who enjoy themselves while gathering presents from a Mexican market for Mama's birthday. This is not a simple counting book; rather, it is a joyous celebration of Mexican folk arts through luminous watercolors, which feature Mexican-type designs and characters with an intermingling of Spanish and English words and phrases.

Oppenheimer, Andres. *Bordering on Chaos: Guerrillas, Stockbrokers, Politicians and Mexico's Road to Prosperity.* Boston: Little, Brown, 1996. 367p. ISBN: 0-316-65095-1. $25.95. Gr. 10-adult.

Mexico's political and economic crises of the mid-1990s are described in a fast-paced narrative that highlights the inefficiencies and corruption of the Mexican government and questions the responsibility of the United States government, Wall Street executives, and the United States media in many of Mexico's recent turbulent events. In a forthright manner, Oppenheimer, a senior Latin American correspondent for the *Miami Herald*, depicts a "system without checks and balances, where the government had always been able to buy off the most influential media and write history at its will" (p.36); and "Mexico's autocratic system, its lack of transparency, and the gullibility of international money managers had ended up deceiving everybody—except for the small group of Mexican insiders who made millions from being in the right government office at the right time" (p.234). Serious students of contemporary Mexico will value Oppenheimer's insights, analysis, and reports as he notes the growing disputes between Mexico and the United States.: "Virtually every major United States newspaper had written long exposés on Mexico's increasingly powerful drug cartels in recent times, but there were few—if any—references to their United States counterparts" (p.312).

Parker, Edward. *Mexico.* (Country Insights) Austin, TX: Raintree Steck-Vaughn, 1998. 48p. ISBN: 0-8172-4791-2. $17.48. Gr. 4-6.

By contrasting life in Puebla, a city in central Mexico, and in Celestún, a fishing village on the Yucatán Peninsula, readers are exposed to many aspects about the land, climate, home life, work, education, recreation, and future of Mexico. Numerous color photos and an easy-to-read text make this well-designed book a good choice for readers interested in an overview of Mexico in the late 1990s.

Pascoe, Elaine. *Mexico and the United States: Cooperation and Conflict.* New York: Twenty-First Century Books, 1996. 126p. ISBN: 0-8050-4180-X. $17.98. Gr. 7-12.

In a most readable and objective manner, Pascoe describes the important conflicts and issues that have existed between the United States and Mexico, beginning with a Spanish settlement on the banks of the Rio Grande in 1598 up to 1996 when illegal immigration and drug trafficking take center stage. By reviewing key historical controversies, the author explains how unfair stereotypes continue to color relations between the two countries: "To many Americans, Mexicans were backward revolutionaries and bandits who needed to be 'saved'—rich, brash, arrogant, and domineering" (p.55). Readers interested in understanding the complex issues facing this difficult relationship should definitely start here. Six color photos, a chronology, and suggestions for further reading are also included.

Patent, Dorothy Hinshaw. *Quetzal: Sacred Bird of the Cloud Forest.* Illus.: Neil Waldman. New York: Morrow, 1996. 40p. ISBN: 0-688-12662-6. $16.00. Gr. 5-8.

Combining the story of the beautiful Quetzal, a unique bird with impressive tail feathers and brilliant iridescence, with the history of the Maya and other cultures of Mesoamerica, ancient beliefs about the god Quetzalcoatl, and the quetzal's life cycle, daily existence, and dangers for survival results in a narrative brimming with natural and pre-Columbian history. The softly shaded, colored-pencil drawings definitely blend well with the tone and spirit of this tribute to the quetzal. It is unfortunate that a photograph of the beautiful quetzal is not included. Nonetheless, this appealing blend of nature, history, and lore will strike a chord with naturalists-to-be as well as historians-to-be.

Platt, Richard. *Aztecs: The Fall of the Aztec Capital.* Illus.: Peter Denis. (DK Discoveries) New York: DK Ink, 1999. 48p. ISBN: 0-7894-3957-3. $14.95. Gr. 4-8.

Beginning with the Spanish conquest of Mexico in 1519, this handsomely illustrated book narrates the dramatic encounter between the Spaniards and the Aztecs that resulted with the end of the Mexica Empire and describes the Aztec way of life: social structure, life at court, war, religion, and writing. The sharp, clear, color photographs and drawings and the brief text highlighting the main characters and events make this a most accessible introduction to the Aztecs and the Spaniards in sixteenth-century Mexico.

Pohl, John M. D. *The Legend of Lord Eight Deer: An Epic of Ancient Mexico.* Illus.: the author. New York: Oxford University Press, 2002. 64p. ISBN: 0-19-514019-2. $17.95. Gr. 5-8.

The Mixtecs of ancient Mexico are introduced to young people through Pohl's vivid retelling of their great epic saga and stunning color illustrations based on their ancient codices. Interspersed in the narrative are informative overviews about the Mixtec nation, ritual dress, personal adornment, codices, and battles, followed by an author's afterword explaining his work. A cast of characters and a chronology will assist readers as they relive Lord Eight Deer's quest to rule his kingdom amid cruel battles, family murders, bloody tyrants, and noble women.

Pringle, Laurence. *An Extraordinary Life: The Story of a Monarch Butterfly.* Illus.: Bob Marstall. New York: Orchard Books, 1997. 32p. ISBN: 0-531-30002-1. $18.95; lib. ed. ISBN: 0-531-33002-8. $19.99. Gr. 3-7.

Through the everyday life of one monarch butterfly, readers are introduced to the butterfly's migratory route from Massachusetts to the mountains of central Mexico. The author explains that due to the poverty of nearby communities, the Mexican overwintering sites, where millions of monarchs gather, are in grave danger. But the main focus of this most informative book is to highlight one monarch's life from an egg's translucent shell through her metamorphosis to her flight south, her mating, migration, and death. Marstall's colorful paintings, numerous sidebars, and maps add further to this engrossing narrative about the life cycle, feeding habits, migration, predators, and mating of the monarch butterfly.

Serrano, Francisco. *Our Lady of Guadalupe*. Illus.: Félipe Dávalos. Toronto: Groundwood Books/Distributed by Publishers Group West, 1998. 14p. ISBN: 0-88899-335-8. $16.95. Gr. 3-6.

The miraculous appearance of the Virgin Mary to Juan Diego, a humble Mexican Indian, in 1531 is narrated in this simple English rendition. Of special interest to children are the strikingly elaborate full-page pop-ups, pullouts, and other illustrated devices that burst open to depict well-known episodes of this popular tradition-legend of all Catholics of Mexico. In contrast to the more intricate Spanish adaptation from the original Nican Mopohua, this English rendition is perfectly understandable by young readers as they discover the legend of the Lady of Guadalupe who, adorned with gold and precious gems, asked Juan Diego to tell the bishop in Mexico City to build a church in her honor.

Stanley, Diane. *Elena*. New York: Hyperion Books for Children, 1996. 55p. ISBN: 0-7868-0256-1. $13.95. Gr. 3-5.

Set in Mexico around the time of the Mexican Revolution, this story recounts Elena's life as a wealthy, proper, young lady who prefers to read and to study rather than to serve and marry a rich man. Despite her father's opposition, she chooses to marry Pablo, the son of a poor Tarascan Indian who works on a big hacienda. Later, when the Mexican Revolution slashed its beautiful country, Elena has to save herself and her family by heading north to the United States. Young readers interested in Mexican culture/history will enjoy this fictionalized account in which Mexico, its people, and its history take center stage.

Steele, Philip. *The Aztec News*. Illus.: Katherine Baxter and others. Cambridge, MA: Candlewick Press, 1997. 32p. ISBN: 0-7636-0115-2. $15.99; pap. ISBN: 0-7636-0427-5. $6.99. Gr. 4-7.

Presented as a special edition newspaper including news stories, classified ads, cartoons, cultural reports, and a lifestyle section, this oversized book highlights the achievements, major events, important rulers, and daily life of the Aztecs. Written in colloquial, modern language and heavily illustrated, it is an accessible introduction that begins with the founding of Tenochtitlán and ends with a timeline in 1522 when the city is named Mexico City and declared the capital of New Spain.

Stein, R. Conrad. *The Mexican Revolution: 1910-1920.* (A Timestop
  Book) New York: New Discovery Books/Silver Burdett, 1994.
  160p. ISBN: 0-02-786950-4. $14.95. Gr. 6-9.

  The issues and personalities surrounding the Mexican
Revolution are described in an easy-to-read narrative. Stein
explains the reasons that led to the revolution, the leaders' brutal
struggle for power that resulted in the death of two million
Mexicans, and Obregón's new society with its literary and artistic
renaissance. Numerous black-and-white photos add immediacy to
this tragic time in Mexico's history. Biographical sketches of some
of the main protagonists of the revolution are also included. It is
interesting to note the author's likes and dislikes: He describes
Francisco Villa "as a brute who considered rape to be a legitimate
method of seducing a woman. He was a cold-blooded killer who
was known to laugh while gunning down another man" (p.109).
And, "Emiliano Zapata was the Revolution's shining star.
Unselfish, completely devoted to his followers, and fearless in battle, he is regarded as the upheaval's greatest leader" (p.143). Many
Mexican historians will question these extreme assertions; others
will certainly concur.

Swope, Sam. *Gotta Go! Gotta Go!* Illus.: Sue Riddle. New York:
  Farrar, Straus & Giroux, 2000. 32p. ISBN: 0-374-32757-2. $12.00.
  Gr. K-2.

  A teeny-tiny creepy-crawly bug does not know why or how,
but she is certain that she must make her way to Mexico. In a
rhythmic repetitive text and with simple line-and-watercolor illustrations, Swope and Riddle describe this tiny bug's migration from
the United States to the mountains of Mexico where she and millions of bugs like her mate before flying north to lay their eggs.
This is an ingenuous fictional rendition of the yearly autumnal
migration of monarch butterflies that continues to amaze scientists.
A brief author's note about the monarch butterflies' long journey is
also included.

Tanaka, Shelley. *Lost Temple of the Aztecs.* (I Was There) Illus.: Greg
  Ruhl. New York: Hyperion/Madison Press, 1998. 48p. ISBN: 0-
  7868-0441-6. $16.95. Gr. 4-7.

  The best parts of this book are the wonderful color
photographs and numerous informative sidebars that describe the
discovery of the Great Aztec Temple in Mexico City, the last few
years of Moctezuma's empire, and the Spanish conquest, from

1519 to 1521. Unfortunately, the author's narrative sensationalizes the events and even Moctezuma's thoughts to such an extreme that the compelling story of the conquest of Mexico suffers by this unnecessary dramatization. Despite the regrettable narrative, the color photographs, illustrations, and appealing design make this an enticing introduction to the Aztecs and the Spanish conquest of Mexico.

The United States and Mexico at War. Nineteenth-Century Expansionism and Conflict. Edited by Donald S. Frazier. New York: Macmillan Reference USA, 1998. 584p. ISBN: 0-02-864606-1. $125.00. Gr. 9-adult.
See review p. 118.

Urrea, Luis Alberto. *By the Lake of Sleeping Children: The Secret Life of the Mexican Border.* New York: Anchor/Doubleday, 1996. 256p. ISBN: 0-385-48419-4. pap. $11.00. Gr. 9-adult.

In a vivid, powerful manner, this first-person reportage describes the post-NAFTA and Proposition 187 effects on the life of garbage pickers, dump dwellers, orphans, and unsuspecting women trapped in the Mexican border with the United States. Frankly and candidly, Urrea, an American citizen born in Tijuana, discusses the political and economic issues between the two countries that condone border crossings and the extreme poverty that results in alcoholism, animal cruelty, and child abuse. This is indeed a forceful and distressing view into the lives of many Mexicans who endure alongside the United States border.

Urrutia, María Cristina, and Rebeca Orozco. *Cinco de Mayo: Yesterday and Today.* Toronto: Groundwood Books/Distributed by Publishers Group West, 1999. 32p. ISBN: 0-88899-355-2. $15.95. Gr. 2-4.

Using historical lithographs showing the Battle of Puebla against the French on May 5, 1862, and on facing pages a contemporary reenactment in the village of San Miguel Tlaixpan, this easy-to-read English rendition is drawn from oral accounts of the participants in the modern-day festival as well as reports by generals in the Mexican army. Originally published in Mexico, this is a simple overview for the young of a legendary encounter widely celebrated in Mexico.

Vázquez-Gómez, Juana. *Dictionary of Mexican Rulers, 1325-1997.* Westport, CT: Greenwood, 1997. 191p. ISBN: 0-313-30049-6. $65.00. Gr. 9-adult.

This well-organized guide to the rulers of Mexico—from Tenoch, the first Aztec "Warrior Leader," to President Ernesto Zedillo, whose term expired in 2000—provides an overview to the history of Mexico. Presented in chronological order and organized into four basic chapters that deal with four periods in history, readers in search of basic information about the men who have governed Mexico, either by popular election or by force, will not be disappointed. Perhaps serious students of Mexican history will question some of the author's assertions: for example, in her introduction to the legacy of the Spanish conquest, she states: "The conquest also brought about a much needed change in some of the more barbaric [?] traditions of the Mexicas" (p.15). Nonetheless, this is a useful reference book about Mexican rulers with concise information and elucidative appendixes.

Ward, Karen. *The Young Chef's Mexican Cookbook.* (I'm the Chef!) New York: Crabtree Publishing, 2001. 34p. ISBN: 0-7787-0281-2. $22.60; pap. ISBN: 0-7787-0295-2. $8.95. Gr. 4-7.

A multiethnic cast of boys and girls are shown as they joyfully prepare and savor fifteen common Mexican dishes. Clear, color step-by-step photographs and easy-to-follow directions to such Mexican favorites as *chilaquiles, sopa de tortilla, guacamole,* and *arroz mexicano* are included. A brief introduction on Mexican cooking, head notes highlighting historical information about each dish, and useful sidebars listing "Tips and Tricks," ingredients, and utensils make this a most enticing guide for gourmands or chefs-to-be.

Winter, Jeanette. *Josefina.* Illus.: the author. San Diego, CA: Harcourt Brace, 1996. 36p. ISBN: 0-15-201091-2. $15.00. Gr. Pre-3.

Through Josefina, a Mexican folk artist who makes painted clay figures in Ocotlán, Mexico, young readers/viewers are exposed to the charm, colors, and motifs of Mexican folk art. The vivid acrylic paintings richly illustrate Josefina's life—as a baby who watched as little clay figures filled her patio, to her marriage to José and the birth of her nine children who help paint Josefina's world. This is followed by a bilingual counting book describing Josefina's world: one sun, two angels, three houses . . . concluding with ten stars and a double-page spread that whimsically portrays some of Mexico's popular traditions. Either as a delightful counting book or as an introduction to Mexican folk arts, this picture book vibrates with the magic of Mexico.

Yacowitz, Caryn. *Pumpkin Fiesta*. Illus.: Joe Cepeda. New York: HarperCollins Publishers, 1998. 32p. ISBN: 0-06-027658-4. $14.95. Gr. Pre-1.

Despite the traditional stereotypical illustrations of rural Mexico—barefooted peasants, donkeys, sombreros—this humorous, cautionary tale about Foolish Fernando who tries to beat Old Juana and win the prize for the best pumpkin at the San Miguel fiesta will delight young listeners. Old Juana wins the pumpkin crown every year because of her dedication, hard work, and love of gardening. Foolish Fernando, on the other hand, is just a boastful copycat who does little to care for his pumpkins and ultimately steals Old Juana's biggest pumpkins. But justice and work are rewarded when Old Juana proves that the beautiful pumpkins are hers. Foolish Fernando apologizes to Old Juana and promises to pay attention and learn the secret of Pumpkin Hill. Spanish words sprinkled throughout the lively narrative add to the Mexican flavor of this pumpkin fiesta. It is unfortunate that the colorful oil paintings are caricatures of rural Mexico and its people.

Panama

Berrocal Essex, Olga. *Delia's Way.* Houston, TX: Arte Público Press, 1998. 186p. ISBN: 1-55885-232-8. pap. $12.95. Gr. 9-adult.

Set in Panama in the 1950s amid the prevailing machismo where "women live their lives under the thumb of one man or another. The father, the lover, the husband, the son. The priest that won't marry you . . . ," this evocative, coming-of-age novel tells about nine-year-old Delia, who is constantly bullied and dominated by her older sister, María Elena. In her quiet, resourceful manner, Delia manages to piece together family secrets that explain her mother's sudden anger and her sister's close relationship with their mother. This is indeed a touching Latino family saga with the added flavor of Panamanian politics, *carnaval*-time exuberance, and sibling rivalry.

Chambers, Veronica. *Marisol and Magdalena: The Sound of Our Sisterhood.* New York: Hyperion Books for Children, 1998. 191p. ISBN: 0-7868-2385-2. $20.49. Gr. 6-9.

Thirteen-year-old Marisol lives in Brooklyn with her mother who grew up in Panama, and she can't imagine life without her best friend Magda. Despite both girls' problems with the Spanish language, they enjoy Panamanian food, dances, and other family traditions. Suddenly, Marisol finds out that she will be spending one year in Panama with *Abuela*, her grandmother, whom she has never met. In a lively first-person narrative, this novel recounts Marisol's experiences in her family's homeland as well as her search for her own father, a man who is vilified by both her mother and grandmother. This is indeed a joyous, if somewhat contrived, rose-colored exploration with trite dialogue of a girl as she confronts the best of her black American and Panamanian cultural roots.

Gold, Susan Dudley. *The Panama Canal Transfer: Controversy at the Crossroads.* Austin, TX: Raintree Steck-Vaughn, 1999. 128p. ISBN: 0-8172-5762-4. $25.69. Gr. 7-10.

    Emphasizing the controversies, politics, and challenges to Panama as it assumes control of the canal, this well-documented history of the Panama Canal describes the building, conflicts, and negotiations that have taken place since 1903. In an evenhanded manner, Gold discusses such sensitive issues as corruption fears ("Will profits from the canal be used to modernize it, or will they go into the pockets of corrupt government officials and their friends and family?" [p.17]); the politics behind the ratification treaty; and the controversial United States invasion of Panama that "left Panama in shambles." Black-and-white photos, source notes, a glossary, and a bibliography complement this straightforward account of the transfer of the Panama Canal.

Lindop, Edmund. *Panama and the United States: Divided by the Canal.* New York: Twenty-First Century Books, 1997. 128p. ISBN: 0-8050-4768-9. $17.98. Gr. 6-9.

    Emphasizing the difficult political relations between the United States and Panama, this straightforward narrative discusses the history of the land and people of Panama and the importance of the Panama Canal that was "constructed, financed, operated, and protected by the United States government" (p.9). Included are chapters on the "ruthless dictator" Manuel Noriega, a "despicable criminal," who provoked a serious crisis in the relations between the two countries, and the United States' invasion of Panama in December 1989 that resulted in Noriega's being a federal prisoner in Miami. Lindop concludes that as the time for the evacuation of United States' interests in Panama approaches, there are new discussions "about the possibility of a continued United States military presence in the area of the Panama Canal after the scheduled departure of United States troops" (p.112). The delicate relationship between the two countries is handled here with great tact; hence, students will benefit from the author's evenhanded approach. A chronology and suggestions for further reading are also included.

Markun, Patricia Maloney. *It's Panama's Canal!* North Haven, CT: Linnet Books, 1999. 112p. ISBN: 0-208-02499-9. $22.50. Gr. 6-9.

    In a straightforward text, Markun discusses in the first half of the book the history and operation of the Panama Canal, and in the second half, the "seamless transition of . . . how to move from American management of the Panama Canal to Panamanian control without a difference in the operating efficiency of this waterway, so long respected around the world" (p.61). She explains that a basic change is that the Panama Canal will be run for profit; hence, toll rates have been raised five times since 1978. She questions Latin American nepotism especially when four people named to the Interoceanic Region Authority who "know nothing about handling real estate or selling power plants" (p.93) are relatives of former president Balladares or his wife. Black-and-white photos, a chronology of events, a bibliography, and an index contribute to making this a good introduction to the issues surrounding the new ownership of the Panama Canal.

Parker, Nancy Winslow. *Locks, Crocs, & Skeeters: The Story of the Panama Canal.* New York: Greenwillow Books, 1996. 32p. ISBN: 0-688-12241-8. $16.00. Gr. 3-5.

    The history of the "eighth wonder of the world"—the Panama Canal—is told in an amusing poem, along with brief biographical sketches of individual explorers, engineers, and political leaders, and an informative text about the costs, operation, and uses of the Panama Canal today. Numerous clear, detailed maps and amusing illustrations in black ink, watercolors, and colored pencil on every page add a touch of lightness to this historical overview of one of the greatest engineering achievements of all time.

Presilla, Maricel E. *Mola: Cuna Life Stories and Art.* New York: Henry Holt, 1996. 32p. ISBN: 0-8050-3801-9. $16.95. Gr. 3-6.

    This is a joyous introduction to Cuna people and culture through *molas*—colorful blouses made of many rectangular pieces of fabric of different colors and textures. Excellent full-color photographs of the *molas* and a simple text provide a cheerful overview of the history, customs, daily life, and folklore of these matrilineal people who live on the San Blás Islands off the northern coast of Panama.

Peru

Abelove, Joan. *Go and Come Back*. New York: DK Ink, 1998. 178p. ISBN: 0-7894-2476-2. $16.95. Gr. 8-12.

Set in the Amazonian jungle of Peru, along the eastern slopes of the Andes, this fictional account about two white women anthropologists from New York who lived among the villagers for one year details the clash of cultures between the "Isabos," who live much as their ancestors have for centuries, and the strange white ladies who wear pants, and maybe had sex with dogs. Written from the point of view of one of the Peruvian teenagers, this novel impresses upon the reader that "normal" behavior is only what one is accustomed to and how often what one doesn't know is considered negatively. Hence, the villagers and the New Yorkers have completely different views on sex, marriage, parties, stealing, lying, death, and motherhood. This novel is especially appealing to anthropologists-to-be, who can experience the misunderstandings between two very different cultures.

Aronson, Marc. *Sir Walter Ralegh and the Quest for El Dorado*. New York: Clarion Books, 2000. 222p. ISBN: 0-395-84827-X. $20.00. Gr. 7-10.
See review p. 72.

Hinds, Kathryn. *The Incas*. (Cultures of the Past) New York: Benchmark Books/Marshall Cavendish, 1998. 80p. ISBN: 0-7614-0270-5. $19.95. Gr. 6-9.

Like other titles in this series, this is a sprightly and colorful introduction to the history, culture, religion, and social structure of the ancient Incas. Divided into five chapters, the smooth narrative with well-organized subheadings is further complemented by a most appealing design, excellent graphics, well-selected pictures, and chatty, full- and half-page sidebars on such topics as the Incas'

Sacred Plant (coca) and the Incas' Afterlife. A chronology, glossary, and index are also included.

Jermyn, Leslie. *Peru.* (Festivals of the World) Milwaukee, WI: Gareth Stevens Publishing, 1998. 32p. ISBN: 0-8368-2006-1. $18.60. Gr. 3-5.

The color, excitement, and traditions of festivals in Peru are described through a simple text and colorful photographs on every page. Like other titles in this series, this is not an in-depth discussion of "fiestas" in Peru; rather, it is a vivid introduction for the young to numerous celebrations in Peru such as *Inti Raymi*, the Inca festival of the sun, Corpus Christi, Puno Day, and others. A glossary and craft activities—sun god mask and *natilla* recipe—are also included.

Macdonald, Fiona. *Inca Town.* (Metropolis) Illus.: Mark Bergin. New York: Franklin Watts, 1998. 45p. ISBN: 0-531-14480-1. $24.00. Gr. 4-7.

Through appealing drawings and simple texts, readers are taken on a tour of Cuzco, the Inca capital at the end of the fifteenth century, before the arrival of the Spaniards. They visit the royal palace, a fortress, the Temple of the Sun, the Sun Maidens' house, the main square, roads and bridges, and other highlights of Inca civilization. Two additional guides—a Time-Traveler's and Guided Tours—provide further information about Inca food, clothing, festivals, the empire, etc. A glossary and an index add to the value of this sprightly introduction to Inca people and culture.

Mann, Elizabeth. *Machu Picchu.* Illus.: Amy Crehore. (Wonders of the World) New York: Mikaya Press, 2000. 48p. ISBN: 0-9650493-9-6. $19.95. Gr. 3-5.

In an engrossing narrative, Mann describes the history of the Incas and the construction of Machu Picchu, the ancient Inca fortress city in the Andes. It highlights significant aspects of Inca civilization, such as their "15,000 miles of brilliantly engineering roads," their "ingenious way of keeping records . . . without the use of written language," and their religious beliefs, which "influenced everything they did." Unfortunately, most of the full-page illustrations are either insipid representations or gory scenes of bloody battles often depicting "Inka warriors [which] sounded as fierce as they looked" (p.15). More compelling and educational are the two color photographs. Students will appreciate the glossary, map, and index.

Martell, Hazel Mary. *Civilizations of Peru before 1535.* (Looking Back) Austin, TX: Raintree Steck-Vaughn, 1999. 63p. ISBN: 0-8172-5428-5. $28.55. Gr. 5-8.

In a well-organized and appealing format, this book describes several of the most important ancient civilizations of Peru and parts of what are now Ecuador, Bolivia, Argentina, and Chile. Beginning with the Chavin civilization to the Paraca, Nazca, Moche, Tiahuanaco, Huari, Chimu, and, finally, the Inca, it provides an overview of their archaeological and artistic achievements as well as everyday lives and eventual decline and conquest. Despite a sometimes "text bookish" narrative, students will be attracted by the numerous clear, color photos and "A Closer Look" boxes, which highlight special topics. A timeline, glossary, bibliography, and index make it even more useful to students.

Newman, Shirlee P. *Isabella: A Wish for Miguel, Peru, 1820.* Illus.: Laurie Harden. (Girlhood Journeys) New York: Aladdin Paperbacks/Simon & Schuster, 1997. 70p. ISBN: 0-689-81572-7. pap. $5.99. Gr. 3-6.

Similar in style to the American Girls series, this is a well-done depiction of life in Peru in the 1800s through the tale of Isabella, a young girl, who tries desperately to save a young male servant from being sent to the mines where native Indians are forced to work under inhuman conditions. Despite a few plot contrivances and some unnaturally stiff illustrations, this is an engaging story with pleasing, albeit small, color illustrations about Isabella's struggle upon the death of her mother and her relationship with her still-mourning father. The lack of children's books on Peru during the Spanish colonial period makes this an especially desirable title. An afterword, Journey to 1820, provides further information about the history of Peru.

Reinhard, Johan. *Discovering the Inca Ice Maiden: My Adventures on Ampato.* Washington, DC: National Geographic Society, 1998. 48p. ISBN: 0-7922-7142-4. $17.95. Gr. 6-12.

In an engrossing first-person account, Reinhard, an anthropologist, narrates his 1995 discovery of the approximately 500-year-old Peruvian ice mummy on Mount Ampato and the subsequent retrieval and study of the girl who became known as the

Inca "Ice Maiden." Stunning, full-page color photographs of the
Peruvian Andes and Inca archaeological sites add interest to this
incredible discovery. A timeline, glossary, and index further complement this narrative, which provides interesting background
information on the Inca Empire as well as Inca customs and
beliefs.

Wood, Tim. *The Incas.* (See Through History) New York: Viking,
1996. ISBN: 0-670-87037-4. $16.99. Gr. 6-9.
    The Inca civilization is brought to life through attractive color
illustrations, see-through plastic overlays, and a straightforward
text. Brief, two-page chapters describe the origins, customs, daily
lives, religion, and government of the Incas as well as their significant achievements in the fields of engineering and transportation.
This attractive introduction to the Incas is further enhanced by a
timeline, a glossary, and an index.

Puerto Rico

Fernandez, Ronald, and others. *Puerto Rico Past and Present: An Encyclopedia.* Westport, CT: Greenwood, 1998. 375p. ISBN: 0-313-29822-X. $59.95. Gr. 8-adult.

More than 300 entries emphasizing the history, achievements, and creations of Puerto Rican people in the nineteenth and, particularly, the twentieth century are included in this ready-reference guide. Beginning with a historical introduction and a chronology of important events, readers will find such high-interest topics as *Nuyorican*, *salsa*, and *machismo* as well as the political leaders, poets, novelists, painters, and musicians who are, according to the authors, at the core of Puerto Rican culture.

Foley, Erin. *Puerto Rico.* (Festivals of the World) Milwaukee, WI: Gareth Stevens Publishing, 1997. 32p. ISBN: 0-8368-1687-0. $18.60. Gr. 3-5.

Festival time in Puerto Rico is described through a simple text and clear color photographs on every page. This is not an in-depth discussion of Puerto Rican *fiestas*; rather, it is a colorful invitation for the young to numerous and varied celebrations, such as San Sebastián, Santiago Apostol, *las Navidades* (Christmas season), and others. A glossary, craft activities, and a *Besitos de Coco* recipe add to this joyous view of Puerto Rican culture.

Harlan, Judith. *Puerto Rico: Deciding Its Future.* New York: Twenty-First Century Books, 1996. 127p. ISBN: 0-8050-4372-1. $17.98. Gr. 7-10.

Despite the matter-of-fact narrative, this comprehensive overview of the history of Puerto Rico, with a focus on current issues, provides a well-balanced approach. Beginning with the question, "What does it mean to be Puerto Rican?" to the ongoing political status debate, Harlan discusses such difficult topics as changes on the island, crime, drug trafficking, and AIDS. She also discusses migration to the mainland. A timeline, source notes, and numerous informative charts and inserts complement this introduction to Puerto Rican life, both on the island and on the mainland. Unfortunately, the very small typeface is an unpleasant detractor.

Jaffe, Nina. *The Golden Flower: A Taino Myth from Puerto Rico.* Illus.: Enrique O. Sánchez. New York: Simon & Schuster, 1996. 32p. ISBN: 0-689-80469-5. $16.00. Gr. K-3.

In a simple, flowing text, this retelling of the popular Taino myth explains the origin of the sea, the forest, and the beautiful island of Boriquén (Puerto Rico). Sánchez's glowing, stylized full-color illustrations dramatically convey the pre-Columbian ambiance and mood, which, "as the Taino say, between the sun and the sparkling blue sea, their island home—Boriquén—came to be" (unpaged). A well-written afterword provides further information about Taino people and culture.

London, Jonathan. *Hurricane!* Illus.: Henri Sorensen. New York: Lothrop, Lee & Shepard Books, 1998. 32p. ISBN: 0-688-12977-3. $16.00; lib. ed. ISBN: 0-688-12978-1. $15.95. Gr. K-3.

Exquisite double-spread oil paintings realistically and dramatically convey the experiences of a young boy and his family when a hurricane hits their home on the island of Puerto Rico. Set on El Yunque, the biggest mountain in Puerto Rico, and including such Puerto Rican distinctions as scorpions and *langostas* (lobsters), readers/viewers will sense the power of a hurricane, from crashing waves to strapping winds to a peaceful morning after, when the sky and sea are rosy and calm and the children can return to play at the beach.

Mohr, Nicholasa. *Old Letivia and the Mountain of Sorrows.* Illus.: Rudy Gutierrez. New York: Viking, 1996. 29p. ISBN: 0-670-84419-5. $15.99. Gr. 1-3.

Mohr's original folktale, set on the ancient island of Borinquen, which one day would become Puerto Rico, tells how Old Letivia, a magic healer, and her friends use her supernatural powers to conquer the evil forces of the Mountain of Sorrows. The richly colored, surrealistic illustrations will have a special appeal for older, more sophisticated readers/viewers. All readers, however, will applaud as the story's magical characters—Old Letivia, a healer disguised as a woman; Cervantes, a whistling turtle; and tiny Símon, a boy no bigger than a coffee pot—find a way to win both respect and riches despite Wild Wind's threats. Liberally sprinkled with Spanish words and numerous elements from Puerto Rican culture, this story has a real Puerto Rican aura.

Montes, Marisa. *Juan Bobo Goes to Work: A Puerto Rican Folktale.* Illus.: Joe Cepeda. New York: HarperCollins Publishers, 2000. 32p. ISBN: 0-688-16233-9. $15.95. Gr. Pre-3.

This amusing retelling features Juan Bobo, the foolish folk hero of Puerto Rico, who never gets anything right. Here he manages to repeatedly confuse his mother's instructions and lose all his pay but when he makes the rich girl laugh, her father repays him with a ham every Sunday. Spanish speakers will especially enjoy the wonderful Spanish words and idiomatic expressions that are perfectly understood in context. Cepeda's bright, humorous watercolors, which beautifully depict the highlands of Puerto Rico, add to Juan Bobo's delightful foolishness.

Santiago, Esmeralda. *Almost a Woman.* Reading, MA: Perseus Books/ Merloyd, 1998. 313p. ISBN: 0-7382-0043-3. $24.00. Gr. 9-adult.

Following her engrossing life story, *When I Was Puerto Rican* (1993), Santiago's new coming-of-age memoir begins with her family's arrival in Brooklyn in 1961. It recounts her mother's objections to her children's "Americanized" interests, the junior high school gang that made her life a terrible nightmare, her grandmother's drinking, her mother's constant pregnancies, the embarrassing visits to the welfare office, and her own successes at the Performing Arts High School as well as her first boyfriends and sexual experiences. Especially touching are Santiago's feelings toward her strict mother who, despite adolescent quarrels, she loves and understands. This is indeed a wonderful memoir about an immigrant's family's experiences in New York amid the perils of poverty and the love of family and Puerto Rican culture.

Tamar, Erika. *Alphabet City Ballet.* New York: HarperCollins Publishers, 1996. 168p. ISBN: 0-06-027328-3. $14.95; lib. ed. ISBN: 0-06-027329-1. $14.89. Gr. 5-8.

Ten-year-old Marisol is proud to have won a scholarship to ballet school, but there are too many obstacles to overcome before her dream can come true. Her Puerto Rican father cannot leave work to take her to class, and Luis, her fifteen-year-old brother, is tempted into the world of drugs and violence. Set in New York

City, this well-paced novel will be especially appealing to balleto-
manes, who can empathize with the demands and beauty of this art
form. The Puerto Rican ambiance adds flavor too, except when the
author insists: ". . . his minute was in Puerto Rican time and could
last half an hour" (p.3). And, "They said three-thirty. They were
late. Maybe Haitian time was like Puerto Rican time" (p.58). These
gratuitous observations detract from an otherwise well-told novel
about dreams and life in a big city.

Velasquez, Eric. *Grandma's Records*. Illus.: the author. New York:
    Walker, 2001. 32p. ISBN: 0-8027-8760-6. $16.95. Gr. K-3.
        Brimming with joy and fond memories, Velasquez relates his
summers as a young boy with his music-loving, Puerto Rican
grandmother in El Barrio. From merengue to salsa to Grandma's
special song, music becomes that "magical moment in time" that
both cherished and enjoyed. The expressive double-spread oil
paintings are as warm and affecting as Velasquez's tender feelings
about his grandmother and their musical experiences in New York
City. Puerto Rican children will be especially touched by
grandma's song, *"En mi Viejo San Juan"* ("In My Old San Juan")
that tells about coming to a new country and leaving those you
love behind. Brief notes about the Puerto Rican band members
mentioned in the story and the song, which is reproduced in both
Spanish and English, add to this joyous celebration of Puerto Rican
music with an unforgettable grandma. Also available in Spanish.

South America

Arnold, Caroline. *South American Animals*. New York: Morrow, 1999. 48p. ISBN: 0-688-15564-2. $16.00. Gr. 2-4.

From the forests of the northern half of South America to the chilly southern seas of South America's shorelines, this stunning, high-quality publication highlights seventeen different animals found in its rain forests, mountains, grasslands, and coastal regions. Each expansive double-page photograph features a different animal—for example, a toucan, a spider monkey, an emerald tree boa, a green sea turtle—in its natural habitat and includes a boxed two-paragraph text with general information. This information calls attention to the animal's special characteristics, such as "Good eyesight and hearing, quick reflexes, and sharp teeth and claws help them [jaguars] catch the animals that are their prey" (p. 18). Whether as an overview of South American fauna or as an attractive book to browse and enjoy, this book will appeal to many.

Uribe, Verónica. *Buzz, Buzz, Buzz*. Illus.: Gloria Calderón. Toronto: Douglas McIntyre/Groundwood Books, 1999. 28p. ISBN: 0-88899-430-3. $15.95. Gr. Pre-2.

Two young children, Juliana and Andrés, try to escape a buzzing mosquito that won't let them sleep. The mosquito follows them from their bedroom to a nearby forest to a dark pond. Finally, an owl takes them home, and a helpful toad takes care of the annoying mosquito. Originally published in Venezuela and translated from Spanish, the simple text lacks the joyous spontaneity and charm of the original Spanish version. But youngsters will enjoy the bold, full-page illustrations that beautifully depict a South American rural setting.

Spain

Ada, Alma Flor. *Jordi's Star*. Illus.: Susan Gaber. New York: Putnam, 1996. 32p. ISBN: 0-399-22832-2. $15.95. Gr. K-3.

Set in Catalonia, Spain, on a barren, rocky hillside, this lyrical story tells about Jordi, a solitary shepherd, who, after a thunderstorm, finds a new magical friend—a star shining in the pool—that alters his life forever. To keep his star happy, he sets about gathering the beauty of the mountainside to bring to her—and to himself. The earthy illustrations dramatically depict Jordi's simple dignity, strong beliefs, and happiness in discovering beauty in his surroundings. Of special interest to Catholic Mexican Americans is a touching illustration that shows Jordi sleeping under a cross, and an icon resembling the Virgin of Guadalupe as his star shines through the window.

Ada, Alma Flor, adapter. *The Three Golden Oranges*. Illus.: Reg Cartwright. New York: Atheneum BFYR/Simon & Schuster, 1999. 32p. ISBN: 0-689-80775-9. $16.00. Gr. 2-4.

In Alma Flor Ada's adaptation of the Hispanic folktale, *"Blancaflor,"* the beautiful princess is a strong, independent young woman who insists on a woman's right to choose whom she wants to marry. Similarly, her sisters, Zenaida and Zoraida, reject two suitors as they'd "rather live alone than with a foolish vain man" or "a foolish greedy man." Despite the lengthy text, some children will enjoy this contemporary rendition about three brothers who, on the advice of an old woman, set out in search of three golden oranges with hopes of finding brides. The full-page stylized oil paintings, on the other hand, depict the tone and ambience of the traditional tale set in southern Spain.

Aronson, Marc. *Sir Walter Ralegh and the Quest for El Dorado*. New York: Clarion Books, 2000. 222p. ISBN: 0-395-84827-X. $20.00. Gr. 7-10.

With the flair and passion of a true admirer, Aronson narrates the life of Sir Walter Ralegh, the adventurer, the sea dog, the careful thinker, the great writer, and the man, whose "life suited his era, when men go off questing after dreams" (p.3). Using the search for El Dorado as a metaphor for Ralegh's life and European dreams that became "only tangles of legends and lies in the minds of would-be conquerors" (p.182), this fast-paced biography offers a fascinating view of the Elizabethan age and the Inca hidden kingdom. Some readers may be confused by the sometimes loose connections between the numerous topics covered, but the gripping narrative, well-selected black-and-white reproductions and maps, and appealing design make this a most inviting introduction to this daring adventurer. Serious students of the era will appreciate the endnotes, bibliography, and timeline.

Fradin, Dennis. *Maria de Sautuola: The Bulls in the Cave*. Illus.: Ed Martinez. Parsippany, NJ: Silver Press, 1997. 32p. ISBN: 0-382-39470-4. $15.95; pap. ISBN: 0-382-39471-2. $5.95. Gr. 3-5.

Maria de Sautuola, an eight-year-old Spanish girl who discovered the first known prehistoric cave paintings in 1879, is introduced to readers through sensitive full-page color paintings and a moving text. The drama of the discovery of the now famous Altamira Cave combined with the insults that befell Maria's father, who died a brokenhearted man, result in a captivating true story about injustice and forgiveness. This is indeed a sad but realistic introduction to the study of archaeology and prehistoric art.

Lace, William W. *Defeat of the Spanish Armada*. (Battles of the Middle Ages) San Diego, CA: Lucent Books, 1997. 96p. ISBN: 1-56006-458-7. $19.95. Gr. 7-12.

The importance and consequences of the defeat of the Spanish Armada to the history of Europe and to military history are highlighted in this readable narrative. It presents an overview of the conflicts between Spain and England in the 1500s up to the dawn of the British Empire. Through an engaging text, numerous black-and-white drawings and maps, and informative sidebars, readers are exposed to the leaders, customs, weapons, and strategies that resulted in a turning point, both in world history and in warfare.

Laden, Nina. *When Pigasso Met Mootisse.* San Francisco: Chronicle Books, 1998. 34p. ISBN: 0-8118-1121-2. $15.95. Gr. K-2.

Lighthearted and fun, this is an amusing tale about the conflicts and rivalries between Pigasso, a talented pig, and Mootisse, an artistic bull, who live across the road from one another. They quarrel and criticize each other, but, ultimately, they create a modern art masterpiece and become great friends. Some children will enjoy this as a pig versus bull story in which friendship in due time prevails. Others will appreciate the parody in which Pigasso's cubist creations are contrasted with Mootisse's cattle "moosterpieces." And others will be able to tie the brief afterword, the true story of Picasso and Matisse, with a pig and bull life and conflicts. But all children will enjoy the humorous word play and stunning, double-spread gouache illustrations with fanciful scenes from the two masters' creations and styles.

Lior, Noa, and Tara Steele. *Spain: The Culture.* ISBN: 0-7787-9366-4.
————. *Spain: The Land.* ISBN: 0-7787-9364-8.
————. *Spain: The People.* ISBN: 0-7787-9365-6.
Ea. vol.: 32p. (The Lands, Peoples, and Cultures Series) New York: Crabtree Publishing, 2002. $20.60. Gr. 3-5.

Like other titles in this series, these books introduce young readers to the culture, land, and people of Spain through excellent color photos and a simple text. In a most appealing format and design, such aspects as the arts, traditions, bullfights, and regional specialties of Spain are highlighted.

Marrin, Albert. *Terror of the Spanish Main: Sir Henry Morgan and His Buccaneers.* New York: Dutton, 1999. 240p. ISBN: 0-525-45942-1. $19.99. Gr. 8-12.

Emphasizing Henry Morgan's role in breaking Spain's monopoly in the West Indies in the seventeenth century, Marrin's engrossing portrait of the man and his times provides readers with a realistic depiction of the buccaneer's boundless ambition and reckless imagination. Numerous black-and-white drawings, paintings, and maps add interest to this account of "the most feared person in the New World . . . [who] for nearly two decades on behalf of England" (p.4) terrorized the Spanish colonies on the northeast coast of South America and her mainland possessions. Perhaps some Spanish-speaking historians may disagree with the author's explanation of *La Leyenda Negra* (the Black Legend). Nonetheless, he explains that buccaneers "were men of their time, no better and no worse. . . . So when dealing with the hated Spaniards, they did what came 'naturally'" (p.135). Includes extensive notes, a bibliography, and an index.

Meadows, Matthew. *Pablo Picasso*. (Art for Young People) New York: Sterling Publishers, 1996. 31p. ISBN: 0-8069-6160-0. $14.95. Gr. 5-7.

Originally published in Great Britain, this well-done introduction to Picasso combines personal information with critical commentary as well as original artwork, reproductions, and photographs. From Picasso's growing up years in Spain to his death at the age of ninety-one, readers will follow the artist's constant exploration with new techniques and materials. A timeline, glossary, index, and picture captions add further to the value of this readable presentation of the man and the artist.

Millar, Heather. *Spain in the Age of Exploration*. (Cultures of the Past) New York: Benchmark Books/Marshall Cavendish, 1999. 80p. ISBN: 0-7614-0303-5. $19.95. Gr. 6-9.

Lively and colorful, this introduction to Spain in the Age of Exploration presents the key factors that made Spain "for a time, the richest and most powerful nation on earth." From Columbus's stumble upon the Americas, to Spain's achievements in the arts, to the influence of religion in the lives of the people, the fluent narrative includes a most appealing design, excellent graphics, well-selected pictures, and chatty, easy-to-understand, half-page sidebars that add further information such as "Adventures of a Writer" (Lope de Vega) and "Beware of the Devil!" A chronology, glossary, and index are also included.

Schiaffino, Mariarosa. *Goya*. Illus.: Claudia Saraceni and Thomas Trojer. Translated by Anthony Brierley. (Masters of Art) New York: Peter Bedrick Books, 2000. 64p. ISBN: 0-87226-529-3. $22.50. Gr. 5-10.

Like the previous eleven titles in this outstanding large-format series about the protagonists and great developments in the world of art, this one introduces the life and times of Francisco de Goya. From his exquisite court paintings, to his doleful lithographs, to his vast collection at the Prado Museum in Madrid, this beautifully illustrated guide will provide readers/viewers with an intimate view of Goya's artistic creations. A chronology, world art museum guide, and an index are also included.

Sierra, Judy. *The Beautiful Butterfly: A Folktale from Spain.* Illus.: Victoria Chess. New York: Clarion Books, 2000. 32p. ISBN: 0-395-90015-8. $15.00. Gr. K-3.

Maintaining the joyous spirit of the original Spanish folktale but exercising the storyteller's prerogative to change the usual tragic ending to a happy one in which the king runs around in his underwear, this popular Hispanic folktale is sure to delight all readers/listeners. Chess's inviting gouache-and-sepia pen-and-ink illustrations tenderly highlight the beautiful butterfly, her many suitors, her grief, and ultimate joy as she raises a family of little buttermice. A brief folklore note tells about the hundreds of variants of this folktale that have been collected in Europe and Latin America.

Stewart, Gail B. *Life during the Spanish Inquisition.* (The Way People Live) San Diego, CA: Lucent Books, 1998. 95p. ISBN: 1-56006-346-7. $17.96. Gr. 7-12.

This is not an examination of the daily life in Spain during the Spanish Inquisition; rather, it is a well-written narrative about the political, religious, and economic issues that resulted in the horrors of the Spanish Inquisition. From the making of the Inquisition in France in the early thirteenth century to its gradual demise in Spain in the nineteenth century, this book presents in gruesome detail the tortures and punishments that were inflicted upon hundreds of thousands of people. Numerous black-and-white maps and illustrations, as well as excerpts from personal narratives, make this an even more powerful depiction of the times.

Venezia, Mike. *El Greco.* Illus.: the author. (Getting to Know the World's Greatest Artists) Chicago: Children's Press, 1997. 32p. ISBN: 0-516-20586-2. $11.95. Gr. 3-6.

Like the previous titles in this simply written and profusely illustrated biographical series, this volume introduces readers to the life and work of Doménikos Theotokópoulos, El Greco, the sixteenth-century artist who created his greatest works in Spain. In a lighthearted manner and through amusing cartoons, the author explains important aspects about El Greco's artistic achievements. In addition, the full-color reproductions of the paintings discussed provide youngsters with an inspiring view of El Greco's paintings—from his religious stories, to his wonderful portraits, to his scenes of Spanish court life.

Zamorano, Ana. *Let's Eat.* Illus.: Julie Vivas. New York: Scholastic, 1996. 32p. ISBN: 0-590-13444-2. $15.95. Gr. Pre-2.

Each day Antonio's Mamá tries to get all the family—Mamá, Papá, Granny, Granpa, brother Salvador, sister Alicia, and the youngest, Antonio—to sit down together to eat, but someone is always busy. Despite the wonderful dishes such as *empanadas*, *gazpacho*, *pollo*, and *sardinas*, she always misses someone. This changes on Sunday when Mamá comes home from the hospital with little Rosa and all the family eats together a delicious "paella." The simple repetitive text sprinkled with Spanish words and expressions and the buoyant watercolor illustrations depicting typical Spanish *comidas* will ring true to many Spanish-speaking children who know about happy family dinners.

United States

Alarcón, Francisco X. *Angels Ride Bikes and Other Fall Poems/Los ángeles andan en bicicleta y otros poemas de otoño.* Illus.: Maya Christina Gonzalez. San Francisco: Children's Book Press, 1999. 32p. ISBN: 0-89239-160-X. $15.95. Gr. 1-3.

With the flair and gusto of a Mexican celebration, Alarcón poetically reminisces about sunny Los Angeles, his loud and cheerful family, his kind and loving *abuela,* and other whimsical impressions of his childhood. The colloquial Spanish renditions and the fresh English poems are beautifully immersed in Gonzalez's colorful and expressive double-page paintings, which are indeed a vibrant visual response to the bilingual poems.

Alarcón, Francisco X. *Iguanas in the Snow and Other Winter Poems/Iguanas en la nieve y otros poemas de invierno.* Illus.: Maya Christina Gonzalez. San Francisco: Children's Book Press, 2001. 32p. ISBN: 0-89239-168-5. $15.95. Gr. 1-3.

With the same flair and gusto of its predecessors, Alarcón poetically celebrates in this final bilingual volume the cycle of seasons and the beauty and uniqueness of multiethnic San Francisco and the mountains of Northern California in the winter. Beautiful Mission Dolores, a bilingual school, migrant life, and giant sequoias are depicted through joyous Spanish colloquial expressions and fresh English poems. Gonzalez's bold and fanciful double-page spreads whimsically complement this buoyant tribute to Latinos in Northern California.

Alarcón, Francisco X. *Laughing Tomatoes and Other Spring Poems/ Jitomates risueños y otros poemas de primavera.* Illus.: Maya Christina Gonzalez. San Francisco: Children's Book Press, 1997. 32p. ISBN: 0-89239-139-1. $15.95. Gr. K-3.

Bilingual (Spanish-English) collections of poems for young readers are not easy to find; hence, this celebration of spring and the fruits of family and sunshine by Chicano poet Alarcón is just right for Spanish speakers. The short poems and simple imagistic reflections are exuberantly expanded by Gonzalez in colorful double-page illustrations. Latino children frolicking with their grandmother as well as important events in the history of Mexican Americans are featured and convey a special joy in culture and nature.

Alvarez, Julia. *How Tía Lola Came to (Visit) Stay.* New York: Knopf, 2001. 147p. ISBN: 0-375-80215-0. $15.95. Gr. 4-7.

Latino children will certainly identify with Tía Lola, who just arrived from the Dominican Republic. She is affectionate, loves to dance and party, wears colorful clothes, and cooks wonderful food. Yet ten-year-old Miguel has mixed feelings about her visit. He is unhappy about his parents' recent divorce and does not feel accepted by his new classmates in Vermont. Still Tía Lola is a joy to have at home. Numerous aspects of Dominican culture and acculturation are included, such as *Santería,* the Spanish language, a visit to Santo Domingo to meet the family, and difficulties in learning English, which of course will ring true to many Latinos. Unfortunately, the adult voice is sometimes heavy handed, which detracts from the delightful characters and humorous situations.

Alvarez, Julia. *Something to Declare.* Chapel Hill, NC: Algonquin Books of Chapel Hill, 1998. 312p. ISBN: 1-56512-193-7. $19.95. Gr. 9-adult.

With wit and her unmistakable candor, Alvarez's relates in these twenty-four personal essays her childhood in her native Dominican Republic where grandfather's blessings really made a difference, girls' only aspirations were to be good wives and mothers, and Dominicans learned the habits of repression, censorship, and terror under Trujillo's thirty-one-year dictatorship. Later, as an adolescent in New York, she tells about her experiences with the English language and her adult life as a writer with an American husband in Vermont. Divided into two parts—"Customs" and "Declarations"—adolescents will be inspired as well as entertained by Alvarez's charisma and dedication to her art.

Alvarez, Julia. *¡Yo!* Chapel Hill, NC: Algonquin Books of Chapel Hill, 1997. 309p. ISBN: 1-56512-157-0. $18.95. Gr. 9-adult.

Yolanda García, the now famous and most artistic of the four little girls who emigrated from the Dominican Republic to New York City in the 1950s when the "proper" Garcías fled Trujillo's dictatorship, is the main character in this entertaining, vivid novel about family sensibilities, exile, and life's inconsistencies. Brief episodes, each with a different narrator, present a different perspective—from her mother's, her best friend's, a suitor's, her third husband's—about Yo, the sister who always had to be center stage. Adolescents will particularly enjoy Yo's sexual peccadilloes, which, combined with Alvarez's animated and wonderfully humorous writing style, result in a most delightful novel.

Americanos: Latino Life in the United States/La vida latina en los Estados Unidos. Edited by Edward James Olmos and Lea Ybarra. Translated by Hortencia Moreno-Gonzáles. Boston: Little, Brown, 1999. 176p. ISBN: 0-316-64909-0. pap. $25.00. Gr. 8-adult.

With a deeply felt introduction by Carlos Fuentes, this bilingual portrait of the Latino community resonates with the contributions of Latinos to the culture, beauty, and diversity of life in the United States. More than 200 exquisite black-and-white and color photographs appear in this well-designed photo documentary that highlights the liveliness, traditions, and achievements of Latinos of all ages. This is indeed a joyful, panoramic view of Latinos in the United States.

Anaya, Rudolfo. *Elegy on the Death of César Chávez.* Illus.: Gaspar Enriquez. El Paso, TX: Cinco Puntos Press, 2000. 31p. ISBN: 0-938317-51-2. $16.95. Gr. 4-7.

Anaya's passionate tribute to César Chávez's life and work resonates with the love and devotion of all his admirers. Using elegies by Shelley and Whitman as models, Anaya's poem recounts Chávez's indefatigable spirit as he labored to organize the *campesinos* " . . . in fields and orchards, in community halls, in schools, churches, campesino homes . . . " and urges them to "Rise, mi gente, rise!" Numerous Spanish words and phrases, interspersed throughout, and Enriquez's powerful collages add to the strong emotional tone of this elegy. An author's afterword and a chronology provide further information about the revered leader of the farmworkers.

Anaya, Rudolfo. *Roadrunner's Dance.* Illus.: David Diaz. New York: Hyperion Books for Children, 2000. 32p. ISBN: 0-7868-0254-5. $16.49. Gr. Pre-3.

Anaya's interest in creation stories resulted in this original story about roadrunners, the swift-running crested birds of the Southwest with streaked brownish plumages and long tails. To stand up to Rattlesnake, the self-styled king of the road, Desert Woman enlists the aid of the other animals to create a new bird with the necessary tools to overcome Rattlesnake. Diaz's highly stylized, brightly colored illustrations provide a magical folkloric touch with a high dose of energy and fantasy. Unfortunately, Anaya's prose, which at times resonates with the cadences of oral telling, is often wordy, lengthy, and tries too hard to educate children on the importance of practice, as well as the value of cooperation and helping others. Even in the afterword, Anaya insists on his admonitions to the young. Despite these caveats, this is an amusing introduction to the fauna and flora of the Southwest.

Ancona, George. *Barrio: José's Neighborhood.* San Diego, CA: Harcourt Brace, 1998. 48p. ISBN: 0-15-201049-1. $18.00. Gr. 3-6.

Ancona's characteristic award-winning color photographs depict *barrio* life in the Mission District of San Francisco where the majority of the neighborhood's immigrants have come from Mexico and other countries south of the United States border. Highlighting the murals, fiestas, and special products from Mexico sold in the *barrio*, this photo-essay provides a colorful, upbeat glimpse of life in José's *barrio*. Numerous Spanish words are sprinkled throughout the narrative adding to the Latino flavor. Ancona briefly mentions a few disagreeable aspects of the *barrio*, such as *pandillas* (street gangs), drinking and smoking on the playground, and a memorial to a teacher who died of AIDS. As a positive, mostly rosy view of the Latino experience in the United States, this photo-essay will be enjoyed by many.

Ancona, George. *Harvest.* Photos by the author. New York: Marshall Cavendish, 2001. 48p. ISBN: 0-7614-5086-6. $15.95. Gr. 4-7.

Ancona's characteristic exquisite, full-color photos capture the work and life of the *campesinos* (farmworkers) "who have come to harvest the crops that grow in the rich earth of the Salinas Valley." By intermingling information on how different crops are picked with personal vignettes of migrant workers who tell about their lives, joys, and disappointments, this photo-documentary provides

an engrossing overview of the lushness of the crops—from straw-
berries to lettuce to peppers to broccoli to celery to pears—and the
Mexican men and women who work in the fields.

Atkin, S. Beth. *Voices from the Streets: Young Former Gang Members
Tell Their Stories.* Photos by the author. Boston: Little, Brown,
1996. 131p. ISBN: 0-316-05634-0. $17.95. Gr. 7-12.

Stark black-and-white photographs, sensitive poems, and revealing first-person interviews with nine former gang members
from different regions of the United States honestly depict their
experiences as they try to leave their gangs and improve their lives.
In an optimistic and generally positive tone, the author describes
the struggles of boys and girls of different ages and ethnicities in
their own voices, including slang terms and substandard grammar.
Through the words of four Latino youths—thirteen-year-old Elena
Rojas who lives in Miami, Florida, with her Cuban-born mother,
stepfather, and baby sister; eighteen-year-old Margie Ledezma
who was born in San Jose, California, after her parents immigrated
from Mexico; fifteen-year-old Melissa Sabater, whose parents are
from Puerto Rico, and who became pregnant at thirteen by a rival
gang member; twenty-two-year-old Daniel Villegas, who suffered
a lot of physical abuse from his alcoholic father when he brought
his family to the United Sates from Mexicali, Mexico—readers
will feel the poignant experiences as well as their reasons for
joining street gangs.

Atkins, Jeannine. *Get Set! Swim!* Illus.: Hector Viveros Lee. New
York: Lee & Low Books, 1998. 32p. ISBN: 1-880000-66-0.
$15.95. Gr. 1-3.

Jessenia, a young girl, is tired of hearing her mother talk about
life in her native Puerto Rico. But Mami is loving and supportive,
especially during Jessenia's first year on the swim team. Lively,
double-page spreads, beautifully rendered in watercolor and pencil,
are the perfect complement to this warm story about family support
and teamwork. Swimming fans will be particularly pleased.

Baca, Jimmy Santiago. *A Place to Stand: The Making of a Poet.* New
York: Grove Press, 2001. 264p. ISBN: 0-8021-1602-7. $24.00. Gr.
9-adult.

In an engrossing memoir, Baca, an award-winning poet, recounts his life from his childhood in rural New Mexico where he
was abandoned by his parents and put in an orphanage at age

seven, to detention centers for boys, drug dealing, and years of abuse at a maximum-security state prison in Arizona. Highlighting the impact of the dehumanizing environment of prison, which can "turn a man into a monster," and the effects of learning to read and write, which gave him the resources to understand himself, Baca provides a living testament to the power of literature and a young man's efforts to survive, despite overwhelming odds. Latino adolescents will be touched by Baca's seemingly endless sufferings and his ultimate success.

Calhoun, Mary. *Tonio's Cat*. Illus.: Edward Martinez. New York: Morrow, 1996. 32p. ISBN: 0-688-13314-2. $16.00. Gr. 2-4.

Tonio, a young boy, longs for Cazador, the special dog he left behind in Mexico when his family moved to California. Feeling sad and lonely, he sees an old yellow-striped cat with a torn ear and a hind-leg limp that searches trash cans for food. The developing relationship between this cat and Tonio is sensitively captured in the rich oil paintings on canvas that realistically depict a Mexican American environment in Southern California. Numerous Spanish words and phrases are well integrated in the reassuring story line that brims with the universal appeal of children's love of pets and the need to belong.

Carlson, Lorie Marie. *Hurray for Three Kings' Day!* Illus.: Ed Martinez. New York: Morrow, 1999. 32p. ISBN: 0-688-16239-8. $16.00; lib. ed. ISBN: 0-688-16240-1. $15.93. Gr. Pre-3.

The best parts of this joyous re-creation of the traditional Hispanic celebration, the Three Kings' Day, are Martinez's engaging, light-filled, oil paintings that touchingly reproduce the spirit and tenor of the holiday. Also informative is the author's note explaining the holiday's significance to Latino-heritage people. What mars this straightforward presentation as Anita and her older brothers celebrate the Epiphany are the at-times awkward Spanish words and phrases woven into the text, which immediately add a sense of foreignness to this otherwise jubilant Latino family celebration on the sixth of January.

Castro, Rafaela G. *Dictionary of Chicano Folklore*. Santa Barbara, CA: ABC-CLIO, 2000. 332p. ISBN: 0-87436-953-3. $55.00. Gr. 9-adult.

In a lively and at times snappy manner, Castro provides information about Chicano folklore and culture. Selected from oral narratives, literature, material culture, folk arts, customs, and beliefs, she includes terms, genres, or concepts that pertain to the Chicano or Mexican American people in the United States. From *"El Abuelo"* to *"La Llorona," "La Malinche," "Machismo,"* and *"Zozobra,"* this dictionary assists users in understanding the Chicano cultural experience in the United States. Is is unfortunate that numerous Spanish words are misspelled and Spanish punctuation marks are completely ignored.

Cockcroft, James D. *Latino Visions: Contemporary Chicano, Puerto Rican and Cuban American Artists.* New York: Franklin Watts, 2000. 143p. ISBN: 0-531-11312-4. $26.00. Gr. 8-12.

Cockcroft states that the purpose of this book is to celebrate the artwork of Latinos living on the mainland of the United States. From the *santeros*, one of the oldest artistic traditions from the Southwestern states, to Chicano mural movements (in which he briefly discusses Mexico's "Three Greats"—Diego Rivera, David Siqueiros, and José Clemente Orozco), to avant-garde Puerto Ricans and the conflicts between "right-wing Cuban exiles" and revolutionary Cubans, Cockcroft stresses Latino political struggles and human rights issues. As a dry introduction to the role in which Latino social, political, and cultural events and traditions have shaped selected artists, this book will be welcomed by serious readers. Unfortunately, the mixed quality of the black-and-white photographs and the small number of full-color plates included do not allow readers to appreciate the "aesthetically brilliant, often intricate, and always powerful" Latino art. Chapter notes, a glossary, bibliographies, and a list of websites are included.

Collins, David R. *Farmworker's Friend: The Story of Cesar Chavez.* Minneapolis, MN: Carolrhoda Books, 1996. 80p. ISBN: 0-87614-982-4. $14.96. Gr. 3-5.

The life of Cesar Chavez, from his early years as a child growing up in a poor migrant-worker family to his death in 1993, is narrated in a direct and well-written text. Collins describes Chavez's life as a community organizer, labor leader, political activist, and fighter for the rights of farmworkers. The narrative is further enriched with numerous candid black-and-white photos. A notes section that provides additional information on incidents mentioned in the text is included as well as a bibliography and an index.

Cooper, Martha, and Ginger Gordon. *Anthony Reynoso: Born to Rope.* New York: Clarion Books, 1996. 32p. ISBN: 0-395-71690-X. $14.95. Gr. 2-4.

Clear candid color photographs and a lively, first-person narrative describe the life of Anthony Reynoso, a young Mexican American boy, who enjoys his life in Guadalupe, Arizona—both as a typical American youngster shooting baskets with his father and collecting basketball cards as well as his life as a young *charro*—a Mexican cowboy. Anthony ropes and rides Mexican rodeo style, eats Mexican food, breaks "piñatas" at birthday parties, and enjoys other activities with his family. This is indeed a joyous celebration of the best of Mexican and American cultures through a wonderful, happy young boy.

Cordova, Amy. *Abuelita's Heart.* New York: Simon & Schuster, 1997. 32p. ISBN: 0-689-80181-5. $16.00. Gr. K-3.

Through a young narrator and bold primitive-style paintings done in acrylics, oil pastels, and colored pencils, readers will experience the special bond between a land "the color of sunset, where each day the great sky herds woolly clouds over the mountains to far-off pastures" and the girl's *abuelita* (grandmother) who teaches her that "by reaching out to one another that we, too, create something beautiful to last throughout the ages." In a spiritual/mystical tone sprinkled with numerous Spanish phrases, followed by contextual translations, as well as the special food, plants, and places of the American Southwest make this tender story about love, family, and nature a symbolic, metaphysical blend of the author's Hispanic and Native-American heritage.

Cowley, Joy. *Gracias, the Thanksgiving Turkey.* Illus.: Joe Cepeda. New York: Scholastic, 1996. 32p. ISBN: 0-590-46976-2. $15.95. Gr. Pre-2.

Set in New York City in a loving Latino family, this heartwarming story tells about Miguel and his special attachment to Gracias, a turkey who made it to Thanksgiving dinner, but not as a cooked turkey. Miguel's understanding grandparents, impatient *Tía* Rosa, and friendly neighbors provide a supporting cast to this humorous story that intermingles well-known Spanish words and expressions in a fast-moving narrative. Cepeda's colorful oil paintings definitely capture the Latino ambience of New York City and Miguel's unique friendship.

Cozic, Charles P., editor. *Illegal Immigration.* (Opposing Viewpoints) San Diego, CA: Greenhaven Press, 1997. 207p. ISBN: 1-56510-514-1. $19.95; pap. ISBN: 1-56510-513-3. $11.95. Gr. 9-12.

Important issues—both pro and con—regarding illegal immigration are examined from the point of view of politicians, journalists, economists, social activists, and others. The authors debate the fairness of the new measures aimed at illegal immigrants, the effects of illegal immigration on local economies and on United States workers, the fortification of the United States-Mexico border, and the victimization of illegal immigrants. This is indeed a timely overview of the numerous arguments that make this such a controversial and divisive issue that especially affects Hispanics and Mexican nationals.

Crawford, Mark. *Encyclopedia of the Mexican-American War.* Santa Barbara, CA: ABC-CLIO, 1999. 349p. ISBN: 1-57607-059-X. $75.00. Gr. 9-adult.
See review p. 42.

Davis, William C. *Three Roads to the Alamo: The Lives and Fortunes of David Crockett, James Bowie, and William Barret Travis.* New York: HarperCollins Publishers, 1998. 791p. ISBN: 0-06-017334-3. $35.00. Gr. 9-adult.

Serious students of the history of Texas will be enthralled by this accessible biography of the three men—David Crockett, James Bowie, and William Barret Travis—who met their deaths at the Alamo on March 6, 1836, in one of the most famous and tragic battles between Mexico and the United States. Davis, a distinguished historian, depicts Bowie as a man of audacious bravery, Travis as a youthful lawyer and political writer of note "with more libido than conscience," and Crockett as a daring hunter and larger-than-life folk character. He narrates with meticulous detail their lives and the inevitable events that led to the deadly battle at the Alamo. Black-and-white reproductions, extensive historical notes, and a bibliography of primary sources and published works supplement this exhaustive and engrossing narrative.

de Paola, Tomie. *The Night of Las Posadas.* Illus.: the author. New York: Puffin/Penguin, 1999. 32p. ISBN: 0-698-11901-0. pap. $6.99. Gr. K-4.

De Paola's characteristic warm, flat artwork, done in acrylic on handmade watercolor paper in shades of purples, deep greens, and blues, provides the setting to this annual celebration of Las Posadas in Santa Fe, New Mexico. An apparent miracle saves the procession when the couple who was to play Mary and Joseph are delayed by car trouble. Young Latino readers and their parents always rejoice in yet another reenactment of Las Posadas. A simple introduction explains this cherished Mexican/Spanish/Latino custom.

Durán, Miguel. *Don't Spit on My Corner.* Houston, TX: Arte Público Press, 1992. 187p. ISBN: 1-55885-042-2. pap. $9.50. Gr. 9-12.

Based on the author's experiences as a teenage *pachuco* in East Los Angeles, this engrossing novel depicts the feelings, thoughts, and predicaments of Latino youth who struggle with gangs, alcohol, and prejudice. With unrestrained candor, Mike, the protagonist, describes his interest in girls and his special attraction to "manly" activities. Despite several undeveloped characters, this novel about growing up amid drugs, violence, and encounters with the law will ring true to inner-city Latino adolescents.

Elya, Susan Middleton. *Home at Last.* Illus.: Felipe Davalos. New York: Lee & Low Books, 2002. 32p. ISBN: 1-58430-020-5. $16.95. Gr. 2-4.

Eight-year-old Ana Patiño likes her new school in the United States even though life is different from that in her village in Mexico. Papá is also adjusting, but mamá finds learning English very difficult. After several distressing situations, especially when Ana's baby brother becomes ill, mamá agrees to learn English. To celebrate mamá's success, the whole family enjoys a special dinner. Although this story is more about her mother, Elya's upbeat account about adjusting to a new language and culture is beautifully illustrated with Davalos's sensitive double-spread oil paintings with a definite Latino ambiance. Despite the almost predictable message, Latino children will empathize with the frustrations and triumphs of adaptation.

English, Karen. *Speak English for Us, Marisol!* Illus.: Enrique O. Sánchez. Morton Grove, IL: Albert Whitman, 2000. 32p. ISBN: 0-8075-7554-2. $14.95. Gr. Pre-3.

The intimacy and close ties in an extended Latino family are tenderly portrayed through Marisol, whose ability to speak both

Spanish and English is needed by her Uncle Tomás in his shop, by her Auntie Flora on the phone, by Ms. López so she can complete an application form, and by her mother to settle a mistaken phone bill. Although Marisol is rushing home to see her cat who is expecting kittens soon, she takes the time to translate the words and explain the misunderstandings. Highlighting the lively ambience of the American Southwest, Sánchez's gouache and acrylic paintings set the tone and reflect the action.

Espada, Martín. *A Mayan Astronomer in Hell's Kitchen.* New York: Norton, 2000. 85p. ISBN: 0-393-04888-8. $21.00. Gr. 9-adult.

From strong ethnic political poems, to deeply felt poems about family and death, to humorous poems about "a tarantula in the bananas," and how Espada was "convinced" by his father to go to college, this collection of sober pragmatical poems will appeal to sophisticated adolescents who care about contemporary issues. Espada, a Brooklyn-born Puerto Rican, combines in his poetry the ethos of Latin Americans with the perspicacity of Latinos living in the United States.

Ewing, Lynne. *Party Girl.* New York: Knopf, 1998. 110p. ISBN: 0-679-89285-0. $16.00. Gr. 6-9.

Set in Los Angeles where gang members fight over crumbling cement and potholed streets in a neighborhood divided by "hatred stronger than barbed-wire fences," this poignant view of Los Angeles gang life is an eloquent plea for a different lifestyle. When fifteen-year-old Kata questions the death of her best friend, Ana, who had come from Mexico, she is engulfed by her own fears and determined to seek revenge. Amid pregnant teenagers, alcoholic mothers, and vicious boyfriends, this realistic novel will ring true to many adolescents in and out of gangs. The sprinkling of Spanish words and phrases adds a decidedly Latino ambience to this cautionary tale.

Fernández-Shaw, Carlos M. *The Hispanic Presence in North America: From 1492 to Today.* Rev. ed. Translated by Alfonso Bertodano Stourton. New York: Facts on File, 1999. 396p. ISBN: 0-8160-4010-9. $45.00. Gr. 9-adult.

The author's purpose is to show how the United States has been influenced by Spain and to highlight the Spanish presence through the centuries. Divided by geographic region and with separate chapters on the states with significant Hispanic populations—

Florida, Louisiana, Missouri, Texas, New Mexico, Arizona, Colorado, and California—this slightly revised edition will be of special interest to students with a strong interest in the Spanish discovery and Spain's influence in the United States. The author mentions briefly a few facts about the present Hispanic population and ignores the influence of other non-Spaniard Hispanic groups in the United States. Fanatics of Spain will be delighted with the cultural and student exchange information provided as well as the appendixes with historical facts and other useful information.

Ferriss, Susan, and Ricardo Sandoval. *The Fight in the Fields: Cesar Chavez and the Farmworkers Movement.* New York: Harcourt Brace, 1997. 331p. ISBN: 0-15-100239-8. $25.00. Gr. 9-adult.

Written as a companion to the PBS documentary, *The Fight in the Fields*, this well-written narrative relates the story of labor in California through the life of Cesar Chavez, the founder of the United Farm Workers Union. With passion and understanding, the authors describe the racial prejudice Chavez experienced as a child, the loss of the family farm, his first years as an organizer, and the impact he had on American labor politics. Numerous black-and-white candid photos and seventeen essays, letters, and poems by such writers as Ernesto Galarza and Rudolfo Anaya add immediacy to this testament to the life of Cesar Chavez.

Figueredo, D. H. *When This World Was New.* Illus.: Enrique O. Sanchez. New York: Lee & Low Books, 1999. 32p. ISBN: 1-880000-86-5. $15.95. Gr. K-3.

With a tinge of sadness and apprehension, Danilito relates his first day in this country. He tells about being excited and scared as he encounters people who don't smile and don't speak Spanish. Fortunately, Uncle Berto makes the close-knit family feel welcome and helps his father find a factory job. Sanchez's acrylic illustrations beautifully capture the family's anxieties and joys in New York City. This poignant story of immigration, from a child's viewpoint, is further enhanced by a simple text sprinkled with Spanish words.

Fraser, Mary Ann. *A Mission for the People: The Story of La Purísima.* New York: Henry Holt, 1997. 38p. ISBN: 0-8050-5050-7. $15.95. Gr. 4-8.

Simply and succinctly, Fraser relates the story of Mission La Purísima in what is now the Santa Barbara region of California, taking into account the points of view of all its inhabitants—the native Chumash, the Spaniards, the Mexicans, and the Americans. Neither condemning nor criticizing, the author aptly contrasts the Puritans of the Plymouth Plantation to Spanish and Mexican citizens' attitudes toward marriage with the native people. Indeed, this is the strength of this book: It truly presents an objective historical overview of the settlement of the West. "Together these people of many nationalities helped build and preserve Mission La Purísima . . . while the blending of people often brings conflict, it also enriches our lives" (p.36). In addition to the informative text, numerous double-page softly colored acrylic illustrations and boxed sections on every page present scenes of the land, lifestyle, artifacts, and special occurrences. A timeline and a highly selective reading list conclude what is up to now one of the best books on California missions for young readers.

Garland, Sherry. *A Line in the Sand: The Alamo Diary of Lucinda Lawrence.* New York: Scholastic, 1998. 201p. ISBN: 0-590-39466-5. $9.95. Gr. 5-8.

Set in Gonzales, Texas, in 1835, this fictional diary recounts the hardships that thirteen-year-old Lucinda Lawrence, her family, and friends endured during the Texas Revolution. Through Lucinda's own family, readers are exposed to the War Party, which wanted Texas to declare her independence from Mexico, and the Peace Party, which wanted Texas to stay part of Mexico with a democratic constitution. Important people and incidents of the times such as Stephen F. Austin, William Travis, Davy Crockett, the massacres at the Alamo and Goliad, the Battle of San Jacinto, and the capture of General Santa Anna are brought to life through the eyes of a "Texian" adolescent. She concludes: "I have never seen such misery as I saw in Gonzales tonight, and I pray I never see it again. Every house has lost someone, whether it be a father or brother, uncle or son" (p.160). This vivid fictionalized depiction by a fifth generation Texan concludes with a summary of the history of Texas up to 1847 and includes black-and-white illustrations.

Garland, Sherry. *Voices of the Alamo.* Illus.: Ronald Himler. New York: Scholastic, 2000. 40p. ISBN: 0-590-98833-6. $16.95. Gr. 3-6.

From a nameless Payaya maiden from the 1500s, to a bold conquistador, to humble padres, to well-known historical figures such as Antonio López de Santa Anna, David Crockett, and William Barret Travis, this exquisitely designed picture book for older readers recounts in sixteen different voices and from different perspectives the story of the Alamo and its effects on the history of Texas. Himler's double-spread, watercolor-and-gouache illustrations provide engrossing views of the people and ambience. A historical note, glossary, and bibliography add to the value of this passionate tribute to the "defenders of the Alamo."

Gonzales, Manuel G. *Mexicanos: A History of Mexicans in the United States.* Bloomington: Indiana University Press, 1999. 322p. ISBN: 0-253-33520-5. $29.95. Gr. 9-adult.

In a lively and somewhat provocative narrative, Gonzales, a Professor of History at Diablo Valley College, provides a synthesis of the Mexican experience in the United States. His purpose is to offer "a concise and balanced account" by describing "our triumphs as well as our trials and tribulations" (p.7). Despite the obvious detractors, the author should be commended for trying to achieve "objectivity" in such highly politicized areas as "*indigenismo*" vs. "*la leyenda negra*," the role of women in colonial New Mexico, Mexicans during the Texas revolt, life in Mexico vs. racial prejudice and discrimination in the United States, Mexican poverty, and the Catholic Church. The book concludes with a discussion of the effects of the "endless influx" of Mexican immigrants. This is indeed a thoughtful survey of the most important and controversial events in the history of Mexicans in the United States.

Gonzalez, Juan. *Harvest of Empire: A History of Latinos in America.* New York: Viking, 2000. 346p. ISBN: 0-670-86720-9. $27.95. Gr. 10-adult.

Gonzalez, a Puerto Rican columnist for the New York *Daily News*, writes passionately and with great conviction about the history of Latin America and Latinos in the United States and how this has affected their search for survival and for inclusion on an equal basis. He traces the long and difficult relationship between Latin America and the United States. By focusing on a family or a few individuals, he reflects on the general migration stories of the major Latino groups. He highlights the most important issues identified with Latinos—politics, immigration, language, and culture. He argues strongly that the U.S. Congress should "end its colonial control [of Puerto Rico] and authorize a genuine decoloni-

zation plebiscite . . . " (p. xvi). Even though some readers will disagree with the author's assertions, this is an insightful, well-
documented overview about the history, half-truths, and realities of
the Latino experience in the United States. Gonzalez responds to
"nativists and eugenicists" that continue to foster "anti-Latino
fervor with recycled myths and stereotypes" (p. 196).

Harrigan, Stephen. *The Gates of the Alamo*. New York: Knopf, 2000.
581p. ISBN: 0-679-44717-2. $25.00. Gr. 9-adult.
      With the flair of a novelist and the insight of a historian,
Harrigan re-creates the story of the Alamo through tragic characters—both real and fictional—and provides a sense of the powerful
drama and loss that resulted from the Mexican-American War.
From well-known historical figures such as James Bowie, "the
renowned knife-fighter, slave smuggler, and land swindler" (p.58),
to Stephen Austin, "a clearheaded, far-thinking man" (p.63), to
Santa Anna "the most compelling . . . elegantly lean . . . human
being [whose] worldly confidence appeared absolute" (pp.173-
174), to Sam Houston "our noble commander in chief . . . [who] is
always said to be drunk" (p.245), to five captivating fictional characters, this engrossing historical novel provides a sensitive view of
the people and conflict in nineteenth-century Texas. Some adolescents will certainly be discouraged by a 581-page narrative, but the
strong emotions that Santa Anna still elicits on both sides of the
Río Grande make this a historical tour de force. Especially when
due to Santa Anna's "overconfidence and inattention, the army was
overrun, he had abandoned it; and out of his own trembling fear for
his life he had sold Texas—the land that so many Mexican
soldados had shed their blood to rescue—to the norteamericano
pirates" (p.564).

Hayes, Joe. *Juan Verdades: The Man Who Couldn't Tell a Lie*. Illus.:
Joseph Daniel Fiedler. New York: Orchard Books, 2001. 30p.
ISBN: 0-439-29311-1. $16.95. Gr. 2-5.
      Hayes adds a decidedly southwestern/Latino flavor to the
traditional tale about "Juan Verdades," an honest foreman who
couldn't tell a lie. The smooth retelling, sprinkled with Spanish
words and phrases and the vernacular of ranchers, is further em-
bellished with Fiedler's lush earth-tone, double-page spreads,
which perfectly depict the romantic overtones of the tale. Young
readers/listeners will enjoy the humorous dialogue and the sur-
prising conclusion, as they delight in Juan Verdades's ability to

keep the girl, the ranch, and the wealthy farmer's trust without telling a lie. An author's note explains the origin and literary changes.

Henkes, Robert. *Latin American Women Artists of the United States: The Works of 33 Twentieth-Century Women.* Jefferson, NC: McFarland, 1999. 245p. ISBN: 0-7864-0519-8. $40.00. Gr. 9-adult.

The purpose of this book is to identify some of the major Latin American women artists who have lived or worked in the United States. Each of the thirty-three artists' careers, education, solo exhibitions, and group showings is discussed. With the exception of eleven color plates in the middle section, all photographs are black and white. Artists-to-be especially will enjoy the author's well-written discussions that capture the essence of the artists' works while providing significant facts and insights. Very little personal information about the artists is provided. It is interesting to note that the author insists in the preface and concluding remarks that, "Latin American art is frequently referred to as sacred art" (p.1). And, "Devout ties to their faith have led many Latin Americans to depict saintly images . . . " (p.233). Yet, "saintly images" are seldom found in these works.

Herrera, Juan Felipe. *CrashBoomLove.* Albuquerque: University of New Mexico Press, 1999. 155p. ISBN: 0-8263-2114-3. pap. $10.95. Gr. 9-12.

Incorporating the angst and vernacular of California migrant workers, poet Juan Felipe Herrera depicts the alienation of sixteen-year-old César Garcia as he struggles through painful experiences at home and at school. From the ridicule and abuse of his class-mates ("They are laughing at you *chavala*, can you hear them? They are saying you are a *mojado*, a sissy *mojado*" [p.46]), to his experiences with gang members and drugs, this series of free-verse poems describes the difficulties of young people who have been abandoned by their fathers and misunderstood by the educational system. This is not a quixotic novel in verse about growing up Latino in the United States; rather, it is a passionate exposé of the realities of Latino youth that explodes with rage and culminates with hope.

Herrera, Juan Felipe. *Grandma and Me at the Flea/Los meros meros remateros.* Illus.: Anita De Lucio-Brock. San Francisco: Children's Book Press, 2002. 32p. ISBN: 0-89239-171-5. $15.95. Gr. 2-5.

In the easygoing vernacular of Mexican Americans, Juanito recounts his experiences helping *abuelita* at the flea market in California's San Joaquin Valley. From *churros*, to *zarapes*, to *fotonovelas*, and *hierbas*, Juanito finds lots to do and enjoy with *abuelita* and his friends. The colorful double-page spreads provide a joyful tone to this side-by-side bilingual story that has the feel of a Mexican fiesta.

Hill, Christine M. *Ten Hispanic American Authors.* (Collective Biographies) Berkeley Heights, NJ: Enslow Publishers, 2002. 112p. ISBN: 0-7660-1541-6. $20.95. Gr. 6-9.

Highlighting significant aspects in the lives of ten of the greatest contemporary Hispanic American writers, Hill introduces Julia Alvarez, Rudolfo Anaya, Sandra Cisneros, Judith Ortiz Cofer, Oscar Hijuelos, Nicholasa Mohr, Richard Rodriguez, Esmeralda Santiago, Gary Soto, and Piri Thomas. Despite the mostly uninteresting black-and-white photos, the brevity of each biographical sketch and the selected bibliography make this collective biography a useful presentation to the life and works of these Latino writers.

Hoyt-Goldsmith, Diane. *Las Posadas: An Hispanic Christmas Celebration.* Photos by Lawrence Migdale. New York: Holiday House, 1999. 32p. ISBN: 0-8234-1449-3. $16.95; pap. ISBN: 0-8234-1635-6. $6.95. Gr. 4-6.

Through eleven-year-old Kristen and her Hispanic American family, readers/viewers are exposed to the preparations and celebration of *Las Posadas*, the nine-day religious festivities that occur just before Christmas. Set in the town of Española, New Mexico, this appealing photo-essay includes clear, color photos of Kristen at home and at church enjoying the rich folk traditions. Of special interest to serious students are the descriptions of *santeros*, *retablos*, and other activities that make *Las Posadas* such a special occasion in New Mexico and other Latino communities. A well-done glossary and an index will further assist students in understanding the meaning of this popular celebration.

Hoyt-Goldsmith, Diane. *Migrant Worker: A Boy from the Rio Grande Valley.* Photos by Lawrence Migdale. New York: Holiday House, 1996. 32p. ISBN: 0-8234-1225-3. $15.95. Gr. 4-7.

Eleven-year-old Ricky describes his life with his family as migrant agricultural workers in Texas. Clear color photographs on every page show a smiling Ricky at home, at school, and on the job as he explains: "Migrants work long hours. Often we are in the fields for ten, eleven, or twelve hours a day. Most jobs do not pay well. On some farms, people are not even paid a minimum wage" (p.12). And, "Sometimes the plants in the fields have been sprayed with chemicals that kill weeds or insects. My mother worries because these poisons can rub off on us" (p.14). The combination of Ricky's first-person narrative and numerous sidebars and photo captions is at times disturbing, but the generally upbeat tone provides an inside view of the difficulties experienced by migrant families: "Many of the fresh fruits and vegetables that end up on the tables of Americans will be there because of our labor" (p.28).

Jiménez, Francisco. *Breaking Through.* Boston: Houghton Mifflin, 2001. 200p. ISBN: 0-618-01173-0. $15.00. Gr. 7-12.

In this touching autobiographical sequel to *The Circuit*, Jiménez relates his teenage years, beginning with his family's deportation to Mexico up to his admission to college. Especially affecting are Francisco's painful efforts to help his hard-to-please father support the family ("thinning lettuce and picking carrots after school and on weekends"), as he worked hard to keep up with his schoolwork, encouraged by his loving mother and supportive teachers and counselors. In a direct, steady tone without melodrama or didacticism, he achieves his objective: "to voice the experiences of many children and young adults who confront numerous obstacles in their efforts to 'break through . . . and become butterflies'" (p.195). Black-and-white photos of Francisco as a high school student and his family as migrant workers are included.

Jiménez, Francisco. *The Circuit: Stories from the Life of a Migrant Child.* Albuquerque: University of New Mexico Press, 1997. 134p. ISBN: 0-8263-1797-9. pap. $10.95. Gr. 7-12.

In this collection of twelve interconnected stories, the author poignantly relates his life with his family as a migrant agricultural worker. From the kindnesses of a train conductor, to the humiliations by teachers and classmates, to the sorrows of poverty and the fear of *la migra*, these stories depict the sad truth about migrant families in the United States.

Johnston, Tony. *Uncle Rain Cloud*. Illus.: Fabricio Vanden Broeck. Watertown, MA: Charlesbridge, 2001. 32p. ISBN: 0-88106-371-1. $15.95. Gr. Pre-3.

Tío Tomás just arrived from Mexico to Los Angeles where he is constantly frustrated about his inability to speak English. Carlos, his nephew, tries to understand and helps him by translating at the store and at conference time with Carlos's teacher. Although Tío Tomás is grouchy by day, at night he delights in telling Carlos stories about pre-Columbian gods—Tezcatlipoca, Huitzilopochtli, Coyolxauhqui, and, of course, Tláloc, and the famous *aguacerazo* (rainstorm). At the end both are delighted because Tío Tomás is learning English and Carlos learns tales about his ancestors; hence, "we'll know twice as much as everyone else." Johnston's sensitive text imaginatively intermingles Spanish words and expressions that will especially touch former Mexico residents. Vanden Broeck's softly textured acrylic and colored pencil illustrations beautifully capture the frustrations, joy, and affection between uncle and nephew.

Kanellos, Nicolás. *Hispanic Firsts: 500 Years of Extraordinary Achievement*. Detroit, MI: Gale, 1997. 372p. ISBN: 0-7816-0517-4. $44.95. Gr. 8-adult.

This easy-to-use volume summarizes the contributions and achievements of Hispanics as pioneers of American culture. Organized in broad fields (e.g., Art and Design, Business and Commerce, Education, etc.), students will find brief entries of important historical accomplishments, beginning with Ponce de León's colonization of the island of San Juan Bautista (Puerto Rico) in 1509 up to Federico Peña as the first Hispanic United States Secretary of Energy in 1997. A timeline, a calendar, and two indexes complement this useful compendium of *Hispanic Firsts*.

Kenig, Graciela. *Best Careers for Bilingual Latinos: Market Your Fluency in Spanish to Get Ahead on the Job*. Lincolnwood, IL: VGM Career Horizons/NTC, 1999. 238p. ISBN: 0-8442-4541-0. pap. $14.95. Gr. 9-adult.

Latinos looking into career opportunities as well as into choosing, shaping, or changing careers will find much valuable information in this well-written, up-to-date guide. The first part describes the need for bilingual employees, reminds Latino readers of their particular strengths, and describes how to market those skills successfully. The second part includes a well-done survey of the "Best Careers for Bilingual Latinos" and provides such information as education/training, career mobility, desired characteristics, job outlook, earnings, and additional sources. Also included under each career are interviews with practitioners that tell about "passion factor: What do you like most about your occupation?" From lawyers-to-be to engineers-to-be, to careers in government and numerous in-between careers, this guide for Latinos is a real plus.

Kimmel, Eric A. *The Runaway Tortilla.* Illus.: Randy Cecil. Delray Beach, FL: Winslow Press, 2000. 32p. ISBN: 1-890817-18-X. $16.95. Gr. K-2.

Set in Texas, down by the Rio Grande, this cumulative modern tale features *Tía* Lupe and *Tío* José as they pursue the runaway tortilla, who manages to escape two horned toads, three donkeys, four jackrabbits, five rattlesnakes, and six buckaroos. Finally, she is tricked and eaten by *Señor* Coyote. The Texas landscape with humorous Latino motifs is beautifully depicted in a colorful array of yellow, pink, and orange oil illustrations. Inspired by *The Gingerbread Man*, this story maintains the appeal of the traditional tale and combines it with the pace and gusto of a Mexican *taquería*.

King, Elizabeth. *Quinceañera: Celebrating Fifteen.* New York: Dutton, 1998. 40p. ISBN: 0-525-45638-4. 415.99. Gr. 6-9.

The lovely Latino/Mexican rite of passage in which a *quinceañera*, a fifteen-year-old girl, is celebrated with a church ceremony and a big party is touchingly depicted through spectacular candid color photographs that show the elaborate preparations and wonderful fiesta. In an easy-flowing narrative with numerous Spanish words sprinkled throughout, the author provides a bit of the history and significance of the event, highlighting the differences in celebrations in various Central American, Cuban, and Mexican families. This is indeed a warm introduction to this joyous, coming-of-age celebration with an unfortunate caveat that mars this otherwise wonderful scrapbook: The word *Quinceañera* is used for the girl it honors, not for the celebration—it sounds awkward and it is incorrect. Other Spanish-language linguistic aberrations will also irritate Spanish-speaking readers.

Kleven, Elisa. *Hooray, a Piñata!* Illus.: the author. New York: Dutton, 1996. 32p. ISBN: 0-525-45605-8. $15.99. Gr. Pre-2.

Vibrant collages and a warm narrative tell about Clara's upcoming birthday party in which she will have a cake, balloons, and a piñata. Accompanied by her mother and her friend, Samson, Clara chooses a colorful dog *piñata*, which she immediately adopts as her pet. As her party approaches, Clara feels sad about breaking her *piñata*, but Samson saves the day and her special dog *piñata* by giving her another *piñata* that they fill with candy and whack, crack, mask, bash, and, ultimately, break. The festive watercolors as well as the ink and cut paper illustrations definitely depict the joy of Mexican-type celebrations in which piñatas and color take center stage. A brief "Note about Piñatas" follows the text.

Las Christmas: Favorite Latino Authors Share Their Holiday Memories. Edited by Esmeralda Santiago and Joie Davidow. Illus.: José Ortega. New York: Knopf, 1998. 198p. ISBN: 0-375-40151-2. $22.00. Gr. 9-adult.

Twenty-four Latino authors share their memories, thoughts, and favorite recipes about the holiday season—from Gustavo Pérez Firmat's Cuban *Nochebuena* with "an uneven division of festive labor: my mother prepared, and my father partied" (p.25), to Denise Chávez's poignant memories of her mother's death of liver cancer and "then watched the slow, inexorable passage of my brilliant but troubled father into dementia from Alzheimer's disease" (pp.39-40), to Francisco Goldman's intermingling of Christmas and Hanukkah, to Martín Espada who leaves the final word to the great Puerto Rican poet, Walt Whitman. Some memories are joyful, holiday recollections; others are deeply felt accounts of poverty, alienation, and deprivation. The recipes are authentic *Navidades* delicacies such as *tostones, buñuelos, tamales,* and *flan*.

The Latino Reader: An American Literary Tradition from 1542 to the Present. Edited by Harold Augenbraum and Margarite Fernández Olmos. Boston: Houghton Mifflin, 1997. 506p. ISBN: 0-395-76528-5. pap. $16.00. Gr. 9-adult.

Organized into three parts—Encounters, Prelude, and Latino United States—this historical anthology traces the roots of Latino writing both in the United States and internationally. Beginning with Alvar Núñez Cabeza de Vaca's *Account* (1542) and going up to Oscar Hijuelo's "The Handsome Man from Heaven" (1993), it includes more than fifty works from several genres: memoirs, letters, poetry, essays, drama, history, and fiction. The editors explain that the uneven aesthetic quality of the texts reflects various stages in the development of Latino literature. Although no single collection can represent the totality of the Latino tradition, this anthology is an attempt to reclaim a previously dismissed body of writing. Adolescents will enjoy the brevity and high reader appeal of many of these selections.

Lind, Michael. *The Alamo: An Epic.* New York: Houghton Mifflin, 1997. 351p. ISBN: 0-395-82758-2. $25.00. Gr. 9-adult.

Written as an epic poem, this is a fictionalized account about the part played in the Texas Revolution by William Barret Travis and the soldiers he commanded. The author states in a lengthy and comprehensive essay that he tried to follow history closely but, in the interest of drama or clarity, he accepted the devices of historical fiction. As such, he worked into the narrative every Alamo defender, including such legendary figures as Davy Crockett, Jim Bowie, and what he believes "is the fairest and most objective portrait of the "charismatic caudillo," General Antonio López de Santa Anna. Serious students of the Texas Revolution will appreciate this American epic that commemorates in a fresh, heroic poem, the siege and battle of the Alamo.

Lomas Garza, Carmen. *In My Family/En mi familia.* Translated by Francisco X. Alarcón. San Francisco: Children's Book Press, 1996. 32p. ISBN: 0-89239-138-3. $15.95. Gr. 2-4.

Like her successful first book, *Family Pictures/Cuadros de familia* (1990), Lomas Garza uses her sparkling narrative paintings to relate her memories of growing up in Kingsville, Texas, near the Mexican border. The accessible bilingual background stories reflect a joyous view of the Latino cultural experience as lived in the Southwest and the smooth Spanish rendition, peppered with a few colloquialisms, will be especially meaningful to Spanish speakers.

Lourie, Peter. *Rio Grande: From the Rocky Mountains to the Gulf of Mexico.* Honesdale, PA: Boyds Mill Press, 1999. 48p. ISBN: 1-56397-706-0. $17.95. Gr. 4-6.

In a remarkable engaging prose, Lourie, a devoted traveler and lover of the outdoors, recounts his discovery of the Rio Grande from its source in the Colorado Rockies, past New Mexico, to El Paso, Texas, where it becomes the border between Mexico and the United States for the rest of its 1000-mile course, to the crowded lower valley, where the "valiant river [runs] its grand course to the sea." In a brief afterword, the author/photographer explains that he respected the wishes of the Cochiti Pueblo by not including photographs of their annual corn festival. Because the issue of immigration across the Rio Grande border is complex and sensitive, he encourages the reader to read further about the relations between the two countries. Nevertheless, the stunning well-selected photographs, including gorgeous landscapes in full-color and historical shots of such famous characters as Billy the Kid, Pancho Villa, and others, and the measured yet straightforward text ("Trying to stop illegal crossings is like trying to hold a fistful of sand. The border is like a sieve" [p.29]) provide young readers with an enthusiastic overview to the beauty, history, and issues along the Rio Grande.

Love, D. Anne. *I Remember the Alamo.* New York: Holiday House, 1999. 156p. ISBN: 0-8234-1426-4. $15.95. Gr. 4-7.

Through the eyes of eleven-year-old Jessie and her courageous Mexican friend, Angelina, readers are exposed to the prejudices, ethnic tensions, and the Texas Revolution, including the siege of the Alamo, the Runaway Scrape, and the massacre at Goliad. Especially well developed in this action-filled novel are the dreams of wealth, power, and adventure of the Texas settlers. But with the exception of Angelina's kindnesses toward the settlers, there is little that explains the Mexican position. Nonetheless, this historical novel is an absorbing introduction to the main events and characters of this tragic era in United States-Mexican relations.

Love to Mamá: A Tribute to Mothers. Edited by Pat Mora. Illus.: Paula S. Barragán M. New York: Lee & Low Books, 2001. 32p. ISBN: 1-58430-019-1. $16.95. Gr. 2-5.

Intermingling tender Spanish expressions, thirteen Latino poets describe their love for their mothers and grandmothers in this affectionate collection that celebrates their special talents. From Trujillo's audacious *abuela* who rode horses when women didn't ride, to Aguilar's wise and humble *mami*, to Muñiz Mutchler's indefatigable *abuelita*, and Olivas's loving *abuelita* whose soft arms smell like perfume and frijoles and coffee and candy, these poems are sure to evoke memorable feelings that we all cherish. Effervescent full-page illustrations, rendered in pencil, cut paper, gouache, and computer graphics, beautifully complement each poem. Short biographies of the poets and a glossary are included.

Lowell, Susan. *Los tres pequeños jabalíes/The Three Little Javelinas.*
Illus.: Jim Harris. Flagstaff, AZ: Northland Publishing, 1996. 32p.
ISBN: 0-87358-661-1. $14.95. Gr. 2-4.

Based on the *Three Little Pigs,* this humorous bilingual
adaptation with a strong Southwestern motif will delight all readers
as three desert javelinas (extremely bristly relatives of swine from
the New World) trot away to seek their fortunes outsmarting
Coyote and his many magical tricks. The wonderfully amusing
full-page illustrations, rich with the colors and ambiance of the
Southwest, are the perfect background to the well-done Spanish
and English renditions on facing pages.

Marrin, Albert. *Empires Lost and Won: The Spanish Heritage in the
Southwest.* New York: Atheneum BFYR/Simon & Schuster, 1997.
216p. ISBN: 0-689-80414-8. $19.00. Gr. 7-12.

From Cabeza de Vaca's long walk in 1528 to the end of the
Mexican War in 1848, Marrin's engrossing narrative describes
the history of the Southwest in a most vivid text that captures
the thoughts, feelings, and customs of the period. Describing the
Europeans "touchy" honor system, he writes that Pedro de Vaca
took insults "very personally! He knifed the villain, tore out his
tongue, and threw it at the bystanders" (p.21). Not a fan of
Mexico's General Antonio López de Santa Anna, he states: "No
ordinary thug, he was one of history's complete scoundrels. . . . A
liar, a bully, and a thief. . . . Vain and conceited, he demanded his
luxuries, though everyone around him was miserable" (pp.116-
117). Numerous black-and-white maps, portraits, and original
drawings add interest to this history of the United States where
Spaniards, Mexicans, Texans, and Native Americans shared the
stage as they fought for land, gold, and power.

Martinez, Victor. *Parrot in the Oven: Mi Vida.* New York:
HarperCollins Publishers, 1996. 216p. ISBN: 0-06-026704-6.
$14.95. Gr. 7-10.

Written in a series of vignettes, this novel relates Manuel's
growing up years in a poor city project with an alcoholic, unem-
ployed father. The best aspect of this novel is the poetic language
that fluidly depicts the life of poor Mexican American families
amid violence, drinking, lack of money, and other indignities. Also
noteworthy is the author's honesty in depicting his father's feelings
about "white" guys: "My dad had it in for white guys like Mr.

It didn't matter that he was my teacher and that he was nice enough to give me a ride home. . . . Letting Mr. Hart take me home was the worst acid I could have poured into his stomach" (p.46). Despite an uneven character development of some members of Manuel's family and a sometimes confusing story, this is a touching, emotional novel that will ring true to many Latino youths in the United States and abroad.

McGinley, Jerry. *Joaquin Strikes Back.* Greensboro, NC: Tudor Publishers, 1998. 158p. ISBN: 0-936389-58-3. $18.95. Gr. 7-10.

Joaquin Lopez, a sophomore in high school, is passionate about soccer, but his new soccer coach won't give him a chance to play and constantly humiliates him, especially about his Mexican-American heritage. Perhaps it is too much to expect that an adolescent can deal with racist remarks at school by himself and "make the most of it" as Joaquin tries to understand and support his parents' decision to move to Wisconsin. And, perhaps, the author is too eager to show how people's negative attitudes toward Mexican-Americans, farm boys, beautiful girls who want to play soccer; and a sixty-year-old janitor hurt innocent people. Nonetheless, Joaquin is a likable character and the fast-moving plot incorporates enough excitement about soccer and competition in sports to make this novel particularly appealing to soccer fans.

Mora, Pat. *Confetti: Poems for Children.* Illus.: Enrique O. Sanchez. New York: Lee & Low Books, 1996. 28p. ISBN: 1-880000-25-3. $14.95. Gr. 1-3.

With gusto and a vivid imagination, this collection of twelve poems celebrates a Latino child's world by intermingling Spanish words and cheerful Latino culture and scenes beautifully complemented by fanciful acrylic illustrations. Latino children will especially enjoy these poems as they relive the joy of "Castanet Clicks," "Dancing Paper," or the warmth of "Abuelita's Lap." A glossary with a pronunciation guide will assist non-Spanish speakers.

Mora, Pat. *The Rainbow Tulip.* Illus.: Elizabeth Sayles. New York: Viking, 1999. 32p. ISBN: 0-670-87291-1. $15.99. Gr. K-3.

Estelita, a Mexican-American first-grader, is known at school as Stella. In a simple first-person narrative, she tells that her mother is not like other mothers: Her mother doesn't speak English. She doesn't wear makeup. Her hair is tied in a bun and

English. She doesn't wear makeup. Her hair is tied in a bun and she only wears dark long dresses. Estelita likes and participates in various school activities even as she experiences the difficulties and pleasures of being different. Despite the slight story, Latino families will identify with Estelita's close family feelings, especially her mother's affectionate Spanish expression, such as, "'*Ay, que muchacha.*'" Also appealing are the soft-toned pastel illustrations framed in white that show a loving family and a successful, yet different, Estelita at school.

Mora, Pat. *This Big Sky*. Illus.: Steve Jenkins. New York: Scholastic, 1998. 32p. ISBN: 0-590-37120-7. $15.95. Gr. 3-5.

This is a collection of fourteen poems that tell about the landscape, people, and animals of the United States Southwest. Spanish speakers will especially enjoy the interspersed Spanish words that add a Latino ambiance to this lyrical panorama, such as Old *Víbora* (Snake), who says, "Leave those doubts and hurts/buzzing like flies in your ears . . ." *paisano* (fellow countryman or road runner), *bruja* (witch), and *lobo* (wolf). The powerful color artwork, created with cut-paper collages, beautifully captures the space, fauna, and flora of the Southwest.

Mora, Pat. *Tomás and the Library Lady*. Illus.: Raul Colón. New York: Knopf, 1997. 32p. ISBN: 0-679-80401-3. $15.00; lib. ed. ISBN: 0-679-90401-8. $16.99. Gr. 2-4.

Inspired by the real life story of Tomás Rivera, who became chancellor of the University of California at Riverside, Mora relates, in an upbeat and tender manner, one summer in Tomás's childhood as he travels with his migrant family from Texas to Iowa harvesting fruit and vegetables. Especially touching is Tomás's relationship with Papá Grande (Grandfather) who was a wonderful storyteller, and the tall library lady, who welcomed him and introduced him to the library and its books. Colón's sensitive scratchboard illustrations beautifully capture Tomás's apprehensions as he stands in front of the library doors, as well as his fantasies from the world of books. So many of us from Hispanic America, including this reviewer, who did not enjoy the luxuries of school or public libraries in our countries of origin but had wonderfully loving grandparents, will identify with Tomás's story about librarians' kindnesses and a loving grandfather's stories.

Morey, Janet Nomura, and Wendy Dunn. *Famous Hispanic Americans.*
New York: Cobblehill Books/Dutton, 1996. 190p. ISBN: 0-525-
65190-X. $15.99. Gr. 7-10.

In a clear and interesting prose, the authors relate the achievements and contributions of fourteen contemporary Hispanic
Americans. Each chapter—12 to 14 pages—features an accom-
plished Latino/a, three or four black-and-white photos and a selected bibliography. A succinct foreword by Dr. Carlos E. Cortés
provides a basic overview of the Hispanic vs. Latino terminology
debate as well as a synopsis of Latinos in the United States. The
biographees are Felipe Alow, Jaime Escalante, Gloria Estefan,
Gigi Fernandez, Andy Garcia, Roberto Goizueta, Carolina Herrera,
Lourdes Lopez, Antonia Novello, Ellen Ochoa, Federico Peña,
Matt Rodriguez, Paul Rodriguez, and Ileana Ros-Lehtinen.

Murray, Yxta Maya. *What It Takes to Get to Vegas.* New York: Grove
Press, 1999. 308p. ISBN: 0-8021-1642-6. $24.00. Gr. 9-adult.

Set among the gyms and street fights of poverty-stricken East
Los Angeles, this snappy novel about a beautiful Rita Zapata, the
neighborhood's loose young woman, is certainly not for those who
object to descriptive prose with zesty sexual energy; colloquially
vivid dialogue; and a diverse cast of characters—from strippers to
looneytunes to trigger-happy conmen. Mature readers, however,
will find Rita's strong coming-of-age story a gritty tale of survival
and hope, in spite of a promiscuous mother who isn't much help
amid the violence and humiliation.

Nickles, Greg. *The Hispanics.* (We Came to North America) New
York: Crabtree Publishing, 2001. 32p. ISBN: 0-7787-0186-7.
$19.95; pap. ISBN: 0-7787-0200-6. $8.95. Gr. 5-7.

Briefly recounting the history of Hispanics in the United
States, this attractive, large-format publication describes the countries of origin, culture, fiestas, and heroes of the descendants of
Spanish-speaking peoples in North America. It is an easy-to-read
and easy-to-understand appealing introduction to Hispanics with
numerous color and black-and-white photographs, maps, drawings,
and period reproductions. Especially insightful are the "Eyewitness
to History" sections featuring excerpts by Ernesto Galarza,
Guillermo Cotto-Thorner, and a Salvadoran child refugee.

Noche Buena: Hispanic American Christmas Stories. Edited by Nicolás Kanellos. New York: Oxford University Press, 2000. 370p. ISBN: 0-19-513527-X. $32.50. Gr. 9-adult.

Featuring both original Christmas celebrations and beliefs among Hispanics and those that have been adapted from Anglo-American traditions, this collection of stories, poems, and songs depicts the joyous family and religious feelings of the season. From anonymous verses and poems from Mexico, to children's religious recitals, to selections from the works of such contemporary masters as Nicholasa Mohr and Gustavo Pérez-Firmat, this sample of narrative and lyric Hispanic literature highlights the spiritual meaning of Christmas and its effects on the worldview of all Hispanics.

Obejas, Achy. *Days of Awe.* New York: Ballantine, 2001. 371p. ISBN: 0-345-43921-X. $24.95. Gr. 9-adult.

With passion and a deep sense of family and history, Obejas's novel tells about life in Cuba, immigration, and dual identities. Alejandra, the strong and likable protagonist, who is bilingual, bicultural, bireligious, and bisexual, discovers her father's Jewish and Spanish roots as she learns about Judaism in Cuba. This is not a simple novel about the Cuban diaspora; rather, it is a provocative narrative about a person's search for her origins, both metaphorically and literally.

Ochoa, George. *The New York Public Library Amazing Hispanic American History: A Book of Answers for Kids.* New York: Wiley, 1998. 192p. ISBN: 0-471-19204-X. $12.95. Gr. 6-12.

This quick-and-handy source of basic facts and frequently asked questions about Hispanic American history, culture, and trivia is just right for those searching for superficial, quickie answers. Organized by geographic area and presented in a question-and-answer format, it provides brief answers to such issues as: Why was Mexico valuable to Spain? What was the result of the Mexican War? or such trivia as, What do you get if you break a piñata? Unfortunately, it also commits such blunders as neglecting to mention Jorge Luis Borges in the brief discussion of great South American writers; yet, Hollywood actors and actresses are overly represented throughout. In addition, the poorly reproduced maps and photos are definitely unappealing.

Olson, Gretchen. *Joyride*. Honesdale, PA: Caroline House/Boyds Mills Press, 1998. 200p. ISBN: 1-56397-687-0. $14.95. Gr. 8-12.

Seventeen-year-old Jeff McKenzie enjoys his life as a tournament tennis player with a beautiful girlfriend and planning for college. But after an unfortunate summer joyride through a local farmer's bean field, he is required to spend his summer working on an Oregon strawberry farm where he is exposed to a new lifestyle, new friends, and old prejudices against Mexican migrant workers. Perhaps the "bad" characters are a bit too contrived, but adolescents will enjoy the fast pace and the deeply felt passion of the American family and their Mexican laborers as they deal with both farm and people problems.

Ortiz Cofer, Judith. *The Year of Our Revolution: New and Selected Stories and Poems*. Houston, TX: Piñata Books/Arte Público Press, 1998. 101p. ISBN: 1-55885-224-7. $16.95. Gr. 9-12.

Much more mature and intense than Ortiz Cofer's previous *An Island Like You: Stories of the Barrio*, this collection of fifteen stories and poems reflects on such personal topics as her parents' marriage, her father's unexpected death and his "demeaning" night job, her Catholic-school education, her first love, and the ever-present tensions with her mother. These are not lighthearted coming-of-age stories and poems; rather, they are interconnected deeply moving reflections focusing on the tensions between Puerto Rican immigrant parents and an American-influenced adolescent who is heavily affected by the trends of the late 1960s.

Pérez, Loida Maritza. *Geographies of Home*. New York: Viking, 1999. 321p. ISBN: 0-670-86889-2. $23.95. Gr. 9-adult.

Compelling and engrossing, this novel by a young author born in the Dominican Republic narrates with painful honesty the problems of a large family as it deals with life in New York City. Iliana, the youngest of fourteen children, experiences prejudice at the university and returns home to confront a violent father, an alienated mother, a sister who is suffering a mental breakdown, another sister who is abused by her husband, and brothers who are finding life equally difficult. This is a remarkably insightful depiction of family life in a new country where being a Spanish-speaking black Hispanic makes poverty an even more formidable obstacle. Yet, a mother and her daughters reach out to each other despite the brutality, violence, sexual exploitations, unspoken truths, and many resentments.

Quiñonez, Ernesto. *Bodega Dreams.* New York: Vintage/Random, 2000. 213p. ISBN: 0-375-70589-9. pap. $12.00. Gr. 10-adult.

Set in Spanish Harlem in the midst of drug dealers and murderers, this powerful novel tells about Chino, an intelligent man, who is torn between his college education and the fast promises of Willie Bodega. Using the invigorating dialogue and vernacular of urban Latinos and the voice of a conflicted young man, Quiñonez depicts the poverty and temptations in their lives. Murder, romance, and passion provide the action; politics and deprivation set the tone.

Ramirez, Juan. *A Patriot after All: The Story of a Chicano Vietnam Vet.* Albuquerque: University of New Mexico Press, 1999. 180p. ISBN: 0-8263-1959-9. pap. $15.95. Gr. 9-adult.

Feeling compelled to make a statement about his experiences "as a grunt, especially as a Chicano" during the Vietnam War, Ramirez examines in a brutally honest voice the effects of his family, alcoholism, and drug abuse on his own life before, during, and after his service in Vietnam. From an abusive, alcoholic father who often beat him, to scurrilous experiences at boot camp, to distressing combat during and after the Tet offensive, readers will share the author's ultimate hope for a "spiritual, productive, loving existence." This is indeed a touching examination of the Vietnam War and a frank exploration of a troubled Mexican-American family. Some readers will applaud the author's openness about his personal problems; others may be bothered by his endless capacity to endure great suffering.

Ramos, Manuel. *Blues for the Buffalo.* New York: St. Martin's, 1997. 215p. ISBN: 0-312-15480-1. $21.95. Gr. 9-adult.

Luis Montez, a Chicano Denver attorney, is relaxing on a Mexican beach where he meets Rachel, a young and mysterious woman. Later he learns about Rachel's disappearance in a world of drugs, alcohol, and murder. Set in the heart of the Chicano community in Denver's northwest quadrant, this engrossing novel with a definite Latino/Hispanic ambiance includes enough action and excitement to appeal to previous readers of the three Luis Montez mysteries.

Reeve, Kirk. *Lolo & Red-Legs.* Flagstaff, AZ: Rising Moon/Northland, 1998. 111p. ISBN: 0-87358-683-2. $12.95; pap. ISBN: 0-87358-684-0. $6.95. Gr. 4-6.

When eleven-year-old Lolo García captures a Mexican red leg tarantula with the help of his grandfather, his mother and sister are horrified, his friends are impressed, and, surprisingly, his classmate Lisa Gomez is delighted. A most sympathetic pet storeowner gives him excellent advice and invites him to the Los Angeles County Fair. In a fast-moving pace and with the Mexican-American ambiance of East Los Angeles, this story will appeal to pet lovers and others as they sympathize with Lolo's disappointment upon the disappearance of his special tarantula. To add authenticity to the story, the author includes numerous expressions in Spanish that he states "reflects the language used in that region." But in fact some of the expressions are Anglicisms used by English speakers with a smattering of Spanish—not by Spanish speakers of the region. Nonetheless, this is an engaging story about a boy's experiences with his tarantula as well as with his Latino family, friends, and enemies.

Rice, David. *Crazy Loco*. New York: Dial Books, 2001. 135p. ISBN: 0-8037-2598-1. $16.99. Gr. 7-10.
　　With verve and gusto, Rice depicts everyday life in a border town in South Texas in this collection of nine stories that resonate with the ambivalent feelings of many Mexican Americans. In "Her Other Son," he speaks for many Mexican Americans when he states, "Though we had grown up listening to Spanish all our lives, we didn't speak the language very well. . . . " (p.18) And, "My Spanish was very Tex-Mex, and I thought he probably would laugh at me" (p.25). Other stories tell about family tensions, the prevalence of maids from Mexico, the pain of first love, the duties of altar boys, and other aspects that add a distinctive flair to life lived in two very different cultures.

Rodríguez, Luis J. *América Is Her Name*. Illus.: Carlos Vázquez. Willimantic, CT: Curbstone Press, 1998. 30p. ISBN: 1-880684-40-3. $15.95. Gr. 2-4.
　　Nine-year-old América Soliz, a Mixteca Indian from Oaxaca, Mexico, lives with her family in the crime-infected Pilsen barrio of Chicago. She is unhappy in school where she constantly experiences prejudice and rejection. But her attitude changes when a Puerto Rican poet visits her school and tells the children about the great Spanish-language poets. He encourages the children to write about their lives, their memories, and their feelings. Despite an intrusive adult voice and illustrations featuring an adult woman

rather than a nine-year-old girl, this story with striking full-color illustrations full of fantastic imagery and incongruous juxtaposition of folk and realistic elements honestly depicts the feelings, ambiance, and thoughts of many Mexicans who are struggling in a new culture.

Rosales, Francisco Arturo. *Chicano!: The History of the Mexican American Civil Rights Movement.* Houston, TX: Arte Público Press, 1996. 304p. ISBN: 1-55885-152-6. $45.00. Gr. 10-adult.

Designed to accompany a television documentary by the same name, this large-format publication strives "to remind not only students but the nation that, during the turbulent 1960s, Chicanos also struggled for justice and equality" (p.xxii). Beginning with the efforts of the "lost-land" generation in the mid-nineteenth century, the author describes early attempts by Mexican immigrants to protect themselves and examines the evolution, promises, and discontent of the Chicano Movement. Passionately, the author argues that the "conditions that led to the inequality of Mexican Americans are steeped first in a legacy of conquest and then in labor exploitation with little regard to their welfare" (p.xxi). Despite several unclear photos, this illustrated history will be treasured by supporters of the Mexican civil rights struggle in the United States.

Ryan, Pam Muñoz. *Esperanza Rising.* New York: Scholastic, 2000. 262p. ISBN: 0-439-12041-1. $15.95. Gr. 6-9.

Set first in Mexico in 1930 amid the turbulence of the Mexican Revolution and later in a company-owned farm labor camp in Southern California during the Great Depression, this poignant novel tells how thirteen-year-old Esperanza and her mother are forced to leave their wealthy ranch in Aguascalientes, Mexico. After enjoying a life of luxuries and servants, Esperanza and her mother must adapt to a life of poverty and hard work. This affecting novel will especially touch immigrants who know about the abuses and lack of opportunities in their home countries and the difficult process of adjusting to many different situations without the comfort of family and close friends. In a brief author's note, Ryan honestly discusses the sensitive "voluntary repatriation" that affected so many Mexicans and Mexican Americans in the 1930s.

Ryan, Pam Muñoz. *Mice and Beans.* Illus.: Joe Cepeda. New York: Scholastic, 2001. 32p. ISBN: 0-439-18303-0. $15.95. Gr. Pre-2.

With the warmth and bustle of a Mexican fiesta, grandmother Rosa María looks forward to celebrating Little Catalina's seventh birthday. As she plans a typical Mexican menu, buys a piñata, orders a cake, and decorates her house, she makes sure that mice are excluded. But when she realizes that thanks to the helpful mice that had filled the empty piñata, Little Catalina enjoyed the candy, she opens her heart even to them. Ryan's vibrant repetitive text, liberally sprinkled with Spanish words is accompanied by Cepeda's exuberant double-page spreads, which joyfully depict the color, fun, and humor of a Mexican family fiesta.

Salcedo, Michele. *Quinceañera!: The Essential Guide to Planning the Perfect Sweet Fifteen Celebration.* New York: Henry Holt, 1997. 239p. ISBN: 0-8050-4465-5. $25.00. Gr. 8-adult.

Discussing the Latina's popular *Quince* celebrations—from its historical and cultural traditions to the "Big Day's" elaborate festivities to other ways to come of age—this well-organized book offers detailed information to the *quinceañera*-to-be and her mother as they question: Why is it important to celebrate a fifteenth birthday? and What does it mean? Numerous details that need to be considered such as the honor escort, the court of honor, the *padrinos*, the religious celebration, and the reception are discussed. It is important to note that the author definitely considered minor differences among Latinos, such as *un chambelán* (among Mexicans), *escorte* (among Puerto Ricans), *galán* (Dominican), and other customs. The only fact that the author overlooked is the popular song "*Las mañanitas*," which is always an important "Happy Birthday" song for all Mexicans and Mexican Americans. Despite this caveat, this is a most comprehensive guide for all Latinas.

San Souci, Robert D. *Little Gold Star: A Spanish American Cinderella Tale.* Illus.: Sergio Martinez. New York: HarperCollins Publishers, 2000. 32p. ISBN: 0-688-14780-1. $15.95. Gr. 2-4.

Maintaining the charm of the popular Cinderella story, this adaptation with a Southwestern flavor replaces the Virgin Mary for the traditional fairy godmother and punishes the vain sisters with ugly horns and donkey's ears. Teresa, the always-kind and hard-working heroine, is rewarded by Virgin Mary with a gold star on her forehead. After a chance encounter, Don Miguel, a handsome young man whose mansion overlooks the plaza, is determined to find her, even though he does not know her name. Martinez's exquisitely styled watercolors depict a joyously romanticized Hispanic setting with elegant protagonists and comically exaggerated mean stepsisters and stepmother. Brimming with the aura of the United States, Spanish colonial era, and the magic of Cinderella, San Souci's wonderful adaptation concludes with everlasting happiness and kind stepsisters.

Sanchez, Reymundo. *My Bloody Life: The Making of a Latin King.* Chicago: Chicago Review Press, 2000. 299p. ISBN: 1-55652-401-3. $24.00. Gr. 9-adult.

This powerful firsthand account of a young Puerto Rican boy, who was raped by a male cousin at age five, denied food by his stepfather at age eight, and beaten by his abusive mother and second stepfather at age ten, is not for the fainthearted. After the family moves to Chicago, he escapes to the street to avoid their vicious beatings. Soon he joins the Latin Kings, the largest and most violent gang in the city. Henceforth, his life revolves around drugs, guns, violence, alcohol, sex, and constant brutality. As an insider's view of the terrible sadism inflicted on children by adults, Sanchez's story offers insights into the abuse and danger of gang life for the young. Despite the brutality, graphic violence, and sex, readers will empathize with Sanchez's dream of going to college, getting his degree, and putting his gang-infested life behind him.

Sandler, Martin W. *Vaqueros: America's First Cowmen.* New York: Henry Holt, 2001. 120p. ISBN: 0-8050-6019-7. $18.00. Gr. 6-9.

With gusto and admiration, Sandler reviews the history of vaqueros—"Hispanic cowmen," who invented "the art of being a cowboy by passing all they knew to the American cowpunchers" (p.viii). Beginning with the arrival of cattle and horses in the New World, he describes the work, clothing, equipment, and deeply held values of these often ignored victims of discrimination as well as racial and ethnic prejudice. Numerous black-and-white photographs and historic prints, informative inserts, source notes, a glossary, and a bibliography add to the value of this wonderful tribute to Hispanic vaqueros and their contributions to the knowledge, skills, and values of American cowboys.

Santella, Andrew. *The Battle of the Alamo.* (Cornerstones of Freedom) New York: Children's Press, 1997. 32p. ISBN: 0-516-20293-6. $18.00. Gr. 3-6.

The story of the infamous Battle of the Alamo in San Antonio, Texas, on March 5, 1836, is recounted through numerous color and black-and-white period photographs, drawings and maps, and an easy-to-read text. The participation of the American heroes of the conflict—Colonel William B. Travis, Colonel David Crockett, Colonel Jim Bowie, General Sam Houston—is highlighted as they fought a much greater Mexican force headed by General Antonio Lopez de Santa Anna. Readers interested in the United States perspective of this unsuccessful attempt to gain independence from Mexico where the 184 United States defenders lost their lives will not be disappointed.

Slate, Joseph. *The Secret Stars.* Illus.: Felipe Dávalos. New York: Marshall Cavendish, 1998. 30p. ISBN: 0-7614-5027-0. $15.95. Gr. K-2.

In New Mexico on a rainy, icy night, Sila and Pepe are sleeping with their grandmother. The children are worried that the Three Kings will not be able to find their baby manger in their little rancho. So their grandmother takes them on a magical journey to see how the secret stars ("Reeds sparkle and bend . . . frostflowers twinkle and chime. . . . The icy nest glistens. . . . The horns glitter with frost. . . .") help the Three Kings navigate. Happily, the morning of the day of the Three Kings, Pepe and Sila find a piñata, toys, and candy in the hay box. Despite a slight story, Dávalos's acrylic illustrations convey the Southwestern motif amid the magic realism and fantasy of the holiday.

Soto, Gary. *Buried Onions.* San Diego, CA: Harcourt Brace, 1997. 149p. ISBN: 0-15-201333-4. $17.00. Gr. 8-12.

Nineteen-year-old Eddie, a college dropout, is struggling to find a job in his violent barrio in Fresno, California. Despite numerous murders including those of his best friend and his cousin, Eddie does not want revenge. But finding a way out for a young Mexican American is not easy. Violence pervades and young men are the victims. In contrast to his popular, humorous style of many of Soto's previous stories and novels, *Buried Onions* depicts the harsh reality of life in the barrio, where random bloodshed triumphs amid vengeance and distrust. How real and how sad.

Soto, Gary. *Chato and the Party Animals.* Illus.: Susana Guevara. New York: Putnam, 2000. 32p. ISBN: 0-399-23159-5. $15.99. Gr. K-3.

Chato, the coolest cat of the barrio first applauded in *Chato's Kitchen* (1995), is now engaged in celebrating the birthday of his best friend, Novio Boy, who was raised in a pound and has never had a party. Because everybody needs a birthday party, Chato decides to organize a truly special *pachanga* for his friend with a *piñata, refritos, "Las mañanitas,"* cake, guacamole, tortillas, and, of course, lots of friends. But Chato forgot to invite the birthday boy, whom no one can find. Happily, at the last minute he appears, ready to eat and join the *pachanga,* which lasted until the sun went down. Soto's delightfully flowing language, peppered with the rich vernacular of Mexican Americans, sounds like a wonderful combination of salsa and friendship. Guevara's festive acrylic-on-scratchboard illustrations resonate with the folklore and traditions of Latino people.

Soto, Gary. *If the Shoe Fits.* Illus.: Terry Widener. New York: G.P. Putnam's, 2002. 32p. ISBN: 0-399-23420-9. $15.99. Gr. K-3.

As the youngest of three brothers and one sister, Rigo unhappily wears mostly hand-me-down clothes. So he is especially delighted when he gets a brand-new pair of loafers for his ninth birthday. But when the neighborhood's rascal makes fun of his shoes, he throws them in the closet. Of course by the end of the summer they were too tight. Fortunately, his uncle is more than happy to wear Rigo's almost-new hand-me-down shoes to his job. Soto's always-amusing depictions of Mexican-American family dynamics are enhanced by Widener's full-page, cartoon-style, stylized illustrations depicting farfetched family and social situations.

Soto, Gary. *Jessie De La Cruz: A Profile of a United Farm Worker.* New York: Persea Books/Braziller, 2000. 116p. ISBN: 0-89255-253-0. $17.95. Gr. 7-12.

The sorrow and numerous adversities in the life of Jessie De La Cruz, the United Farm Worker's first female organizer, are narrated by Gary Soto. He is a true admirer who attempts "to show how one woman's life became a part of *la Causa.*" This is not written in Gary Soto's relaxed, easy-going style; rather, it is a somber biography that tells about De La Cruz's poverty, death of family members, harsh working conditions, and the numerous injustices she constantly experienced. Readers interested in the political history of the farmworker movement will be especially interested in the black-and-white photos and her Congressional Testimony, Will the Family Farm Survive in America?

Soto, Gary. *Nerdlandia: A Play.* New York: PaperStar/Penguin, 1999. 88p. ISBN: 0-698-11784-0. pap. $5.99. Gr. 8-12.

Martin, a Chicano nerd who wears glasses and pants hiked up to his chest, is utterly in love with Ceci, the coolest *chola* in school. Enter their well-meaning friends with lots of "expert" advice to help them transform themselves—Martin becomes a cool *vato* and Ceci becomes a stunning nerd, now interested in a sweet, intelligent geek. Brimming with the vernacular of Chicano teenagers, including common Spanish slang expressions, this humorous urban comedy depicts the honesty and foolishness of love to which all teenagers can relate. Some Spanish-speaking adults might be taken aback by the "colorful" vernacular, but Latino teenagers will definitely enjoy it. A selected glossary with sanitized informal definitions is included.

Soto, Gary. *Novio Boy: A Play.* San Diego, CA: Harcourt Brace, 1997. 78p. ISBN: 0-15-201531-0. pap. $7.00. Gr. 6-9.

Rudy, a small, sweet, and funny ninth grader, anxiously prepares for his first date with Patricia, a tall romantic eleventh grader. With wit and charm, Soto describes the doubts and apprehensions of a first date, which only get worse when his mother, his uncle, and others offer opinions on the matter. The lighthearted dialogue liberally sprinkled with Spanish words and phrases, makes this play even more enjoyable, especially to Latino adolescents, who know about *chones* and *novios;* others may need to use the extensive glossary at the end. As a joyous comedy with a strong Latino flavor, this play is hard to beat.

Soto, Gary. *Off and Running.* Illus.: Eric Velasquez. New York: Delacorte Press, 1996. 136p. ISBN: 0-385-32181-3. $15.95. Gr. 4-6.

Fifth-grader Miata Ramirez (heroine of *The Skirt*) is running for class president and her best friend, Ana, is her running mate. They promise to clean up the school, plant flowers, and involve the parents. Their opponents are Rudy Herrera (last seen in *Boys at Work*) and his friend Alex, who propose more recess and ice cream every day. The serious girls worry about competing with the loud, funny, and popular boys. In a warm and lighthearted manner, Soto describes student politics amid cordial Latino family members and teachers. Despite the loosely connected chapters, young Latino readers will empathize with several embarrassing situations such as spilling *mole* sauce on your party dress at a *quinceañera*. The sprinkling of Spanish expressions adds authenticity to the dialogue and the characters.

Soto, Gary. *The Old Man and His Door*. Illus.: Joe Cepeda. New York: Putnam, 1996. 32p. ISBN: 0-399-22700-8. $15.95. Gr. Pre-2.

An old man in a little village was good at working in the garden but terrible at listening to his wife. So begins this amusing wise-fool story about an old man who doesn't listen to his wife's instructions and gets in trouble by taking *la puerta* (the door) to a barbecue party instead of *el puerco* (the pig). But all ends well due to his generosity and good intentions. The bold, bright illustrations depicting a kindly old man, a feisty old woman in red tennis shoes, and other hearty characters add to the humor and enjoyment of this story. The underlying Mexican ambiance and numerous Spanish words and phrases scattered throughout the text make this an especially fun story for Mexican American children to listen to or to read. A glossary of Spanish terms will assist non-Spanish speakers.

Soto, Gary. *Petty Crimes*. San Diego, CA: Harcourt Brace, 1998. 157p. ISBN: 0-15-201658-9. $16.00. Gr. 5-7.

In a poignant and sometimes pathetic manner, Soto describes the life of Latino youth as they confront numerous petty crimes in California's Central Valley. Subjects range from fourteen-year-old Priscilla, who takes what she wants whenever she wants it, to fourteen-year-old Alma, who tries desperately to buy back her dead mother's clothes, to thirteen-year-old Mario, who is still an infant in the art of scamming, to José, a born worker, who finally realizes that there are many liars like his cousin Arnie. This collection of ten stories will certainly ring true to many adolescents. In Soto's wonderful style, he condenses the pathos of life amid the trials of adolescence.

Soto, Gary. *Snapshots from the Wedding*. Illus.: Stephanie Garcia. New York: Putnam, 1997. 32p. ISBN: 0-399-22808-X. $14.95. Gr. K-3.

The joy and special events at a Mexican American wedding celebration are warmly described by Maya, a flower girl. She tells about Danny, who bears the rings; Father Jaime; a yawning altar boy with a dirty tennis shoe; the long wedding kiss; the special food; the toast; the mariachis; and the dancing. Soto's delightful and simple free verse, which is beautifully illustrated with amusing three-dimensional artwork created with sculpy clay, acrylic paints, wood, and lace, definitely convey the cheerfulness of family weddings as enshrined in a beautiful family album.

Spurr, Elizabeth. *Mama's Birthday Surprise*. Illus.: Felipe Dávalos. New York: Hyperion Books for Children, 1996. 57p. ISBN: 0-7868-0265-0. $13.95; pap. ISBN: 0-7868-1124-2. $3.95. Gr. 3-4.

Mamá loves to tell her three children—Pepe, Pablo, and Rosa—stories about wealthy *Tío* César, who lives in a faraway hacienda in Guadalajara, Mexico. Every Sunday, she writes him long letters full of only good news and lights a candle in his honor. Despite constantly changing stories, the children plan to surprise Mamá with money for four tickets to Guadalajara. And, to their surprise, a mantel portrait in their uncle's hacienda confirms Mamá's often-told story. The story seems a little far-fetched, but the appealing characters with a distinct Mexican-American flavor make this a pleasant story about a close relationship between a Latino mother and her children. Unfortunately, many of the numerous Spanish words sprinkled throughout are misspelled, including those in the glossary.

Stewart, Sue. *Musica!: Salsa, Rumba, Merengue and More*. San Francisco: Chronicle Books, 1999. 176p. ISBN: 0-8118-2566-3. pap. $22.95. Gr. 10-adult.

From the origins of the salsa orchestra in Cuba at the turn of the 1900s to "Africando" and the Dark Latin Groove of the late 1990s, this well-done survey of the world of Latin dance music will satisfy serious fans of the genre. In a fluid yet comprehensive narrative, it describes Salsa's immediate ancestors—*son, guaracha, mambo, guajira*—and highlights the contributions of such legends as Tito Puente, Celia Cruz, Ruben Blades, Gloria Estefan, and other lesser-known musicians. This is not a lighthearted overview of the "unsexy 'Latin Music'"; rather, it is a thorough depiction of the world of salsa, including its musical styles, instruments, and dances with numerous color and black-and-white photos, a discography, a bibliography, and an index.

Talbert, Marc. *Star of Luís*. New York: Clarion Books, 1999. 181p. ISBN: 0-395-91423-X. $15.00. Gr. 5-9.

Set in Los Angeles and New Mexico during World War II, this novel exposes the prejudices of the times amid unspoken family secrets and the power of religion and traditions. Luís, a Mexican American boy, and his mother move from East Los Angeles to New Mexico. It is here that he discovers that he is not Catholic, but Jewish and, because "it's always been dangerous to be a Jew," it's best to keep his Jewish identity as a family secret. Many allusions to Latino culture seem as contrived as the numerous misused or misspelled Spanish words and phrases used throughout. Nevertheless, Luís's story, with many unresolved pieces, will ring true to adolescents who have experienced discrimination for religious, ethnic, or national reasons.

Torres, Leyla. *Liliana's Grandmothers*. Illus.: the author. New York: Farrar, Straus & Giroux, 1998. 32p. ISBN: 0-374-35105-8. $16.00. Gr. Pre-2.

In a sweet and simple tone, the reader is introduced to Liliana's grandmothers: Mima, who lives down the street in the United States, and Mama Gabina, who lives in South America and speaks only Spanish. Despite superficial differences between the two grandmothers, children will identify with the warm feelings elicited by both grandmothers as they do yoga exercises, feed the birds, eat a peanut butter and jelly sandwich, or prepare a big Latin American lunch. Torres's pastel, double-page spreads affectionately convey the heartfelt bonds between Liliana and her two loving grandmothers, whether close or far away. This title is also available in Spanish.

Touching the Fire: Fifteen Poets of Today's Latino Renaissance. Edited by Ray González. New York: Anchor/Doubleday, 1998. 304p. ISBN: 0-385-47862-3. pap. $12.95. Gr. 9-adult.

By focusing on the fifteen poets (including himself) who González considers the major contemporary Latino poets, this anthology presents a wide diversity of voices and emotions. Topics range from a young girl's feelings as she vies for her father's attention, to a lawyer's instructions to culturally adapt, to tuberculosis, to the nightmare of the poor. These 150 poems will appeal to sophisticated adolescents as they encounter the expressive literary works of such poets as Judith Ortiz Cofer, Victor Hernández Cruz, Silvia Curbelo, Juan Delgado, Martín Espada, and Diana García.

Tripp, Valerie. *Again, Josefina!* Illus.: Jean-Paul Tibbles. (The American Girls Collection) Middleton, WI: Pleasant Co. Publications, 2000. 46p. ISBN: 1-58485-032-9. $3.95. Gr. 3-5.

In this newest title about life on the New Mexican frontier, nine-year-old Josefina struggles with her piano lessons but is delighted to see how much her baby nephew enjoys her music. The "Peek in the Past" section describes the importance of music, the joy of a *fandango*, and how to dance "*La Vaquerita*." As an introduction to "rancho" life in the early 1800s, this series is hard to beat.

Tripp, Valerie. *Changes for Josefina: A Winter Story.* ISBN: 1-56247-592-4. $12.95; pap. ISBN: 1-56247-551-6. $5.95.
————. *Happy Birthday, Josefina!* ISBN: 1-56247-588-6. $12.95; pap. ISBN: 1-56247-587-8. $5.95.
————. *Josefina Saves the Day: A Summer Story.* ISBN: 1-56247-590-8. $12.95; pap. ISBN: 1-56247-589-4. $5.95.
Ea. vol.: 70p. Illus.: Jean-Paul Tibbles. (American Girl) Middleton, WI: Pleasant Co. Publications, 1998. Gr. 3-5.

Like the previous three titles in this engaging American Girls series about the life and times of early New Mexico inhabitants, these easy-to-read stories with pleasing Latino characters and fast-moving plots provide the right amount of background information without overwhelming readers. In *Changes for Josefina*, Josefina and her sisters try to find a way to keep their beloved *Tía* Dolores from leaving their ranch amid the excitement of the Feast of the Three Kings, the last day of the Christmas season. In *Happy Birthday, Josefina!* Josefina learns she can become a *curandera* (healer) when she saves the life of a friend who has been bitten by a rattlesnake. Josefina's quick wits are especially important when her father must decide whether to trust an American trader in *Josefina Saves the Day.* Further historical information about New Mexico in 1824 is provided in "Peek into the Past" sections. Also included are glossaries of Spanish words.

Tripp, Valerie. *Josefina Learns a Lesson: A School Story.* 70p. ISBN: 1-56247-517-7.
————. *Josefina's Surprise: A Christmas Story.* 69p. ISBN: 1-56247-519-3.
————. *Meet Josefina: An American Girl.* 85p. ISBN: 1-56247-515-0.
Ea. vol.: (American Girl) Middleton, WI: Pleasant Co. Publications, 1997. pap. $5.95. Gr. 3-5.

Through nine-year-old Josefina, the youngest of four sisters, children are exposed to the life of a Mexican family who lives in New Mexico in 1824. In *Meet Josefina*, Josefina and her three sisters struggle with the endless chores of life in a Mexican rancho near present-day Santa Fe as well as the loss of their beloved mother. Fortunately, *Tía* Dolores, a strong and intelligent woman, comes to live with them and helps them overcome the effects of a flood in *Josefina Learns a Lesson*. The traditional Christmas *Posadas* are joyfully re-created in *Josefina's Surprise*. As engaging, easy-to-read stories with pleasing Latino characters and fast-moving plots, these stories will find grateful readers, especially among Latinas interested in the life and times of early New Mexico inhabitants. "Peek into the Past" sections and glossaries of Spanish words provide further historical information about New Mexico in 1824.

The United States and Mexico at War. Nineteenth-Century Expansionism and Conflict. Edited by Donald S. Frazier. New York: Macmillan Reference USA, 1998. 584p. ISBN: 0-02-864606-1. $125.00. Gr. 9-adult.

More than two hundred scholars from Mexico, the United States, and other countries contributed six hundred articles to produce this one-volume encyclopedia highlighting the important events—from 1821 to 1854—that resulted in the Mexican War, the Treaty of Guadalupe Hidalgo, and United States expansionism. Designed as a concise, first source for generations of future scholars, the editors endeavored to reflect an inclusive and balanced perspective of the numerous issues sensitive to readers on both sides of the United States-Mexico border. Hence, most entries reflect differing perspectives on such controversial topics as Claims and Damages, Camp Followers, Legacy of the War, James K. Polk, and Antonio López de Santa Anna. Especially noteworthy are the more than 50 black-and-white line-drawn maps and numerous illustrations taken from daguerreotypes of the 1840s. Also useful are the informative appendixes and exhaustive index.

Velásquez, Gloria. *Rina's Family Secret.* (Roosevelt High School Series) Houston, TX: Piñata Books/Arte Público Press, 1998. 151p. ISBN: 1-55885-233-6. pap. $9.95. Gr. 8-12.

Rina, the oldest of three children, lives with her Puerto Rican mother and alcoholic stepfather, who frequently and viciously beats her mother. Despite his horrible abuse, Rina's mother constantly forgives him. Told in the alternating voices of Rina and Ms. Martínez, a sympathetic counselor, who also suffered with a violent, alcoholic father, this intense, realistic novel is a haunting narrative about the pain and effects of domestic violence on women and children. Although a glossary is provided, English-speaking readers might be frustrated by the Spanish words and phrases scattered throughout, but this only adds to the Latino ambiance and characterizations. Certainly the pain and anguish of innocent victims of abusive fathers are universal, even if Rina's inner conflicts are solved a little too easily at the end.

Weaver, Beth Nixon. *Rooster.* Delray Beach, FL: Winslow Press, 2001. 301p. ISBN: 1-58837-001-1. $16.95. Gr. 7-12.

Set in rural Florida in the late 1960s, this highly packed novel includes family conflict, social clashes, and political disagreements, along with a touch of teenage romance and drugs. Through her Cuban refugee neighbors, fifteen-year-old Kady is exposed to the travails of families who had to flee Castro's Cuba. Tony, her neighbor, explains, "Fidel is the tyrannical king of his island castle, surrounded by a ninety-mile wide moat. And those still trapped inside those castle walls are his captives" (p.141). Especially appealing to adolescents is Kady's romance with seventeen-year-old Jon, a wealthy boy who showers her with gifts and delights her with marijuana brownies. Numerous incidents make this an overly long novel, but Kady's dilemmas and feelings about her mother and her young brain-damaged neighbor are honest and touching.

Welcome to Josefina's World, 1824: Growing Up on America's Southwest Frontier. (The American Girls Collection) Middleton, WI: Pleasant Co. Publications, 1999. 58p. ISBN: 1-56247-769-2. $14.95. Gr. 4-6.

Using parts of previous titles from the engaging American Girls series about the life and times of early New Mexico inhabitants, this handsomely illustrated large-format publication describes the history and daily activities of Mexican Americans in New Mexico during the 1800s. The brief easy-to-understand text and lively layout and design with numerous color drawings, period photographs, and maps on every page make this a most enjoyable introduction to the rich heritage of New Mexico. Included is information about women's rights, the Santa Fe Trail, El Camino Real, courtship and marriage, and other subjects.

Welter, John. *I Want to Buy a Vowel: A Novel of Illegal Alienation.* Chapel Hill, NC: Algonquin Books of Chapel Hill, 1996. 314p. ISBN: 1-56512-118-X. $18.95. Gr. 9-12.

Alfredo Santayana, an illegal alien from Guatemala who is learning to speak English by watching TV commercials, is eager to start a new life in Waxahachie, a small Texas town. Even though he had so little in Guatemala, he has even less in the United States. Enter Eva and Ana, two adorable American girls who befriend him and who try to make sense out of immigration laws, satanism, religion, bad marriages, the Spanish language, and other important considerations. This is indeed a wonderfully entertaining satire of American life, especially of current United States immigration laws that, had they existed in the 1700s and 1800s, would have certainly punished most ancestors of today's Americans.

Willard, Nancy. *The Tortilla Cat.* Illus.: Jeanette Winter. San Diego, CA: Harcourt Brace, 1998. 48p. ISBN: 0-15-289587-6. $15.00. Gr. 3-5.

Doctor Romero, who can cure anything, loves his five children but refuses to consider any pets in the home except goldfish. When a bad fever kills his wife Catherine, he does his best to be both father and mother. As one by one the children get sick with the deadly fever, they are saved by a little gray cat carrying a tray with a single tortilla. Rational Doctor Romero refuses to believe in the magic cat until he too gets sick. Winter's framed acrylic illustrations perfectly complement the magical realism in which this loving Latino family constantly experiences serious sickness and fears death. Some children (and their parents) may be bothered by the ever-present afflictions and preoccupations with losing a family member; others will enjoy the magical cat's tortillas that even defeat Papa's logic.

Wing, Natasha. *Jalapeño Bagels.* Illus.: Robert Casilla. New York: Atheneum BFYR/Simon & Schuster, 1996. 24p. ISBN: 0-689-80530-6. $15.00. Gr. Pre-2.

Pablo can't decide what to take to school for International Day from his parents' *panadería* (bakery). He helps his mother prepare *pan dulce*, *empanadas*, and *chango bars* and also helps his father with bagels, cream cheese, and lox. He decides on the jalapeño bagels because they are a mixture of both of them—just like him. Soft, full-page watercolor illustrations definitely convey the warm feelings in this ethnically diverse family in which both cultures have something to share and savor. A well-done glossary of Spanish and Yiddish terms adds further to its international/intercultural appeal.

Winick, Judd. *Pedro and Me: Friendship, Loss, and What I Learned.* New York: Henry Holt, 2000. 187p. ISBN: 0-8050-6403-6. $15.00. Gr. 8-12.

With candor and warmth, Winick uses his talents as a cartoonist to relate the life of Pedro Zamora, a Cuban immigrant who became HIV-positive as a teenager and dedicated his life to educate people about being gay and living with AIDS. Especially appealing to adolescents will be the graphic-novel format that combines an honest depiction of feelings with a sensitive narrative that deals with personal prejudices, confronting family about being gay, the importance of condoms and safe sex, mutual masturbation, and, ultimately, the death of his dear friend. Winick deftly integrates Zamora's Cuban background and close family ties with his own life as a cartoonist and their joint appearance on the 1993 MTV's *The Real World*, San Francisco. Adolescents will appreciate the forthright discussion .

Winter, Jonah. *¡Béisbol! Latino Baseball Pioneers and Legends.* New York: Lee & Low Books, 2001. 32p. ISBN: 1-58430-012-4. $16.95. Gr. 3-8.

Highlighting basic facts and the contributions of fourteen Latino baseball superstars, Winter celebrates the accomplishments of such champions as José Méndez (Cuba), who played between 1908-1927; Martín Dihigo (Cuba), considered "the greatest baseball player of all time"; Bobby Avila (Mexico), "the first Mexican player in the major leagues"; and Felipe Alou (Dominican Republic), whose success as a major league manager "was one of the last frontiers for Latin American ball players." In a double-spread format, full-page acrylic portraits of each player on the right page face the easy-to-read narrative on the opposite page. Baseball fans will rejoice in the groundbreaking achievements of these Latino stars.

Uruguay

Bridal, Tessa. *The Tree of Red Stars*. Minneapolis, MN: Milkweed
Editions, 1997. 287p. ISBN: 1-5131-013-4. $21.95. Gr. 9-adult.

In a moving, sometimes witty, account, Magdalena Ortega
Grey tells about her growing up years in Montevideo, where she,
her family, and friends enjoyed a life of privilege and luxuries that
included travel abroad, tea parties, and elaborate birthday and
wedding celebrations. With gusto and a refreshing perspective, she
describes the roles of women and men: "'. . . in Uruguay a woman
can't walk down the street without every male out of diapers feeling it his God-given right to comment on her appearance. Without,
of course, her having the right to reciprocate'" (p.36). The tone
changes when she joins the guerrilla Tupamaro movement and she
is confronted with the terror and brutality of a repressive regime
and the imprisonment and torture of innocent people. Despite oc-
casional intrusive social and political commentary, this tender
story of love and friendship provides an insightful view into the
realities of Latin American politics and life.

Venezuela

Horenstein, Henry. *Baseball in the Barrios*. San Diego, CA: Gulliver Books/Harcourt Brace, 1997. 36p. ISBN: 0-15-200499-8. $16.00; pap. ISBN: 0-15-200504-8. $8.00. Gr. 3-6.

Hubaldo, a fifth-grader who lives in Caracas, the capital of Venezuela, tells about his love for baseball and why he and his friends would rather play baseball than do anything else. Candid full-color photographs and an engaging text follow Hubaldo at his favorite pastime with his friends and at home with his family. Baseball fans will compare and enjoy this book, which includes the baseball Spanish vocabulary; others will be interested in this refreshing view of Venezuelan children engrossed in this "all-American sport."

Rawlins, Carol B. *The Orinoco River*. (Watts Library) New York: Franklin Watts, 1999. 63p. ISBN: 0-531-11740-5. $24.00. Gr. 4-7.

The location, origin, history, and uses of the Orinoco River, one of the five largest river systems in South America, are examined in a straightforward narrative. Highlighting the influence of the Orinoco on Venezuela's people and ecosystem, this appealing publication includes numerous large color photographs and sidebars. A glossary, bibliography, and online sites provide additional information for students interested in learning more about this up-to-now pristine river.

St. Aubin de Terán, Lisa. *The Hacienda*. Boston: Little, Brown, 1997. 342p. ISBN: 0-316-81634-5. $23.95. Gr. 9-adult.

Life in a Venezuelan hacienda is poignantly recounted in this engrossing memoir that tells about wealthy landowners whose lives focused on *Qué dirán?* [sic] (What will people say?) It was all about not losing face and about hacienda workers who could not read or write and who barely survive. Married at the age of

123

seventeen to a schizophrenic Venezuelan twenty years her senior, she leaves England to settle in her husband's sugarcane and avocado plantation, where she is constantly exposed to his abuses, violence, and neglect. As an extraordinary tale of survival, in which fantasy and romantic notions eventually result in an assertive woman who escapes to London with her child, this deeply felt memoir has the pace and setting of magical realism at its best.

Series Roundup

In addition to the books previously reviewed, these nonfiction series books offer overviews about the various countries, people, and cultures of Latinos. Books are grouped under series title and listed alphabetically by author. Full imprint information and tentative grade levels are provided.

Each title listed is recommended. Asterisk (*) denotes that the book is reviewed in the corresponding chapter.

AlphaBasiCs
Kalman, Bobbie, and Jane Lewis. *Mexico from A to Z*. New York: Crabtree Publishing, 1999. 32p. ISBN: 0-86505-382-0. $20.60; pap. ISBN: 0-86505-412-6. $14.97. Gr. 3-5.

America the Beautiful
Davis, Lucile. *Puerto Rico*. Danbury, CT: Children's Press, 2000. 144p. ISBN: 0-516-21042-2. $33.00. Gr. 4-7.

American Profiles
Oleksy, Walter. *Hispanic-American Scientists*. New York: Facts on File, 1998. 120p. ISBN: 0-8160-3704-3. $19.95. Gr. 7-10.

American War Series
Carey, Jr., Charles W. *The Mexican War: "Mr. Polk's War."* 2002. ISBN: 0-7660-1853-9.
Somerlott, Robert. *The Spanish-American War: "Remember the Maine!"* 2002. ISBN: 0-7660-1855-5.
Ea. vol.: 128p. Berkeley Heights, NJ: Enslow Publishers. $20.95. Gr. 6-9.

Ancient Civilizations
Deedrick, Tami. *Maya.* Austin, TX: Raintree Steck-Vaughn Publishers, 2001. 48p. ISBN: 0-7398-3585-8. $22.83. Gr. 2-4.

The Ancient World
Hull, Robert. *The Aztecs.* 1998. ISBN: 0-8172-5056-5.
Sayer, Chloë. *The Incas.* 1999. ISBN: 0-8172-5125-1.
    Ea. vol.: 64p. Austin, TX: Raintree Steck-Vaughn Publishers. $27.12. Gr. 5-9.

Artisans around the World
Franklin, Sharon, and others. *Mexico & Central America.* Austin, TX: Raintree Steck-Vaugh Publishers, 2000. 48p. ISBN: 0-7398-0121-X. $25.69. Gr. 3-6.

Baseball's New Wave
Stewart, Mark. *Alex Rodriguez: Gunning for Greatness.* Brookfield, CT: Millbrook Press, 1999. 48p. ISBN: 0-7613-1515-2. $22.90; pap. ISBN: 0-7613-1040-1. $6.95. Gr. 4-6.

Biography
Benson, Michael. *Gloria Estefan.* 2000. ISBN: 0-8225-4982-4; pap. ISBN: 0-8225-9692-X.
Márquez, Herón. *Latin Sensations.* 2001. ISBN: 0-8225-4993-X; pap. ISBN: 0-8225-9695-4.
    Ea. vol.: 112p. Minneapolis, MN: Lerner Publications. $25.26. ($7.95. pap.) Gr. 5-8.

Book Report Biographies
Gourse, Leslie. *Gloria Estefan: Pop Sensation.* New York: Franklin Watts, 2000. 112p. lib. ed. ISBN: 0-531-11569-0. $21.85; pap. ISBN: 0-531-16457-8. $12.95. Gr. 9-12.

Building History
McNeese, Tim. *The Panama Canal.* San Diego, CA: Lucent Books, 1997. 96p. ISBN: 1-56006-425-0. $16.95. Gr. 5-8.

Celebrity Bios—High Interest Books
Parker, Judy. *Mariah Carey.* 2001. ISBN: 0-516-23425-0.
————. *Ricky Martin.* 2001. ISBN: 0-516-23427-7; pap. ISBN: 0-516-29602-7.

Talmadge, Morgan. *Christina Aguilera.* 2001. ISBN: 0-516-23422-6; pap. ISBN: 0-516-23584-2.
————. *Enrique Iglesias.* 2001. ISBN: 0-516-23417-X; pap. ISBN: 0-516-23579-6.
Ea. vol.: 48p. Danbury, CT: Children's Press. $19.00. ($6.95. pap.) Gr. 4-9.

Cities of the World
Kent, Deborah. *Buenos Aires.* 1998. ISBN: 0-516-20592-7.
————. *Madrid.* 2000. ISBN: 0-516-20783-0.
Stein, R. Conrad. *Mexico City.* 1996. ISBN: 0-516-00352-6.
Ea. vol.: 64p. Danbury, CT: Children's Press/Grolier. $26.00. Gr. 3-5.

Cities through Time
Cory, Steve. *Daily Life in Ancient and Modern Mexico City.* Minneapolis, MN: Runestone Press/Lerner Publications, 1999. 64p. ISBN: 0-8225-3212-3. $17.95. Gr. 3-6.

Community Builders
George, Linda, and Charles George. *Luis Muñoz Marín: Father of Modern Puerto Rico.* New York: Children's Press, 1999. 48p. ISBN: 0-516-21586-8. $17.25. Gr. 3-5.

Contemporary Hispanic Americans
Carrillo, Louis. *Edward James Olmos.* 1997. ISBN: 0-8172-3989-8; pap. ISBN: 0-8172-6878-2.
————. *Oscar de la Renta.* 1996. ISBN: 0-8172-3980-4; pap. ISBN: 0-8114-9787-9.
Ling, Bettina. *José Canseco.* 1996. ISBN: 0-8172-3983-9; pap. ISBN: 0-8114-9790-9.
Pérez, Frank. *Dolores Huerta.* 1996. ISBN: 0-8172-3981-2; pap. ISBN: 0-8114-9789-5.
Pérez, Frank, and Ann Weil. *Raul Julia.* 1996. ISBN: 0-8172-3984-7; pap. ISBN: 0-8114-9786-0.
Rodriguez, Janel. *Gloria Estefan.* 1996. ISBN: 0-8172-3982-0; pap. ISBN: 0-8114-9786-0.
————. *Nely Galan.* 1997. ISBN: 0-8172-3991-X; pap. ISBN: 0-8172-6879-0.
Schwartz, Michael. *Luis Rodriguez.* 1997. ISBN: 0-8172-3990-1; pap. ISBN: 0-8172-6879-0.

Ea. vol.: 48p. Austin, TX: Raintree Steck-Vaughn Publishers. $24.26. ($7.95. pap.) Gr. 4-7.

Cornerstones of Freedom

Collins, Mary. *The Spanish-American War.* 1998. ISBN: 0-516-20759-8; pap. ISBN: 0-516-26337-4.

*Santella, Andrew. *The Battle of the Alamo.* 1997. ISBN: 0-516-20293-6; pap. ISBN: 0-516-26135-5. *See review p. 111.*

Winkelman, Barbara Gaines. *The Panama Canal.* 1999. ISBN: 0-516-21142-0; pap. ISBN: 0-516-26460-5.

Ea. vol.: 32p. New York: Children's Press. $19.50. ($5.95. pap.) Gr. 3-6.

Countries of the World—Bridgestone Books

Dahl, Michael. *Guatemala.* 1998. ISBN: 1-56065-738-3.

———. *Mexico.* 1997. ISBN: 1-56065-476-7.

Deady, Kathleen W. *Spain.* 2001. ISBN: 0-7368-0816-7.

Dubois, Muriel L. *Argentina.* 2001. ISBN: 0-7368-0811-6.

———. *Dominican Republic.* 2001. ISBN: 0-7368-0812-4.

Mara, William P. *Cuba.* 1999. ISBN: 0-7368-0068-9.

Riehecky, Janet. *Nicaragua.* 2002. ISBN: 0-7368-1107-9.

Thoennes, Kristin. *Peru.* 1999. ISBN: 0-7368-0155-3.

Ea. vol.: 24p. Mankato, MN: Bridgestone Books/Capstone Press. $14.60. Gr. 2-4.

Countries of the World—Gareth Stevens Publishing

Cramer, Mark. *Cuba.* 2000. ISBN: 0-8368-2316-8.

Daniels, Amy S. *Ecuador.* 2002. ISBN: 0-8368-2343-5.

Frank, Nicole. *Argentina.* 2000. ISBN: 0-8368-2315-X.

———. *Costa Rica.* 2000. ISBN: 0-8368-2323-0.

Grinsted, Katherine. *Spain.* 1999. ISBN: 0-8368-2312-5.

Heisey, Janet. *Peru.* 2001. ISBN: 0-8368-2333-8.

Jermyn, Leslie. *Colombia.* 1999. ISBN: 0-8368- 2308-7.

———. *Mexico.* 1998. ISBN: 0-8368-2127-0.

Ea. vol.: 96p. Milwaukee, WI: Gareth Stevens Publishing. $26.60. Gr. 4-7.

Country Insights

Morrison, Marion. *Cuba.* 1998. ISBN: 0-8172-4796-3.

*Parker, Edward. *Mexico.* 1998. ISBN: 0-8172-4791-2. *See review p. 52.*

Ea. vol.: 48p. Austin, TX: Raintree Steck-Vaughn Publishers. $17.48. Gr. 4-6.

Crafts from the Past
Chapman, Gillian. *The Aztecs*. Des Plaines, IL: Heinemann Interactive Library, 1997. 39p. ISBN: 1-57572-555-X. $25.64. Gr. 2-4.

Culture and Customs of Latin America and the Caribbean
Brown, Isabel Zakrzewski. *Culture and Customs of the Dominican Republic*. 1999. 198p. ISBN: 0-313-30314-2.

Foster, David William, and others. *Culture and Customs of Argentina*. 1998. 173p. ISBN: 0-313-30319-3.

Handelsman, Michael. *Culture and Customs of Ecuador*. 2000. 154p. ISBN: 0-313-30244-8.

Williams, Raymond Leslie, and Kevin C. Guerrieri. *Culture and Customs of Colombia*. 1999. 148p. ISBN: 0-313-30405-X.
   Ea. vol.: Westport, CT: Greenwood. $45.00. Gr. 9-adult.

Cultures of the Past
Galvin, Irene Flum. *The Ancient Maya*. 1997. ISBN: 0-7614-0091-5.

*Hinds, Kathryn. *The Incas*. 1998. ISBN: 0-7614-0270-5. *See review pp. 62-63.*

*Millar, Heather. *Spain in the Age of Exploration*. 1999. ISBN: 0-7614-0303-5. *See review p. 74.*

Stein, R. Conrad. *The Aztec Empire*. 1996. ISBN: 0-7614-0072-9.
   Ea. vol.: 80p. Tarrytown, NY: Benchmark Books/Marshall Cavendish. $19.95. Gr. 6-9.

Cultures of the World
Jermyn, Leslie. *Paraguay*. 2000. ISBN: 0-7614-0979-3.

———. *Uruguay*. 2000. ISBN: 0-7614-0873-3.

Kohen, Elizabeth. *Spain*. 1996. ISBN: 1-85435-451-5.

McGaffey, Leta. *Honduras*. 2000. ISBN: 0-7614-0955-6.

Pateman, Robert. *Bolivia*. 1996. ISBN: 0-7614-0178-4.

Sheehan, Sean. *Guatemala*. 1999. ISBN: 0-7614-0812-6.
   Ea. vol.: 128p. New York: Marshall Cavendish. $24.95. Gr. 6-10.

Daily Life through History
Carrasco, David. *Daily Life of the Aztecs: People of the Sun and Earth*. 1998. 282p. ISBN: 0-313-29558-1.

Malpass, Michael A. *Daily Life in the Inca Empire.* 1996. 164p. ISBN: 0-313-29390-2.

Sharer, Robert J. *Daily Life in Maya Civilization.* 1996. 236p. ISBN: 0-313-29342-2.

Ea. vol.: Westport, CT: Greenwood. $45.00. Gr. 9-adult.

Discover the Life of an Explorer
Kline, Trish. *Christopher Columbus.* 2002. ISBN: 1-58952-066-1.

———. *Francisco Coronado.* 2002. ISBN: 1-58952-428-4.

———. *Francisco Pizarro.* 2002. ISBN: 1-58952-297-4.

———. *Francisco Vázquez de Coronado.* 2002. ISBN: 1-58952-294-X.

———. *Hernán Cortés.* 2002. ISBN: 1-58952-293-1.

———. *Ponce de León.* 2001. ISBN: 1-58952-068-8.

Ea. vol.: 24p. Vero Beach, FL: Rourke Publishing. $18.60. Gr. 2-4.

DK Discoveries
Chrisp, Peter. *Christopher Columbus: Explorer of the New World.* 2001. ISBN: 0-7894-7936-2.

*Platt, Richard. *Aztecs: The Fall of the Aztec Capital.* 1999. ISBN: 0-7894-3957-3. *See review p. 53.*

Ea. vol.: 48p. New York: DK Ink. $14.95. Gr. 4-8.

The Drama of American History
Collier, Christopher, and James Lincoln Collier. *Hispanic America, Texas, and the Mexican War, 1835-1850.* Tarrytown, NY: Benchmark Books, 1999. 94p. ISBN: 0-7614-0780-4. $29.93. Gr. 6-9.

Enchantment of the World, Second Series
Augustin, Byron. *Bolivia.* 2001. ISBN: 0-516-21050-0.

Hintz, Martin. *Argentina.* 1998. ISBN: 0-516-20647-8.

McNair, Sylvia. *Chile.* 2000. ISBN: 0-516-21007-6.

Morrison, Marion. *Colombia.* 1999. ISBN: 0-516-21106-4.

———. *Costa Rica.* 1998. ISBN: 0-516-20469-6.

———. *Cuba.* 1999. ISBN: 0-516-21051-3.

———. *Ecuador.* 2000. ISBN: 0-516-21544-2.

———. *El Salvador.* 2001. ISBN: 0-516-21118-8.

———. *Nicaragua.* 2002. ISBN: 0-516-20963-9.

———. *Peru.* 2000. ISBN: 0-516-21545-0.

Rogers, Lura. *Spain.* 2001. ISBN: 0-516-21123-4.

Rogers, Lura, and Barbara Radcliffe. *The Dominican Republic*. 1999. ISBN: 0-516-21125-0.

Stein, R. Conrad. *Mexico*. 1998. ISBN: 0-516-20650-8.

Ea. vol.: 144p. New York: Children's Press. $32.00. Gr. 5-9.

Exploring Cultures of the World

Chicoine, Stephen. *Spain: Bridge between Continents*. 1997. ISBN: 0-7614-0143-1.

Kent, Deborah. *Mexico: Rich in Spirit and Tradition*. 1996. ISBN: 0-7614-0187-3.

King, David C. *Peru: Lost Cities, Found Hopes*. 1998. ISBN: 0-7614-0396-5.

Markham, Lois. *Colombia: The Gateway to South America*. 1997. ISBN: 0-7614-0140-7.

Pickering, Marianne. *Chile: Where the Land Ends*. 1997. ISBN: 0-7614-0333-7.

Ea. vol.: 64p. Tarrytown, NY: Benchmark Books/Marshall Cavendish. $17.95. Gr. 4-7.

Exploring the World

Doak, Robin Santos. *Francisco Vázquez de Coronado: Exploring the Southwest*. 2001. ISBN: 0-75670-123-7.

Heinrichs, Ann. *De Soto: Hernando de Soto Explores the Southeast*. 2002. ISBN: 0-75650-179-2.

————. *Ponce de León: Juan Ponce de León Searches for the Fountain of Youth*. 2002. ISBN: 0-75650-181-4.

Ea. vol.: 48p. Minneapolis, MN: Compass Point Books. $21.26. Gr. 4-6.

Faces and Places

*Berendes, Mary. *Mexico*. 1998. ISBN: 1-56766-372-9. *See review p. 39.*

————. *Spain*. 1999. ISBN: 1-56766-518-7.

Ea. vol.: 32p. Chanhassen, MN: Child's World. $22.79. Gr. 2-5.

Festivals of the World

Berg, Elizabeth. *Mexico*. 1997. ISBN: 0-8368-1686-2.

Fisher, Frederick. *Costa Rica*. 1999. ISBN: 0-8368-2022-3.

*Foley, Erin. *Puerto Rico*. 1997. ISBN: 0-8368-1687-0. *See review p. 66.*

Furlong, Arlene. *Argentina*. 1999. ISBN: 0-8368-2030-4.

*Jermyn, Leslie. *Peru*. 1998. ISBN: 0-8368-2006-1. *See review p. 63.*

McKay, Susan. *Spain*. 1999. ISBN: 0-8368-2035-5.

Roraff, Susan. *Chile*. 1998. ISBN: 0-8368-2012-6.
  Ea. vol.: 32p. Milwaukee, WI: Gareth Stevens Publishing. $18.60.
  Gr. 3-5.

Fiesta!
Bolivia. 1999. ISBN: 0-7172-9325-4.
Chile. 1999. ISBN: 0-7172-9327-0.
Guatemala. 1999. ISBN: 0-7172-9332-7.
Peru. 1999. ISBN: 0-7172-9106-5.
Puerto Rico. 1999. ISBN: 0-7172-9337-8.
Spain. 1999. ISBN: 0-7172-9338-6.
  Ea. vol.: 32p. Danbury, CT: Grolier Educational. $18.22. Gr. 3-5.

Finding Out about Holidays
Gnojewski, Carol. *Cinco de Mayo: Celebrating Hispanic Pride.*
  Berkeley Heights, NJ: Enslow Publishers, 2002. 48p. ISBN: 0-
  7660-1575-0. $18.95. Gr. 1-4.

First Battles
McNeese, Tim. *Remember the Main: The Spanish-American War*
  Begins. Greensboro, NC: Morgan Reynolds Publishers, 2002.
  112p. ISBN: 1-883846-79-X. $20.95. Gr. 5-8.

First Peoples
Eagen, James. *The Aymara of South America*. 2002. ISBN: 0-8225-
  4174-2.
Tahan, Raya. *The Yanomami of South America*. 2002. ISBN: 0-8225-
  4851-8.
  Ea. vol.: 48p. Minneapolis, MN: Lerner Publications. $23.93. Gr. 4-7.

First Reports
Gray, Shirley W. *Mexico*. 2001. ISBN: 0-75650-031-1.
Klingel, Cynthia Fitterer, and Robert Noyed. *Bolivia*. 2002. ISBN: 0-
  7560-182-2.
————. *Chile*. 2002. ISBN: 0-75650-183-0.
Press, Petra. *The Maya*. 2001. ISBN: 0-75650-081-8.
  Ea. vol.: 48p. Minneapolis, MN: Compass Point Books. $21.26.
  Gr. 3-5.

Footsteps in Time
Hewitt, Sally. *The Aztecs*. 1996. ISBN: 0-516-08071-1.
Thomson, Ruth. *The Rainforest Indians*. 1996. ISBN: 0-516-08074-1.
  Ea. vol.: 24p. Danbury, CT: Children's Press. $18.00. Gr. 2-5.

Frozen in Time

Patent, Dorothy Hinshaw. *Treasures of the Spanish Main.* Tarrytown, NY: Benchmark Books/Marshall Cavendish, 1999. 64p. ISBN: 0-7614-0786-3. $18.95. Gr. 5-7.

Getting to Know the World's Greatest Artists

*Venezia, Mike. *El Greco.* 1999. ISBN: 0-516-20586-2. *See review p. 75.*

———. *Frida Kahlo.* 1999. ISBN: 0-516-20975-2.

———. *Rivera.* 1999. ISBN: 0-516-42299-5.

Ea. vol.: 32p. Chicago: Children's Press. $11.95. Gr. 3-6.

Globe-Trotters Club

Dell'Oro, Suzanne Paul. *Argentina.* 1998. ISBN: 1-57505-114-1.

Jones, Helga. *Venezuela.* 2000. ISBN: 1-57505-122-2.

Milivojevic, JoAnn. *Puerto Rico.* 2000. ISBN: 1-57505-119-2.

Streissguth, Tom. *Mexico.* 1997. ISBN: 1-57505-100-1.

West, Tracey. *Costa Rica.* 1999. ISBN: 1-57505-109-5.

Ea. vol.: 48p. Minneapolis, MN: Carolrhoda Books. $22.60. Gr. 4-6.

Great Hispanics of Our Time

Romero, Maritza. *Joan Baez: Folksinger for Peace.* 1997. ISBN: 0-8239-5084-0.

———. *Ellen Ochoa: The First Hispanic Woman Astronaut.* 1997. ISBN: 0-8239-5087-5.

———. *Henry Cisneros: A Man of the People.* 1997. ISBN: 0-8239-5082-4.

———. *Jaime Escalante: Inspiring Educator.* 1997. ISBN: 0-8239-5085-9.

———. *Roberto Clemente: Baseball Hall of Famer.* 1997. ISBN: 0-8239-5083-2.

———. *Selena Perez: Queen of Tejano Music.* 1997. ISBN: 0-8239-5086-7.

Ea. vol.: 24p. New York: PowerKids Press/Rosen Publishing Group. $13.95. Gr. 2-4.

Great Journeys

Perl, Lila. *North across the Border: The Story of Mexican Americans.* Tarrytown, NY: Benchmark Books/Marshall Cavendish, 2001. 112p. ISBN: 0-7614-1266-3. $21.95. Gr. 5-9.

The Greenwood Histories of the Modern Nations
Kirkwood, Burton. *The History of Mexico*. 2000. 245p. ISBN: 0-313-30351-7.
Pierson, Peter. *The History of Spain*. 1999. 223p. ISBN: 0-313-30272-3.
Ea. vol.: Westport, CT: Greenwood. $35.00. Gr. 9-adult.

Groundbreakers
Manning, Ruth. *Francisco Pizarro*. Chicago: Heinemann Library, 2001. 48p. ISBN: 1-57572-369-7. $25.64. Gr. 3-5.

Hello U.S.A.
Johnston, Joyce. *Puerto Rico*. Minneapolis, MN: Lerner Publications, 2002. 84p. ISBN: 0-8225-4058-4. $25.26; pap. ISBN: 0-8225-4150-5. $6.95. Gr. 3-5.

Hispanic Biographies
Byers, Ann. *Jaime Escalante: Sensational Teacher*. 1996. 128p. ISBN: 0-89490-763-8.
Cruz, Bárbara C. *Frida Kahlo: Portrait of a Mexican Painter*. 1996. 112p. ISBN: 0-89490-765-4.
———. *José Clemente Orozco: Mexican Artist*. 1998. 128p. ISBN: 0-7660-1041-4.
———. *Raúl Julia: Actor and Humanitarian*. 1998. 128p. ISBN: 0-7660-1040-6.
———. *Rubén Blades: Salsa Singer and Social Activist*. 1997. 128p. ISBN: 0-89490-893-6.
Genet, Donna. *Father Junípero Serra: Founder of California Missions*. 1996. 128p. ISBN: 0-89490-762-X.
Gonzales, Doreen. *Cesar Chavez: Leader for Migrant Farm Workers*. 1996. 128p. ISBN: 0-89490-760-3.
———. *Diego Rivera: His Art, His Life*. 1996. 128p. ISBN: 0-89490-764-6.
———. *Gloria Estefan: Singer and Entertainer*. 1998. 128p. ISBN: 0-89490-890-1.
———. *Richard "Pancho" Gonzalez: Tennis Champion*. 1998. 128p. ISBN: 0-89490-891-X.
Goodnough, David. *José Martí: Cuban Patriot and Poet*. 1996. 128p. ISBN: 0-89490-761-1.
———. *Pablo Casals: Cellist for the World*. 1997. 128p. ISBN: 0-89490-889-8.

————. *Pablo Neruda: Nobel Prize-Winning Poet.* 1998. 128p. ISBN: 0-7660-1042-2.

————. *Plácido Domingo: Opera Superstar.* 1997. 104p. ISBN: 0-89490-892-8.

————. *Simón Bolívar: South American Liberator.* 1998. 112p. ISBN: 0-7660-1044-9.

Mirriam-Goldberg, Caryn. *Sandra Cisneros: Latina Writer and Activist.* 1998. 112p. ISBN: 0-7660-1045-7.

Ea. vol.: Springfield, NJ: Enslow Publishers. $18.95. Gr. 6-9.

History Beneath Your Feet
Chrisp, Peter. *The Aztecs.* Austin, TX: Raintree Steck-Vaughn Publishers, 1999. 48p. ISBN: 0-8172-5753-5. $27.12. Gr. 4-6.

History's Great Defeats
Barghusen, Joan D. *The Aztecs: End of a Civilization.* San Diego, CA: Lucent Books, 2000. 112p. ISBN: 1-56006-620-2. $24.95. Gr. 6-9.

Holidays and Celebrations
Schaefer, Lola M. *Cinco de Mayo.* Mankato, MN: Pebble Books, 2001. 24p. ISBN: 0-7368-0661-X. $13.25. Gr. Pre-2.

How It Was
Young, Robert. *A Personal Tour of La Purisima.* Minneapolis, MN: Lerner Publications, 1999. 64p. ISBN: 0-8225-3576-9. $23.95. Gr. 3-6.

How We Lived
Stein, R. Conrad. *In the Spanish West.* Tarrytown, NY: Benchmark Books/Marshall Cavendish, 2000. 120p. ISBN: 0-7614-0906-8. $18.95. Gr. 5-7.

The Importance of
Altman, Linda Jacobs. *Cesar Chavez.* 1996. ISBN: 1-56006-071-9.
Carroll, Bob. *Pancho Villa.* 1996. ISBN: 1-56006-069-7.
Lilley, Stephen R. *Hernando Cortes.* 1996. ISBN: 1-56006-066-2.
Ea. vol.: 111p. San Diego, CA: Lucent Books. $16.95. Gr. 7-9.

In American History
Brubaker, Paul. *The Cuban Missile Crisis in American History.* 2001. ISBN: 0-7660-1414-2.
Gaines, Ann Graham. *The Panama Canal in American History.* 1999. ISBN: 0-7660-1216-6.

Green, Carl R. *The Mission Trails in American History.* 2001. ISBN: 0-7660-1349-9.

Sorrels, Roy. *The Alamo in American History.* 1996. ISBN: 0-89490-770-0.

Ea. vol.: 128p. Springfield, NJ: Enslow Publishers. $20.95. Gr. 6-9.

In Their Own Voices

Hadden, Gerry. *Teenage Refugees from Guatemala Speak Out.* 1997. ISBN: 0-8239-2436-4.

———. *Teenage Refugees from Mexico Speak Out.* 1997. ISBN: 0-8239-2441-6.

Ea. vol.: 64p. New York: Rosen Publishing Group. $15.95. Gr. 5-8.

In World History

Flowers, Charles. *Cortés and the Conquest of the Aztec Empire.* 2001. ISBN: 0-7660-1395-2.

Worth, Richard. *Pizarro and the Conquest of the Incan Empire.* 2000. ISBN: 0-7660-1396-0.

Ea. vol.: 128p. Berkeley Heights, NJ: Enslow Publishers. $20.95. Gr. 6-9.

Jam Session

Dougherty, Terri. *Sammy Sosa.* Minneapolis, MN: Abdo Publishing, 1999. 32p. ISBN: 157765-348-3. $22.78; pap. ISBN: 157765-346-7. $6.95. Gr. 3-5.

Journey between Two Worlds

Malone, Michael R. *A Guatemalan Family.* 1996. ISBN: 0-8225-3400-2.

———. *A Nicaraguan Family.* 1998. ISBN: 0-8225-3412-6.

Ea. vol.: 64p. Minneapolis, MN: Lerner Publications. $22.60. Gr. 4-7.

Latinos at Work

Bankston, John. *Careers in Community Service.* 2002. ISBN: 1-58415-082-3.

Garcia, Kimberly. *Careers in Technology.* 2001. ISBN: 1-58415-087-4.

Menard, Valerie. *Careers in Sports.* 2001. ISBN: 1-58415-086-6.

Torres, John Albert. *Careers in the Music Industry.* 2001. ISBN: 1-58415-085-8.

Wade, Linda R. *Careers in Law and Politics*. 2002. ISBN: 1-58415-085-8.

Wilson, Wayne. *Careers in Entertainment*. 2002. ISBN: 1-58415-083-1.

———. *Careers in Publishing and Communications*. 2001. ISBN: 1-58415-088-2.

Zannos, Susan. *Careers in Education*. 2001. ISBN: 1-58415-081-5.

———. *Careers in Science and Medicine*. 2001. ISBN: 1-58415-084-X.

———. *Latino Entrepreneurs*. 2001. ISBN: 1-58415-089-0.

   Ea. vol.: 96p. Bear, DE: Mitchell Lane Publishers. $22.95. Gr. 5-8.

Latinos in American History

Roberts, Russell. *Pedro Menéndez de Avilés*. 2002. ISBN: 1-58415-150-1.

Whiting, Jim. *Francisco Vásquez de Coronado*. 2002. ISBN: 1-58415-146-3.

   Ea. vol.: 48p. Bear, DE: Mitchell Lane Publishers. $19.95. Gr. 5-8.

Latinos in Baseball

DeMarco, Tony. *Ivan Rodriguez*. 2000. ISBN: 1-58415-006-8.

———. *Vinny Castilla*. 2000. ISBN: 1-58415-008-4.

Gallagher, Jim. *Alex Rodriguez*. 2000. ISBN: 1-58415-010-6.

———. *Pedro Martinez*. 1999. ISBN: 1-883845-85-8.

———. *Ramon Martinez*. 2000. ISBN: 1-58415-009-2.

Macht, Norman L. *Roberto Alomar: An Authorized Biography*. 1999. ISBN: 1-883845-84-X.

Muskat, Carrie. *Bernie Williams*. 2000. ISBN: 1-58415-011-4.

———. *Moises Alou: An Authorized Biography*. 1999. ISBN: 1-883845-86-6.

———. *Sammy Sosa: An Authorized Biography*. 1999. ISBN: 1-883845-92-0.

Torres, John Albert. *Bobby Bonilla*. 1999. ISBN: 1-883845-83-1.

———. *Tino Martinez*. 1999. ISBN: 1-883845-82-3.

Vascellaro, Charlie. *Manny Ramirez*. 2000. ISBN: 1-58415-020-3.

   Ea. vol.: 64p. Childs, MD: Mitchell Lane Publishers. $18.95. Gr. 4-8.

Letters Home from

Gresko, Marcia S. *Mexico*. 1999. ISBN: 1-56711-402-4.

Halvorsen, Lisa. *Peru*. 2000. ISBN: 1-56711-414-8.

   Ea. vol.: 32p. Woodbridge, CT: Blackbirch Press. $16.95. Gr. 3-5.

Look What Came From

Harvey, Miles. *Look What Came from Mexico.* Danbury, CT: Franklin Watts, 1998. 32p. ISBN: 0-531-11496-1. $23.00. Gr. 2-4.

Lost Civilizations

Kallen, Stuart A. *The Mayans.* San Diego, CA: Lucent Books, 2001. 112p. ISBN: 1-56006-757-8. $27.45. Gr. 7-10.

Mapping Our World

Sammis, Fran. *South America.* Tarrytown, NY: Benchmark Books/ Marshall Cavendish, 2000. 64p. ISBN: 0-7614-0369-8. $27.07. Gr. 5-7.

Modern Nations of the World

Corona, Laurel. *Peru.* 2001. 112p. ISBN: 1-56006-862-0.
Fox, Mary Virginia. *Cuba.* 1999. 112p. ISBN: 1-56006-474-9.
Goodwin, William. *Mexico.* 1999. 128p. ISBN: 1-56006-351-3.
Grabowski, John F. *Spain.* 2000. 112p. ISBN: 1-56006-602-4.
    Ea. vol.: San Diego, CA: Lucent Books. $23.70. Gr. 8-12.

Nations of the World

Dalal, Anita. *Argentina.* 2001. ISBN: 0-7398-1279-3.
Green, Jen. *Mexico.* 2000. ISBN: 0-8172-5779-9.
    Ea. vol.: 128p. Austin, TX: Raintree Steck-Vaughn Publishers. $34.26. Gr. 4-7.

The New Americans

González-Pando, Miguel. *The Cuban Americans.* 1998. 184p. ISBN: 0-313-29824-6.
Torres-Saillant, Silvio, and Ramona Hernández. *The Dominican Americans.* 1998. 185p. ISBN: 0-313-29839-4.
    Ea. vol.: Westport, CT: Greenwood. $39.95. Gr. 9-adult.

Our Neighborhood

Flanagan, Alice K. *Buying a Pet from Ms. Chavez.* 1998. Illus.: Romie Flanagan. ISBN: 0-516-20773-3; pap. ISBN: 0-516-26293-9.
    ———. *Call Mr. Vasquez, He'll Fix It.* 1996. Illus.: Christine Osinski. ISBN: 0-516-20045-3; pap. ISBN: 0-516-26062-6.
    ———. *Riding the Ferry with Captain Cruz.* Illus.: Christine Osinski. ISBN: 0-516-20046-1; pap. ISBN: 0-516-26059-6.
    Ea. vol.: 32p. Danbury, CT: Children's Press. $20.00. ($6.95. pap.) Gr. K-2.

Port Cities of North America
Márquez, Herón. *Destination San Juan.* 1999. 80p. ISBN: 0-8225-2792-8.
————. *Destination Veracruz.* 1998. 72p. ISBN: 0-8225-2791-X.
    Ea. vol.: Minneapolis, MN: Lerner Publications. $23.93. Gr. 5-8.

Read and Discover
Davis, Lucile. *Cesar Chavez: A Photo-Illustrated Biography.* 1998. ISBN: 1-56065-569-0.
O'Mara, Anna. *Rain Forests.* 1996. ISBN: 1-56065-336-1.
    Ea. vol.: 24p. Mankato, MN: Bridgestone Books/Capstone Press. $14.60. Gr. 2-4.

A Real-Life Reader Biography
Boulais, Sue. *Andres Galarraga.* 1998. 32p. ISBN: 1-883845-61-0.
————. *Gloria Estefan.* 1998. 32p. ISBN: 1-883845-62-9.
Boulais, Sue, and Barbara J. Marvis. *Tommy Nuñez.* 1998. 32p. ISBN: 1-883845-52-1.
Cole, Melanie. *Jimmy Smits.* 1998. 32p. ISBN: 1-883845-59-9.
————. *Mariah Carey.* 1998. 32p. ISBN: 1-883845-51-3.
————. *Mary Joe Fernandez.* 1997. 32p. ISBN: 1-883845-63-7.
Granados, Christine. *Christina Aguilera.* 2001. 32p. ISBN: 1-58415-044-0.
————. *Enrique Iglesias: Latino Pop Star.* 2000. 32p. ISBN: 1-58415-045-9.
————. *Sheila E.* 2000. 32p. ISBN: 1-58415-019-X.
Marvis, Barbara J. *Rafael Palmeiro.* 1998. 32p. ISBN: 1-883845-49-1.
————. *Robert Rodriguez.* 1998. 24p. ISBN: 1-883845-48-3.
————. *Selena.* 1998. 24p. ISBN: 1-883845-47-5.
Menard, Valerie. *Cheech Marin: Actor, Comedian.* 2002. 32p. ISBN: 1-58415-070-X.
————. *Cristina Saralegui.* 1998. 32p. ISBN: 1-883845-60-2.
————. *Jennifer Lopez: Latina Singer/Actress.* 2000. 32p. ISBN: 1-58415-025-4.
————. *Oscar De la Hoya.* 1998. 24p. ISBN: 1-883845-58-0.
————. *Ricky Martin.* 2000. 32p. ISBN: 1-58415-059-9.
————. *Salma Hayek.* 2000. 32p. ISBN: 1-58415-018-1.
Menard, Valerie, and Sue Boulais. *Trent Dimas.* 1998. 32p. ISBN: 1-883845-50-5.
Muskat, Carrie. *Sammy Sosa.* 2000. 32p. ISBN: 1-883845-96-3.
Torres, John Albert. *Marc Anthony: Latino Recording Artist.* 2002. 32p. ISBN: 1-58415-069-6.

Wilson, Wayne. *Shakira: Latina Pop Rock Artist/Actress.* 2002. 32p. ISBN: 1-58415-071-8.

Zannos, Susan. *Cesar Chavez.* 1999. 32p. ISBN: 1-883845-71-8.
Ea. vol.: Childs, MD: Mitchell Lane Publishers. $15.95. Gr. 3-8.

Rookie Read-About Geography

Fowler, Allan. *South America.* 2001. ISBN: 0-516-21672-4; pap. ISBN: 0-516-27300-0.

Marx, David F. *Mexico.* 2000. ISBN: 0-516-22041-1; pap. ISBN: 0-516-27086-9.
Ea. vol.: 32p. Danbury, CT: Children's Press. $19.00. ($6.95. pap.) Gr. 1-3.

Rulers and Their Times

Mann, Kenny. *Isabel, Ferdinand and Fifteenth-Century Spain.* Tarrytown, NY: Benchmark Books/Marshall Cavendish, 2001. 80p. ISBN: 0-7614-1030-9. $19.95. Gr. 6-9.

Sports Great

Macnow, Glen. *Alex Rodriguez.* 2002. ISBN: 0-7660-1845-8.

Savage, Jeff. *Rebecca Lobo.* 2001. ISBN: 0-7660-1466-5.

Torres, John Albert. *Oscar De la Hoya.* 1999. ISBN: 0-7660-1066-X.
Ea. vol.: 64p. Berkeley Heights, NJ: Enslow Publishers. $17.95. Gr. 5-8.

Sports Stars

MacLean, Caleb. *Sammy Sosa: Cubs Clubber.* 1999. ISBN: 0-516-21662-7.

Stewart, Mark. *Andres Galarraga: The Big Cat.* 1997. ISBN: 0-516-20483-1.

———. *Ivan Rodriguez: Armed and Dangerous.* 1999. ISBN:0-516-21220-6.

———. *Pedro Martinez: Pitcher Perfect.* 2000. ISBN: 0-516-22048-9.

———. *Ramon Martinez: Master of the Mound.* 1997. ISBN: 0-516-20699-0.
Ea. vol.: 48p. New York: Children's Press. $19.50. Gr. 3-5.

The States and Their Symbols

Feeney, Kathy. *Puerto Rico: Facts and Symbols.* Mankato, MN: Hilltop Books/Capstone Press, 2001. 24p. ISBN: 0-7368-0644-X. $18.60. Gr. 2-4.

A Ticket To

Dell'Oro, Suzanne Paul. *Argentina*. 1998. ISBN: 1-57505-139-7.

Jones, Helga. *Venezuela*. 2000. ISBN: 1-57505-146-X.

Milivojevic, JoAnn. *Puerto Rico*. 2000. ISBN: 1-57505-144-3.

Streissguth, Tom. *Mexico*. 1997. ISBN: 1-57505-125-7.

West, Tracey. *Costa Rica*. 1999. ISBN: 1-57505-134-6.

> Ea. vol.: 48p. Minneapolis, MN: Carolrhoda Books. $22.60. Gr. 2-4.

A True Book (About Primates)

Martin, Patricia A. Fink. *Monkeys of Central and South America*. New York: Children's Press, 2000. 48p. ISBN: 0-516-21574-4. $21.50; pap. ISBN: 0-516-27017-6. $6.95. Gr. 3-5.

A True Book (Countries of the World)

Burgan, Michael. *Argentina*. 1999. ISBN: 0-516-21188-9; pap. ISBN: 0-516-26490-7.

Heinrichs, Ann. *Mexico*. 1997. ISBN: 0-516-20337-1; pap. ISBN: 0-516-26173-8.

———. *Venezuela*. 1997. ISBN: 0-516-20344-4.

Landau, Elaine. *The Dominican Republic*. 2000. ISBN: 0-516-1171-4; pap. ISBN: 0-516-27022-2.

———. *Peru*. 2000. ISBN: 0-516-1174-9; pap. ISBN: 0-516-27019-2.

———. *Puerto Rico*. 1999. ISBN: 0-516-20986-8.

Peterson, David. *Cuba*. 2001. ISBN: 0-516-27358-2.

———. *South America*. 1998. ISBN: 0-516-20769-5; pap. ISBN: 0-516-26440-0.

Rau, Dana Meachen. *Panama*. 1999. ISBN: 0-516-21189-7; pap. ISBN: 0-516-26497-4.

> Ea. vol.: 48p. New York: Children's Press. $21.50. ($6.95. pap.) Gr. 3-5.

Turning Points in World History

Stalcup, Brenda, ed. *The Inquisition*. San Diego, CA: Greenhaven Press, 2001. 267p. ISBN: 0-7377-0486-1. $22.96; ISBN: 0-7377-0485-3. pap. $14.96. Gr. 10-adult.

Understanding People in the Past

Rees, Rosemary. *The Aztecs*. 1999. ISBN: 1-57572-888-5.

———. *The Incas*. 1999. ISBN: 1-57572-889-3.

> Ea. vol.: 64p. Des Plaines, IL: Heinemann Library. $15.95. Gr. 3-6.

A Visit to
Alcraft, Rob. *A Visit to Mexico*. 1999. ISBN: 1-57572-848-6.
Foster, Leila Merrell. A *Visit to Puerto Rico*. 2001. ISBN: 1-57572-381-6.
Fox, Mary Virginia. *A Visit to Colombia*. 2001. ISBN: 1-57572-378-6.
———. *A Visit to Costa Rica*. 2001. ISBN: 1-57572-379-4.
Gillis, Jennifer. *A Visit to Cuba*. 2000. ISBN: 1-57572-380-8.
    Ea. vol.: 32p. Chicago: Heinemann Library. $21.36. Gr. 2-4.

Visual Geography Series
Argentina in Pictures. 1999. ISBN: 0-8225-1807-4.
Bolivia in Pictures. 1998. ISBN: 0-8225-1808-2.
Chile in Pictures. 1999. ISBN: 0-8225-1809-0.
Colombia in Pictures. 1996. ISBN: 0-8225-1810-4.
Costa Rica in Pictures. 1997. ISBN: 0-8225-1805-8.
Guatemala in Pictures. 1997. ISBN: 0-8225-1803-1.
Haverstock, Nathan A. *Cuba in Pictures*. 1997. ISBN: 0-8225-1811-2.
———. *Dominican Republic in Pictures*. 1997. ISBN: 0-8225-1812-0.
———. *Nicaragua in Pictures*. 1998. ISBN: 0-8225-1817-1.
———. *Paraguay in Pictures*. 1995. ISBN: 0-8225-1819-8.
Mexico in Pictures. 1999. ISBN: 0-8225-1801-5.
Panama in Pictures. 1996. ISBN: 0-8225-1818-X.
Peru in Pictures. 1997. ISBN: 0-8225-1820-1.
Puerto Rico in Pictures. 1995. ISBN: 0-8225-1821-X.
Sumwalt, Martha Murray. *Ecuador in Pictures*. 1998. ISBN: 0-8225-1813-9.
Uruguay in Pictures. 1999. ISBN: 0-8225-1823-6.
Venezuela in Pictures. 1998. ISBN: 0-8225-1824-4.
    Ea. vol.: 64p. Minneapolis, MN: Lerner Publications. $21.27. Gr. 5-9.

Viva Mexico!
Ancona, George. *The Fiestas*. 2001. ISBN: 0-7614-1327-1.
———. *The Folk Arts*. 2001. ISBN: 0-7614-1326-X.
———. *The Foods*. 2001. ISBN: 0-7614-1328-6.
———. *The Past*. 2001. ISBN: 0-7614-1330-8.
———. *The People*. 2001. ISBN: 0-7614-030-X.
    Ea. vol.: 48p. Tarrytown, NY: Benchmark Books. $16.95. Gr. 3-5.

The Way People Live
Kallen, Stuart A. *Life in the Amazon Rain Forest*. 1999. ISBN: 1-56006-387-4.

*Stewart, Gail B. *Life during the Spanish Inquisition.* 1998. ISBN: 1-56006-346-7. *See review p. 75.*
Ea. vol.: 96p. San Diego, CA: Lucent Books. $17.96. Gr. 7-12.

We the People
Burgan, Michael. *The Alamo.* 2001. ISBN: 0-75650-097-4.
Heinrichs, Ann. *California Missions.* 2002. ISBN: 0-75650-208-X.
Ea. vol.: 48p. Minneapolis, MN: Compass Point Books. $21.26. Gr. 3-6.

Welcome to My Country
Garret, Rosalie, and Nicole Frank. *Welcome to Costa Rica.* 2001. ISBN: 0-8368-2523-3.
Jermyn, Leslie, and Fiona Conboy. *Welcome to Mexico.* 1999. ISBN: 0-8368-2398-2.
Lim, Bee Hong. *Welcome to Colombia.* 2000. ISBN: 0-8368-2508-X.
Mesenas, Geraldine. *Welcome to Spain.* 2000. ISBN: 0-8368-2512-8.
Mesenas, Geraldine, and Nicole Frank. *Welcome to Argentina.* 2001. ISBN: 0-8368-2515-2.
Yip, Dora, and Janet Heisey. *Welcome to Peru.* 2002. ISBN: 0-8368-2533-0.
Yip, Dora, and Mark Cramer. *Welcome to Cuba.* 2001. ISBN: 0-8368-2516-0.
Ea. vol.: 48p. Milwaukee, WI: Gareth Stevens Publishing. $22.60. Gr. 2-4.

Women Changing the World
Silverstone, Michael. *Rigoberta Menchu: Defending Human Rights in Guatemala.* New York: Feminist Press, 1999. 112p. ISBN: 1-55861-198-3. pap. $9.95. Gr. 5-8.

World History
Frost, Mary Pierce, and Susan Keegan. *The Mexican Revolution.* 1997. ISBN: 1-56006-292-4.
Gow, Catherine Hester. *The Cuban Missile Crisis.* 1997. ISBN: 1-56006-289-4.
Lace, William W. *The Alamo.* 1998. ISBN: 1-56006-450-1.
Lilley, Stephen R. *The Conquest of Mexico.* 1997. ISBN: 1-56006-298-3.
The Mexican War of Independence. 1997. ISBN: 1-56006-297-5.
Nardo, Don. *The Mexican-American War.* 1999. 1-56006-495-1.
Nishi, Dennis. *The Inca Empire.* 2000. ISBN: 1-56006-538-9.
Ea. vol.: 112p. San Diego, CA: Lucent Books. $23.70. Gr. 7-12.

World in Maps
Bramwell, Martyn. *Central and South America*. 2000. ISBN: 0-8225-2912-2.
———. *North America and the Caribbean*. 2000. ISBN: 0-8225-2911-4.
    Ea. vol.: 56p. Minneapolis, MN: Lerner Publications. $29.93. Gr. 4-7.

A World of Holidays
Chambers, Catherine. *All Saints, All Souls, and Halloween*. 1997. ISBN: 0-8172-4606-1.
———. *Carnival*. 1998. ISBN: 0-8172-4613-4.
Vázquez, Sarah. *Cinco de Mayo*. 1999. ISBN: 0-8172-5562-1.
    Ea. vol.: 31p. Austin, TX: Raintree Steck-Vaughn Publishers. $22.83. Gr. 3-5.

The World's Children
Beirne, Barbara. *Children of Ecuadorean Highlands*. 1996. ISBN: 1-57505-000-5.
Hermes, Jules. *The Children of Bolivia*. 1996. ISBN: 0-87614-935-2.
———. *Children of Guatemala*. 1997. ISBN: 0-87614-994-8.
Ross, Michael Elsohn. *Children of Puerto Rico*. 2002. ISBN: 1-57505-522-8.
*Staub, Frank J. *Children of Cuba*. 1996. ISBN: 0-87614-989-1. *See review p. 15.*
———. *The Children of Sierra Madre*. 1996. ISBN: 0-87614-943-3.
———. *Children of Yucatán*. 1996. ISBN: 0-87614-984-0.
    Ea. vol.: 48p. Minneapolis, MN: Carolrhoda Books. $22.60. Gr. 3-5.

Author Index

Abelove, Joan, 62
Ada, Alma Flor, 25, 71
Aira, César, 1
Alarcón, Francisco X., 37, 77
Alcraft, Rob, 142
Alphin, Elaine Marie, 21
Altman, Linda Jacobs, 135
Alvarez, Julia, 16, 78
Amado, Elisa, 23
Anaya, Rudolfo, 37, 79, 80
Ancona, George, 9, 38, 80, 142
Appelbaum, Diana, 16
Arnold, Caroline, 70
Aronson, Marc, 62, 72
Atkin, S. Beth, 81
Atkins, Jeannine, 81
Augustin, Byron, 130

Baca, Jimmy Santiago, 81
Bankston, John, 136
Barghusen, Joan D., 135
Beirne, Barbara, 144
Benítez, Sandra, 21
Benson, Michael, 126
Berendes, Mary, 39, 131
Berg, Elizabeth, 131
Berrocal Essex, Olga, 59
Blum, Mark, 19
Borges, Jorge Luis, 1
Boulais, Sue, 139
Bramwell, Martyn, 144

Bridal, Tessa, 122
Brill, Marlene Targ, 23
Brown, Isabel Zakrzewski, 129
Brubaker, Paul, 135
Bunting, Eve, 39
Burgan, Michael, 141, 143
Burr, Claudia, 39, 40
Byers, Ann, 134

Calhoun, Mary, 82
Carey, Jr., Charles W., 125
Carlson, Lorie Marie, 82
Carrasco, David, 129
Carrillo, Louis, 127
Carroll, Bob, 135
Castillo, Ana, 40
Castro, Rafaela G., 82
Chambers, Catherine, 144
Chambers, Veronica, 59
Chapman, Gillian, 129
Chicoine, Stephen, 131
Chin-Lee, Cynthia, 25
Chrisp, Peter, 130, 135
Christopher, Matt, 17
Climo, Shirley, 41
Coburn, Jewell Reinhart, 41
Cockcroft, James D., 83
Cole, Melanie, 139
Collard, Sneed B., 7
Collier, Christopher, 130
Collier, James Lincoln, 130

Collins, David R., 83
Collins, Mary, 128
Conboy, Fiona, 143
Cooper, Martha, 84
Cordova, Amy, 84
Corona, Laurel, 138
Cory, Steve, 127
Courgeon, Rémi, 46
Cowan, Catherine, 41
Cowley, Joy, 84
Cozic, Charles P., 85
Cramer, Mark, 128, 143
Crawford, Mark, 42, 85
Cruz, Bárbara C., 134

Dahl, Michael, 128
Dalal, Anita, 138
Daniels, Amy S., 128
Davis, Lucile, 125, 139
Davis, William C., 85
Day, Nancy, 42
de Paola, Tomie, 85
Deady, Kathleen W., 128
Deedrick, Tami, 126
Delacre, Lulu, 25
Dell'Oro, Suzanne Paul, 133,
    141
DeMarco, Tony, 137
Dent, David W., 26
Doak, Robin Santos, 131
Dougherty, Terri, 136
Dubois, Muriel L., 128
Dujovne Ortiz, Alicia, 1
Dunn, Wendy, 102
Durán, Miguel, 86

Eagen, James, 132
Eboch, Chris, 42
Ehlert, Lois, 26, 43
Elya, Susan Middleton, 43, 86
English, Karen, 86
Ephron, Amy, 9

Espada, Martín, 87
Ewing, Lynne, 87

Feeney, Kathy, 140
Fernandez, Ronald, 66
Fernandez Barrios, Flor, 10
Fernández-Shaw, Carlos M.,
    87
Ferriss, Susan, 88
Figueredo, D. H., 88
Fine, Edith Hope, 44
Fisher, Frederick, 131
Fisher, Leonard Everett, 44
Flanagan, Alice K., 138
Flowers, Charles, 136
Foley, Erin, 66, 131
Foss, Clive, 10
Foster, David William, 129
Foster, Leila Merrell, 142
Fowler, Allan, 140
Fox, Mary Virginia, 138, 142
Fradin, Dennis, 72
Frank, Nicole, 128, 143
Franklin, Sharon, 126
Fraser, Mary Ann, 88
Frost, Mary Pierce, 143
Furlong, Arlene, 131

Gage, Amy Glaser, 24
Gaines, Ann Graham, 135
Gallagher, Jim, 137
Galvin, Irene Flum, 129
García, Cristina, 10
Garcia, Kimberly, 136
Garland, Sherry, 89
Garret, Rosalie, 143
Geeslin, Campbell, 45
Genet, Donna, 134
George, Charles, 127
George, Linda, 127
Gerson, Mary-Joan, 24, 45
Gibb, Tom, 11

Gillis, Jennifer, 142
Gnojewski, Carol, 132
Gold, John C., 28
Gold, Susan Dudley, 28, 60
Goldstein, Ernest, 46
Gollub, Matthew, 46
Gonzales, Doreen, 134
Gonzales, Manuel G., 90
Gonzalez, Juan, 90
González, Lucía M., 29
Gonzalez, Ralfka, 46
González-Pando, Miguel, 138
Goodnough, David, 134, 135
Goodwin, William, 138
Gordon, Ginger, 84
Gorkin, Michael, 22
Gourse, Leslie, 126
Gow, Catherine Hester, 143
Grabowski, John F., 138
Granados, Christine, 139
Gray, Shirley W., 132
Green, Carl R., 136
Green, Jen, 138
Gresko, Marcia S., 137
Grinsted, Katherine, 128
Guerrieri, Kevin C., 129

Hadden, Gerry, 136
Hall, Diane, 4
Halvorsen, Lisa, 137
Handelsman, Michael, 129
Harlan, Judith, 66
Harrigan, Stephen, 91
Harvey, David Alan, 11
Harvey, Miles, 138
Haverstock, Nathan A., 142
Hayes, Joe, 91
Heinrichs, Ann, 131, 141, 143
Heisey, Janet, 128, 143
Heller, Ruth, 19
Helly, Mathilde, 47
Henderson, James D., 29

Henkes, Robert, 92
Hermes, Jules, 144
Hernández, Ramona, 138
Herrera, Juan Felipe, 92, 93
Hewitt, Sally, 132
Hill, Christine M., 93
Hinds, Kathryn, 62, 129
Hintz, Martin, 130
Hoepker, Thomas, 24
Hoff, Rhoda, 11
Horenstein, Henry, 123
Hoyt-Goldsmith, Diane, 93, 94
Hull, Robert, 126

Jaffe, Nina, 67
Jenkins, Lyll Becerra de, 6
Jermyn, Leslie, 63, 128, 129, 131, 143
Jiménez, Francisco, 94
Johnson, Sylvia, 30
Johnston, Joyce, 134
Johnston, Tony, 47, 95
Jones, Helga, 133, 141
Joose, Barbara M., 47
Joseph, Lynn, 17

Kallen, Stuart A., 138, 142
Kalman, Bobbie, 125
Kanellos, Nicolás, 95, 103
Keegan, Susan, 143
Kenig, Graciela, 95
Kent, Deborah, 127, 131
Kimmel, Eric A., 48, 96
King, David C., 131
King, Elizabeth, 96
Kirkwood, Burton, 134
Kleven, Elisa, 97
Kline, Trish, 130
Klingel, Cynthia Fitterer, 132
Kohen, Elizabeth, 129
Kohli, Eddy, 12
Krauze, Enrique, 48

Kroll, Virginia, 49

Lace, William W., 72, 143
Laden, Nina, 73
Lamazares, Ivonne, 12
Landau, Elaine, 141
Leiner, Katherine, 13
Leonard, Elmore, 13
Levitt, Helen, 49
Lewin, Ted, 19
Lewis, Jane, 125
Lilley, Stephen R., 135, 143
Lim, Bee Hong, 143
Lind, Michael, 98
Lindop, Edmund, 60
Ling, Bettina, 127
Lior, Noa, 73
Lomas Garza, Carmen, 98
London, Jonathan, 67
Lourie, Peter, 20, 49, 50, 98
Love, D. Anne, 99
Lowell, Susan, 100

Macdonald, Fiona, 50, 63
Macht, Norman L., 137
MacLean, Caleb, 140
Macnow, Glen, 140
Malone, Michael R., 136
Malpass, Michael A., 130
Mann, Elizabeth, 63
Mann, Kenny, 140
Manning, Ruth, 134
Mara, William P., 128
Markham, Lois, 131
Markun, Patricia Maloney, 60
Marley, David F., 31
Márquez, Herón, 126, 139
Marrin, Albert, 73, 100
Martell, Hazel Mary, 64
Martí, José, 13
Martin, Patricia A. Fink, 141
Martinez, Victor, 100

Marvis, Barbara J., 139
Marx, David F., 140
Marzollo, Jean, 50
McDermott, Gerald, 50
McGaffey, Leta, 129
McGinley, Jerry, 101
McKay, Susan, 131
McNair, Sylvia, 130
McNeese, Tim, 126, 132
Meadows, Matthew, 74
Menard, Valerie, 136, 139
Mesenas, Geraldine, 143
Milivojevic, JoAnn, 133, 141
Millar, Heather, 74, 129
Mirriam-Goldberg, Caryn, 135
Missen, François, 14
Mohr, Nicholasa, 67
Montes, Marisa, 68
Mora, Pat, 51, 101, 102
Morey, Janet Nomura, 103
Morrison, Marion, 128, 130
Murray, Yxta Maya, 103
Muskat, Carrie, 137, 139

Nardo, Don, 143
Newhouse, Elizabeth, 11
Newman, Shirlee P., 64
Nickles, Greg, 2, 22, 103
Nishi, Dennis, 143
Noyed, Robert, 132

O'Mara, Anna, 139
Obejas, Achy, 104
Ochoa, George, 104
Oleksy, Walter, 125
Olson, Gretchen, 105
Oppenheimer, Andres, 51
Orozco, José-Luis, 32
Orozco, Rebeca, 56
Ortiz Cofer, Judith, 105

Parker, Edward, 52, 128

Parker, Judy, 126
Parker, Nancy Winslow, 61
Pascoe, Elaine, 52
Pateman, Robert, 129
Patent, Dorothy Hinshaw, 4,
    52, 133
Peña, Terri de la, 25
Pérez, Frank, 127
Pérez, Loida Maritza, 105
Perl, Lila, 133
Peterson, David, 141
Pickering, Marianne, 131
Pierson, Peter, 134
Pitcher, Caroline, 5
Platt, Richard, 53, 130
Pohl, John M. D., 53
Pomerantz, Charlotte, 33
Preller, James, 17
Presilla, Maricel E., 61
Press, Petra, 132
Pringle, Laurence, 53

Quiñonez, Ernesto, 106

Radcliffe, Barbara, 131
Ramirez, Juan, 106
Ramos, Manuel, 106
Rau, Dana Meachen, 141
Rawlins, Carol B., 6, 123
Rees, Rosemary, 141
Reeve, Kirk, 106
Regler, Margaret, 11
Reinhard, Johan, 64
Rice, David, 107
Riehecky, Janet, 128
Roberts, Russell, 137
Rodriguez, Janel, 127
Rodríguez, Luis J., 107
Rogers, Lura, 130, 131
Romero, Maritza, 133
Roraff, Susan, 132
Rosales, Francisco Arturo, 108

Ross, Michael Elsohn, 144
Ryan, Pam Muñoz, 108, 109

Salas, Osvaldo, 14
Salas, Roberto, 14
Salcedo, Michele, 109
Sammis, Fran, 138
San Souci, Robert D., 109
Sanchez, Reymundo, 110
Sandler, Martin W., 110
Sandoval, Ricardo, 88
Santella, Andrew, 111, 128
Santiago, Esmeralda, 68
Savage, Jeff, 18, 140
Sayer, Chloë, 126
Schaefer, Lola M., 135
Schiaffino, Mariarosa, 74
Schwartz, Michael, 127
Serrano, Francisco, 54
Sharer, Robert J., 130
Sheehan, Sean, 129
Shirey, Lynn, 34
Sierra, Judy, 75
Silverstone, Michael, 143
Sinclair, Andrew, 2, 14
Skármeta, Antonio, 34
Slate, Joseph, 111
Somerlott, Robert, 125
Sorrels, Roy, 136
Soto, Gary, 111, 112, 113, 114
Spurr, Elizabeth, 115
St. Aubin de Terán, Lisa, 123
Stalcup, Brenda, 141
Stanley, Diane, 54
Staub, Frank J., 15, 144
Steele, Philip, 54
Steele, Tara, 73
Stein, R. Conrad, 55, 127, 129,
    131, 135
Stewart, Gail B., 75, 143
Stewart, Mark, 126, 140
Stewart, Sue, 115

Strauss, Susan, 7
Streissguth, Tom, 133, 141
Sumwalt, Martha Murray, 142
Swope, Sam, 55
Symmes, Patrick, 3

Tagliaferro, Linda, 20
Tahan, Raya, 132
Talbert, Marc, 115
Talmadge, Morgan, 127
Tamar, Erika, 68
Tanaka, Shelley, 55
Thoennes, Kristin, 128
Thomson, Ruth, 132
Torres, John Albert, 136, 137,
    139, 140
Torres, Leyla, 34, 116
Torres-Saillant, Silvio, 138
Tripp, Valerie, 117

Uribe, Verónica, 70
Urrea, Luis Alberto, 56
Urrutia, María Cristina, 56

Vargo, Sharon Hawkins, 35
Vascellaro, Charlie, 137
Vázquez, Sarah, 144
Vázquez-Gómez, Juana, 57
Velasquez, Eric, 69
Velásquez, Gloria, 118
Venezia, Mike, 75, 133

Viesti, Joe, 4

Wade, Linda R., 137
Ward, Karen, 57
Weaver, Beth Nixon, 119
Weil, Ann, 127
Welter, John, 120
West, Tracey, 133, 141
Whiting, Jim, 137
Willard, Nancy, 120
Williams, Raymond Leslie,
    129
Wilson, Wayne, 137, 140
Wing, Natasha, 120
Winick, Judd, 121
Winkelman, Barbara Gaines,
    128
Winter, Jeanette, 57
Winter, Jonah, 121
Winther, Barbara, 35
Wolf, Bernard, 15
Wood, Tim, 65
Worth, Richard, 136

Yacowitz, Caryn, 58
Yip, Dora, 143
Young, Robert., 135

Zamorano, Ana, 76
Zannos, Susan, 137, 140

Title Index

A Is for the Americas, 25
Abuelita's Heart, 84
Again, Josefina!, 116
Agüero Sisters, The, 10
Alamo, The, 143
Alamo: An Epic, The, 98
Alamo in American History, The, 136
Alex Rodriguez, 137, 140
Alex Rodriguez: Gunning for Greatness, 126
All Saints, All Souls, and Halloween, 144
Almost a Woman, 68
Alphabet City Ballet, 68
América Is Her Name, 107
Americanos: Latino Life in the United States/La vida latina en los Estados Unidos, 79
Ancient Aztecs: Secrets of a Lost Civilization to Unlock and Discover, The, 50
Ancient Maya, The, 129
Andres Galarraga, 139
Andres Galarraga: The Big Cat, 140
Angels Ride Bikes and Other Fall Poems/Los ángeles andan en bicicleta y otros poemas de otoño, 77
Anthony Reynoso: Born to Rope, 84
Argentina, 128, 130, 131, 133, 138, 141
Argentina in Pictures, 142
Argentina: The Culture, 2
Argentina: The Great Estancias, 1
Argentina: The Land, 2
Argentina: The People, 2
At the Plate with . . . Sammy Sosa, 17
Aymara of South America, The, 132

Aztec Empire, The, 129
Aztec News, The, 54
Aztecs, The, 126, 129, 132, 135, 141
Aztecs: End of a Civilization, The, 135
Aztecs: The Fall of the Aztec Capital, The, 52, 130

Barrilete: A Kite for the Day of the Dead, 23
Barrio: José's Neighborhood, 80
Baseball in the Barrios, 123
Battle of the Alamo, The, 110, 128
Bear for Miguel, A, 21
Beautiful Butterfly: A Folktale from Spain, The, 75
¡Béisbol! Latino Baseball Pioneers and Legends, 121
Bernie Williams, 137
*Best Careers for Bilingual Latinos: Market Your Fluency in Spanish
     to Get Ahead on the Job*, 95
Bitter Grounds, 21
Blessed by Thunder: Memoir of a Cuban Girlhood, 10
Blues for the Buffalo, 106
Bobby Bonilla, 137
Bodega Dreams, 105
Bolivia, 129, 130, 132
Bolivia in Pictures, 142
*Bordering on Chaos: Guerrillas, Stockbrokers, Politicians and
     Mexico's Road to Prosperity*, 51
Breaking Through, 94
Broken Shields, 39
Buenos Aires, 127
Buried Onions, 111
Butterfly Boy, 49
Buying a Pet from Ms. Chavez, 138
Buzz, Buzz, Buzz, 70
*By the Lake of Sleeping Children: The Secret Life of the Mexican
     Border*, 56

California Missions, 143
Call Mr. Vasquez, He'll Fix It, 138
*¡Cámara! Ciudad de México: Monumentos de una nueva
     generación/Picture Mexico City: Landmarks of a New
     Generation*, 40
Careers in Community Service, 136
Careers in Education, 137

Careers in Entertainment, 137
Careers in Law and Politics, 137
Careers in Publishing and Communications, 137
Careers in Science and Medicine, 137
Careers in Sports, 136
Careers in Technology, 136
Careers in the Music Industry, 136
Carnival, 144
Celebrate! in Central America, 4
Central and South America, 144
Cesar Chavez, 135, 140
Cesar Chavez: A Photo-Illustrated Biography, 139
Cesar Chavez: Leader for Migrant Farm Workers, 134
Changes for Josefina: A Winter Story, 116
Charro: The Mexican Cowboy, 38
Chasing Che: A Motorcycle Journey in Search of the Guevara Legend, 3
Chato and the Party Animals, 111
Che Guevara, 2, 15
Cheech Marin: Actor, Comedian, 139
Chicano!: The History of the Mexican American Civil Rights Movement, 107
Children of Bolivia, The, 144
Children of Cuba, 15, 144
Children of Ecuadorean Highlands, 144
Children of Guatemala, 144
Children of Puerto Rico, 144
Children of Sierra Madre, The, 144
Children of Yucatán, 144
Chile, 130, 132
Chile in Pictures, 142
Chile: Where the Land Ends, 131
Christina Aguilera, 127, 139
Christopher Columbus, 130
Christopher Columbus: Explorer of the New World, 130
Cinco de Mayo, 135, 144
Cinco de Mayo: Celebrating Hispanic Pride, 132
Cinco de Mayo: Yesterday and Today, 56
Circuit: Stories from the Life of a Migrant Child, The, 94
Civilizations of Peru before 1535, 64
Cocoa Ice, 16
Colombia, 128, 130

Colombia in Pictures, 142
Colombia: The Gateway to South America, 131
Color of My Words, The, 17
Composition, The, 34
Confetti: Poems for Children, 101
Conquest of Mexico, The, 143
Cortés and the Conquest of the Aztec Empire, 136
Costa Rica, 128, 130, 131, 133, 141
Costa Rica in Pictures, 142
CrashBoomLove, 92
Crazy Loco, 107
Cristina Saralegui, 139
Cuba, 11, 12, 128, 130, 138, 141
Cuba: After the Revolution, 15
Cuba in Pictures, 142
Cuba Libre, 13
Cuban Americans, The, 138
Cuban Kids, 9
Cuban Missile Crisis, The, 143
Cuban Missile Crisis in American History, The, 135
Cuckoo/Cucú, 43
Culture and Customs of Argentina, 129
Culture and Customs of Colombia, 129
Culture and Customs of Ecuador, 129
Culture and Customs of the Dominican Republic, 129

Daily Life in Ancient and Modern Mexico City, 127
Daily Life in Maya Civilization, 130
Daily Life in the Inca Empire, 130
Daily Life of the Aztecs: People of the Sun and Earth, 129
Days of Awe, 104
De Soto: Hernando de Soto Explores the Southeast, 131
Defeat of the Spanish Armada, 72
Delia's Way, 59
Destination San Juan, 139
Destination Veracruz, 139
Dictionary of Chicano Folklore, 82
Dictionary of Mexican Rulers, 1325-1997, 57
Diego Rivera: His Art, His Life, 134
Diez deditos/Ten Little Fingers and Other Play Rhymes and Action Songs from Latin America, 32
Discovering the Inca Ice Maiden: My Adventures on Ampato, 64

Dolores Huerta, 127
Dominican Americans, The, 138
Dominican Republic, 128
Dominican Republic, The, 131, 141
Dominican Republic in Pictures, 142
Domitila: A Cinderella Tale from the Mexican Tradition, 41
Don't Spit on My Corner, 86

Ecuador, 128, 130
Ecuador in Pictures, 142
Edward James Olmos, 127
Eight Animals on the Town, 43
El Greco, 75, 133
El Salvador, 130
El Salvador: The Land, 22
El Salvador: The People and Culture, 22
Elegy on the Death of César Chávez, 79
Elena, 54
Ellen Ochoa: The First Hispanic Woman Astronaut, 133
Empires Lost and Won: The Spanish Heritage in the Southwest, 100
Encyclopedia of Contemporary Latin American and Caribbean Cultures, 27
Encyclopedia of Latin American and Caribbean Art, 27
Encyclopedia of Latin American History and Culture, 27
Encyclopedia of Latin American Literature, 28
Encyclopedia of Mexico: History, Society & Culture, 44
Encyclopedia of the Mexican-American War, 42, 85
Enrique Iglesias, 127
Enrique Iglesias: Latino Pop Star, 139
Environments of the Western Hemisphere, 28
Esperanza Rising, 108
Eva Perón, 1
Extraordinary Life: The Story of a Monarch Butterfly, An, 53

Famous Hispanic Americans, 102
Farmworker's Friend: The Story of Cesar Chavez, 83
Father Junípero Serra: Founder of California Missions, 134
Fidel Castro, 10
Fidel Castro: Leader of Cuba's Revolution, 11
Fidel's Cuba: A Revolution in Pictures, 14
Fiesta Femenina: Celebrating Women in Mexican Folktale, 45
Fiesta Fireworks, 38

Fiestas, The, 142

Fight in the Fields: Cesar Chavez and the Farmworkers Movement, The, 88

Folk Arts, The, 142

Foods, The, 142

Francisco Coronado, 130

Francisco Pizarro, 130, 134

Francisco Vásquez de Coronado, 137

Francisco Vázquez de Coronado, 130

Francisco Vázquez de Coronado: Exploring the Southwest, 131

Frida Kahlo, 133

Frida Kahlo: Portrait of a Mexican Painter, 134

From Grandmother to Granddaughter: Salvadoran Women's Stories, 22

From the Bellybutton of the Moon and Other Summer Poems/Del ombligo de la luna y otros poemas de verano, 37

Galápagos in 3-D, 19

Galápagos Islands: Nature's Delicate Balance at Risk, 20

Galápagos Means "Tortoises," 19

Gates of the Alamo, The, 91

Gathering the Sun: An Alphabet in Spanish and English, 25

Geographies of Home, 105

Get Set! Swim!, 81

Ghost Wings, 47

Gloria Estefan, 126, 127, 139

Gloria Estefan: Pop Sensation, 126

Gloria Estefan: Singer and Entertainer, 134

Go and Come Back, 62

Gods and Goddesses of the Ancient Maya, 44

Going Home, 39

Golden Flower: A Taino Myth from Puerto Rico, The, 67

Golden Tales: Myths, Legends and Folktales from Latin America, 25

Gotta Go! Gotta Go!, 55

Governments of the Western Hemisphere, 28

Goya, 74

Gracias, the Thanksgiving Turkey, 84

Grandma and Me at the Flea/Los meros meros remateros, 92

Grandma's Records, 69

Guatemala, 128, 129, 132

Guatemala in Pictures, 142

Guatemalan Family, A, 136

Hacienda, The, 123
Happy Birthday, Josefina!, 116
Harvest, 38, 80
Harvest of Empire: A History of Latinos in America, 90
Henry Cisneros: A Man of the People, 133
Hernán Cortés, 130
Hernando Cortes, 135
Hispanic America, Texas, and the Mexican War, 1835-1850, 130
Hispanic Firsts: 500 Years of Extraordinary Achievement, 95
Hispanic Presence in North America: From 1492 to Today, The, 87
Hispanic-American Scientists, 125
Hispanics, The, 103
History of Mexico, The, 134
History of Spain, The, 134
Home at Last, 86
Honduras, 129
Hooray, a Piñata!, 96
How Nanita Learned to Make Flan, 45
How Tía Lola Came to (Visit) Stay, 78
Hurray for Three Kings' Day!, 82
Hurricane!, 67

I Remember the Alamo, 99
I Want to Buy a Vowel: A Novel of Illegal Alienation, 119
If the Shoe Fits, 112
Iguanas in the Snow and Other Winter Poems/Iguanas en la nieve y otros poemas de invierno, 77
Illegal Immigration, 85
In My Family/En mi familia, 98
In the Spanish West, 135
Inca Empire, The, 143
Inca Town, 63
Incas, The, 62, 65, 126, 129, 141
Inquisition, The, 141
Isabel, Ferdinand and Fifteenth-Century Spain, 140
Isabella: A Wish for Miguel, Peru, 1820, 64
It's Panama's Canal!, 60
Ivan Rodriguez, 137
Ivan Rodriguez: Armed and Dangerous, 140

Jade and Iron: Latin American Tales from Two Cultures, 29
Jaime Escalante: Inspiring Educator, 133

Jaime Escalante: Sensational Teacher, 134

Jalapeño Bagels, 120

Jennifer Lopez: Latina Singer/Actress, 139

Jessie De La Cruz: A Profile of a United Farm Worker, 112

Jimmy Smits, 139

Joan Baez: Folksinger for Peace, 133

Joaquin Strikes Back, 101

Jordi's Star, 71

José Canseco, 127

José Clemente Orozco: Mexican Artist, 134

José Martí: Cuban Patriot and Poet, 134

Josefina, 57

Josefina Learns a Lesson: A School Story, 117

Josefina Saves the Day: A Summer Story, 117

Josefina's Surprise: A Christmas Story, 117

Journey for Peace: The Story of Rigoberta Menchú, 23

Journey of Diego Rivera, The, 46

Joyride, 104

Juan Bobo Goes to Work: A Puerto Rican Folktale, 68

Juan Verdades: The Man Who Couldn't Tell a Lie, 91

Las Christmas: Favorite Latino Authors Share Their Holiday Memories, 97

Las Posadas: An Hispanic Christmas Celebration, 93

Latin American Art in the Twentieth Century, 30

Latin American Folktales: Stories from Hispanic and Indian Traditions, 31

Latin American Women Artists of the United States: The Works of 33 Twentieth-Century Women, 92

Latin American Writers, 34

Latin Sensations, 126

Latino Encyclopedia, The, 31

Latino Entrepreneurs, 137

Latino Reader: An American Literary Tradition from 1542 to the Present, The, 97

Latino Visions: Contemporary Chicano, Puerto Rican and Cuban American Artists, 83

Laughing Tomatoes and Other Spring Poems/Jitomates risueños y otros poemas de primavera, 77

Legacy of the Monroe Doctrine: A Reference Guide to U.S. Involvement in Latin America and the Caribbean, The, 26

Legend of Lord Eight Deer: An Epic of Ancient Mexico, The, 53

Let's Eat, 76
Life during the Spanish Inquisition, 75, 143
Life in the Amazon Rain Forest, 142
Liliana's Grandmothers, 34, 115
Line in the Sand: The Alamo Diary of Lucinda Lawrence, A, 89
Little Gold Star: A Spanish American Cinderella Tale, 109
Little Red Ant and the Great Big Crumb: A Mexican Fable, The, 41
Locks, Crocs, & Skeeters: The Story of the Panama Canal, 61
Lolo & Red-Legs, 106
Look What Came from Mexico, 138
Lost Temple of the Aztecs, 55
Lost Treasure of the Inca, 20
Love to Mamá: A Tribute to Mothers, 99
Luis Muñoz Marín: Father of Modern Puerto Rico, 127
Luis Rodriguez, 127

Machu Picchu, 63
Madrid, 127
Magic Maguey, The, 47
Mama Does the Mambo, 13
Mama's Birthday Surprise, 114
Mangaboom, 33
Manny Ramirez, 137
Marc Anthony: Latino Recording Artist, 139
Maria de Sautuola: The Bulls in the Cave, 72
Mariah Carey, 126, 139
Mariana and the Merchild: A Folk Tale from Chile, 5
Marisol and Magdalena: The Sound of Our Sisterhood, 59
Market Day: A Story Told with Folk Art, 26
Mary Joe Fernandez, 139
Maya, 126
Maya, The, 132
Maya's Children: The Story of La Llorona, 37
Mayan Astronomer in Hell's Kitchen, A, 87
Mayans, The, 138
Mayeros: A Yucatec Maya Family, 38
McGwire & Sosa: A Season to Remember, 17
Meet Josefina: An American Girl, 117
Memories of Cuba, 14
Mexican Revolution, The, 143
Mexican Revolution: 1910-1920, The, 55
Mexican War of Independence, The, 143

Mexican War: "Mr. Polk's War," The, 125

Mexican-American War, The, 143

Mexicanos: A History of Mexicans in the United States, 90

Mexico, 39, 51, 128, 131, 132, 133, 137, 138, 140, 141

Mexico & Central America, 126

Mexico and the United States: Cooperation and Conflict, 52

Mexico, Biography of Power: A History of Modern Mexico, 1810-1996, 48

Mexico City, 49, 127

Mexico from A to Z, 125

Mexico in Pictures, 142

Mexico: Rich in Spirit and Tradition, 131

Mice and Beans, 108

Migrant Worker: A Boy from the Rio Grande Valley, 93

Mission for the People: The Story of La Purísima, A, 88

Mission Trails in American History, The, 136

Moises Alou: An Authorized Biography, 137

Mola: Cuna Life Stories and Art, 61

Monkeys of Central and South America, 141

Monteverde: Science and Scientists in a Costa Rican Cloud Forest, 7

Montezuma and the Aztecs, 46

Montezuma and the Fall of the Aztecs, 48

Musica!: Salsa, Rumba, Merengue and More, 115

Musicians of the Sun, 50

My Bloody Life: The Making of a Latin King, 109

My Daughter, My Son, the Eagle, the Dove: An Aztec Chant, 40

My First Book of Proverbs/Mi primer libro de dichos, 46

My Life with the Wave, 41

Mystery of the Maya: Uncovering the Lost City of Palenque, The, 49

Nely Galan, 127

Nerdlandia: A Play, 112

New York Public Library Amazing Hispanic American History: A Book of Answers for Kids, The, 104

Nicaragua, 128, 130

Nicaragua in Pictures, 142

Nicaraguan Family, A, 136

Night of Las Posadas, The, 85

Nilo and the Tortoise, 19

Noche Buena: Hispanic American Christmas Stories, 104

North across the Border: The Story of Mexican Americans, 133

North America and the Caribbean, 144
Novio Boy: A Play, 113

Off and Running, 113
Old Letivia and the Mountain of Sorrows, 67
Old Man and His Door, The, 113
Orinoco River, The, 6, 123
Oscar De la Hoya, 139, 140
Oscar de la Renta, 127
Our Lady of Guadalupe, 54
Oxford Book of Latin American Short Stories, The, 32
Oxford Encyclopedia of Mesoamerican Cultures: The Civilizations of Mexico and Central America, The, 33

Pablo Casals: Cellist for the World, 134
Pablo Neruda: Nobel Prize-Winning Poet, 135
Pablo Picasso, 74
Panama, 141
Panama and the United States: Divided by the Canal, 60
Panama Canal, The, 126, 128
Panama Canal in American History, The, 135
Panama Canal Transfer: Controversy at the Crossroads, The, 60
Panama in Pictures, 142
Pancho Villa, 135
Paraguay, 129
Paraguay in Pictures, 142
Parrot in the Oven: Mi Vida, 100
Party Girl, 87
Pascual's Magic Pictures, 24
Past, The, 142
Patriot after All: The Story of a Chicano Vietnam Vet, A, 106
Pedro and Me: Friendship, Loss, and What I Learned, 120
Pedro Martinez, 137
Pedro Martinez: Pitcher Perfect, 140
Pedro Menéndez de Avilés, 137
People, The, 142
People of Corn: A Mayan Story, 24, 45
Personal Tour of La Purísima, A, 135
Peru, 63, 128, 130, 131, 132, 137, 138, 141
Peru in Pictures, 142
Peru: Lost Cities, Found Hopes, 131
Petty Crimes, 114

Pizarro and the Conquest of the Incan Empire, 136
Place to Stand: The Making of a Poet, A, 81
Plácido Domingo: Opera Superstar, 135
*Plays from Hispanic Tales: One-Act, Royalty-Free Dramatizations
   for Young People, from Hispanic Stories and Folktales*, 35
Ponce de León, 130
*Ponce de León: Juan Ponce de León Searches for the Fountain of
   Youth*, 131
Puerto Rico, 66, 125, 131, 132, 133, 134, 141
Puerto Rico: Deciding Its Future, 66
Puerto Rico: Facts and Symbols, 140
Puerto Rico in Pictures, 142
Puerto Rico Past and Present: An Encyclopedia, 66
Pumpkin Fiesta, 58

Quetzal: Sacred Bird of the Cloud Forest, 4, 52
Quinceañera: Celebrating Fifteen, 96
*Quinceañera!: The Essential Guide to Planning the Perfect Sweet
   Fifteen Celebration*, 109

Rafael Palmeiro, 139
Rain Forests, 139
Rainbow Tulip, The, 101
Rainforest Indians, The, 132
Ramon Martinez, 137
Ramon Martinez: Master of the Mound, 140
Raul Julia, 127
Raúl Julia: Actor and Humanitarian, 134
Rebecca Lobo, 140
Reference Guide to Latin American History, A, 29
Religions of the Western Hemisphere, 29
Remember the Main: The Spanish-American War Begins, 132
Return of the Maya: Guatemala—a Tale of Survival, 24
Richard "Pancho" Gonzalez: Tennis Champion, 134
Ricky Martin, 126, 139
Riding the Ferry with Captain Cruz, 138
Rigoberta Menchu: Defending Human Rights in Guatemala, 143
Rina's Family Secret, 118
Rio Grande: From the Rocky Mountains to the Gulf of Mexico, 50,
   98
Rivera, 133
Roadrunner's Dance, 80

Robert Rodriguez, 139
Roberto Alomar: An Authorized Biography, 137
Roberto Clemente: Baseball Hall of Famer, 133
Rooster, 118
Rubén Blades: Salsa Singer and Social Activist, 134
Runaway Tortilla, The, 96

Salma Hayek, 139
Sammy Sosa, 136, 139
Sammy Sosa: An Authorized Biography, 137
Sammy Sosa: Cubs Clubber, 140
Sammy Sosa: Home Run Hero, 18
Sandra Cisneros: Latina Writer and Activist, 135
Secret Footprints, The, 16
Secret Stars, The, 111
Selena, 139
Selena Perez: Queen of Tejano Music, 133
Señor Cat's Romance and Other Favorite Stories from Latin America, 29
Señor Felipe's Alphabet Adventure: El alfabeto español, 35
Shakira: Latina Pop Rock Artist/Actress, 140
Sheila E., 139
Simón Bolívar: South American Liberator, 135
Sir Walter Ralegh and the Quest for El Dorado, 62, 72
Snapshots from the Wedding, 114
So Loud a Silence, 6
Soccer Cousins, 50
Something to Declare, 78
South America, 138, 140, 141
South American Animals, 70
Spain, 128, 129, 130, 131, 132, 138
Spain: Bridge between Continents, 131
Spain in the Age of Exploration, 74, 129
Spain: The Culture, 73
Spain: The Land, 73
Spain: The People, 73
Spanish-American War, The, 128
Spanish-American War: "Remember the Maine!," The, 125
Speak English for Us, Marisol!, 86
Star of Luís, 115
Sugar Island, The, 12

Teenage Refugees from Guatemala Speak Out, 136
Teenage Refugees from Mexico Speak Out, 136
Ten Hispanic American Authors, 93
Terror of the Spanish Main: Sir Henry Morgan and His Buccaneers, 73
This Big Sky, 102
This Craft of Verse, 1
Three Golden Oranges, The, 71
Three Roads to the Alamo: The Lives and Fortunes of David Crockett, James Bowie, and William Barret Travis, 85
Tino Martinez, 137
Tomás and the Library Lady, 102
Tomatoes, Potatoes, Corn, and Beans: How the Foods of the Americas Changed Eating around the World, 30
Tommy Nuñez, 139
Tonio's Cat, 82
Tortilla Cat, The, 120
Touching the Fire: Fifteen Poets of Today's Latino Renaissance, 116
Treasures of the Spanish Main, 133
Tree of Red Stars, The, 122
Trent Dimas, 139
Tres pequeños jabalíes, Los/The Three Little Javelinas, 99
Twentieth-Century Latin American Poetry: A Bilingual Anthology, 34

Uncle Rain Cloud, 94
Uncle Snake, 46
Under the Lemon Moon, 44
Uneasy Neighbors: Cuba and the United States, 11
United States and Mexico at War. Nineteenth-Century Expansionism and Conflict, The, 56, 118
Uno, dos, tres, One, Two, Three, 51
Uruguay, 129
Uruguay in Pictures, 142

Vaqueros: America's First Cowmen, 110
Venezuela, 133, 141
Venezuela in Pictures, 142
Versos sencillos/Simple Verses, 13
Vinny Castilla, 137
Visit to Colombia, A, 142

Visit to Costa Rica, A, 142
Visit to Cuba, A, 142
Visit to Mexico, A, 142
Visit to Puerto Rico, A, 142
Voices from the Streets: Young Former Gang Members Tell Their Stories, 81
Voices of the Alamo, 89

Wars of the Americas: A Chronology of Armed Conflict in the New World, 1492 to the Present, 31
Welcome to Argentina, 143
Welcome to Colombia, 143
Welcome to Costa Rica, 143
Welcome to Cuba, 143
Welcome to Josefina's World, 1824: Growing Up on America's Southwest Frontier, 119
Welcome to Mexico, 143
Welcome to Peru, 143
Welcome to Spain, 143
Well of Sacrifice, The, 42
What It Takes to Get to Vegas, 103
When Pigasso Met Mootisse, 73
When the Viceroy Came, 40
When This World Was New, 88
When Woman Became the Sea: A Costa Rican Creation Myth, 7
White Rose/Una rosa blanca, 9

Yanomami of South America, The, 132
Year of Our Revolution: New and Selected Stories and Poems, The, 105
¡Yo!, 78
Young Chef's Mexican Cookbook, The, 57
Your Travel Guide to Ancient Mayan Civilization, 42

Subject Index

ALAMO (SAN ANTONIO, TX)—FICTION
   Garland, *A Line in the Sand: The Alamo Diary of Lucinda Lawrence*, 89
   Harrigan, *The Gates of the Alamo*, 91
   Love, *I Remember the Alamo*, 99

ALAMO (SAN ANTONIO, TX)—HISTORY
   Davis, *Three Roads to the Alamo: The Lives and Fortunes of David Crockett, James Bowie, and William Barret Travis*, 85
   Garland, *Voices of the Alamo*, 89
   Santella, *The Battle of the Alamo*, 111

ALAMO (SAN ANTONIO, TX)—POETRY
   Lind, *The Alamo: An Epic*, 98

ALCOHOLISM
   Atkin, *Voices from the Streets: Young Former Gang Members Tell Their Stories*, 81
   Ramirez, *A Patriot after All: The Story of a Chicano Vietnam Vet*, 106
   Sanchez, *My Bloody Life: The Making of a Latin King*, 110
   Urrea, *By the Lake of Sleeping Children: The Secret Life of the Mexican Border*, 56

ALCOHOLISM—FICTION
   Durán, *Don't Spit on My Corner*, 86
   Ewing, *Party Girl*, 87
   Martinez, *Parrot in the Oven: Mi Vida*, 100
   Ramos, *Blues for the Buffalo*, 106
   Velásquez, *Rina's Family Secret*, 118

ALPHABET—FICTION
   Ada, *Gathering the Sun: An Alphabet in Spanish and English*, 25
   Vargo, *Señor Felipe's Alphabet Adventure: El alfabeto español*, 35

AMERICA
   (*See also individual countries*)
   Bramwell, *North America and the Caribbean*, 144

AMERICA—MILITARY HISTORY
   Marley, *Wars of the Americas: A Chronology of Armed Conflict in the New World, 1492 to the Present*, 31

AMERICA—MISCELLANEA
   Chin-Lee and Peña, *A Is for the Americas*, 25

ANIMALS
   Arnold, *South American Animals*, 70
   Heller, *Galápagos Means "Tortoises,"* 19
   Tagliaferro, *Galápagos Islands: Nature's Delicate Balance at Risk*, 20

ANIMALS—FICTION
   Anaya, *Roadrunner's Dance*, 80
   Calhoun, *Tonio's Cat*, 82
   Cowley, *Gracias, the Thanksgiving Turkey*, 84
   Elya, *Eight Animals on the Town*, 43
   Gage, *Pascual's Magic Pictures*, 24
   Kleven, *Hooray, a Piñata!*, 97
   Laden, *When Pigasso Met Mootisse*, 73
   Lewin, *Nilo and the Tortoise*, 19
   Ryan, *Mice and Beans*, 109
   Soto, *Chato and the Party Animals*, 112
   Vargo, *Señor Felipe's Alphabet Adventure: El alfabeto español*, 35
   Willard, *The Tortilla Cat*, 120

ANIMALS—POETRY
   Mora, *This Big Sky*, 102

ANTHROPOLOGISTS—PERU
   Reinhard, *Discovering the Inca Ice Maiden: My Adventures on Ampato*, 64

ANTIQUITIES
Fradin, *Maria de Sautuola: The Bulls in the Cave*, 72
Lourie, *The Mystery of the Maya: Uncovering the Lost City of Palenque*, 49
Macdonald, *Inca Town*, 63
Mann, *Machu Picchu*, 63
Martell, *Civilizations of Peru before 1535*, 64
Reinhard, *Discovering the Inca Ice Maiden: My Adventures on Ampato*, 64

ARCHEOLOGY
Fradin, *Maria de Sautuola: The Bulls in the Cave*, 72
Lourie, *Lost Treasure of the Inca*, 20

ARCHITECTURE
Aira, *Argentina: The Great Estancias*, 1
¡Cámara! Ciudad de México: Monumentos de una nueva generación/Picture Mexico City: Landmarks of a New Generation, 40

ARGENTINA
Aira, *Argentina: The Great Estancias*, 1
Argentina in Pictures, 142
Burgan, *Argentina*, 141
Dalal, *Argentina*, 138
Dell'Oro, *Argentina*, 133, 141
Dubois, *Argentina*, 128
Foster, *Culture and Customs of Argentina*, 129
Frank, *Argentina*, 128
Furlong, *Argentina*, 131
Hintz, *Argentina*, 130
Kent, *Buenos Aires*, 127
Mesenas and Frank, *Welcome to Argentina*, 143
Nickles, *Argentina: The Culture*, 2
Nickles, *Argentina: The Land*, 2
Nickles, *Argentina: The People*, 2
Symmes, *Chasing Che: A Motorcycle Journey in Search of the Guevara Legend*, 3

ARGENTINA—BIOGRAPHY
Dujovne Ortiz, *Eva Perón*, 1
Sinclair, *Che Guevara*, 2

ARGENTINA—DESCRIPTION
Nickles, *Argentina: The Land*, 2
Nickles, *Argentina: The People*, 2

ARGENTINA—FICTION
Borges, *This Craft of Verse*, 1

ARGENTINA—HISTORY
Dujovne Ortiz, *Eva Perón*, 1
Nickles, *Argentina: The Land*, 2

ARGENTINA—PICTORIAL WORKS
Aira, *Argentina: The Great Estancias*, 1

ARGENTINA—SOCIAL LIFE AND CUSTOMS
Nickles, *Argentina: The Culture*, 2
Nickles, *Argentina: The People*, 2

ART
Fradin, *Maria de Sautuola: The Bulls in the Cave*, 72
Goldstein, *The Journey of Diego Rivera*, 46
Meadows, *Pablo Picasso*, 74

ART—ENCYCLOPEDIAS
Encyclopedia of Latin American and Caribbean Art, 27
Latin American Art in the Twentieth Century, 30

ART—20TH CENTURY
Cockcroft, *Latino Visions: Contemporary Chicano, Puerto Rican and Cuban American Artists*, 83
Henkes, *Latin American Women Artists of the United States: The Works of 33 Twentieth-Century Women*, 92
Latin American Art in the Twentieth Century, 30

ARTISTS—FICTION
Laden, *When Pigasso Met Mootisse*, 73

ARTISTS—MEXICO
Goldstein, *The Journey of Diego Rivera*, 46

ARTISTS—SPAIN
Meadows, *Pablo Picasso*, 74

Schiaffino, *Goya*, 74
Venezia, *El Greco*, 75

ARTISTS—UNITED STATES
Henkes, *Latin American Women Artists of the United States: The Works of 33 Twentieth-Century Women*, 92

AUNTS—FICTION
Tripp, *Changes for Josefina: A Winter Story*, 117
Tripp, *Happy Birthday, Josefina!*, 117
Tripp, *Josefina Learns a Lesson: A School Story*, 117
Tripp, *Josefina Saves the Day: A Summer Story*, 117
Tripp, *Josefina's Surprise: A Christmas Story*, 117
Tripp, *Meet Josefina: An American Girl*, 117

AZTECS (MEXICO)
Burr, *Broken Shields*, 39
Castillo, *My Daughter, My Son, the Eagle, the Dove: An Aztec Chant*, 40
Helly and Courgeon, *Montezuma and the Aztecs*, 47
Kimmel, *Montezuma and the Fall of the Aztecs*, 48
Macdonald, *The Ancient Aztecs: Secrets of a Lost Civilization to Unlock and Discover*, 50
McDermott, *Musicians of the Sun*, 50
Platt, *Aztecs: The Fall of the Aztec Capital*, 53
Steele, *The Aztec News*, 54
Tanaka, *Lost Temple of the Aztecs*, 55

BASEBALL
Horenstein, *Baseball in the Barrios*, 123

BASEBALL PLAYERS
Christopher, *At the Plate with . . . Sammy Sosa*, 17
Preller, *McGwire & Sosa: A Season to Remember*, 17
Savage, *Sammy Sosa: Home Run Hero*, 18
Winter, *¡Béisbol! Latino Baseball Pioneers and Legends*, 121

BILINGUAL BOOKS
Ada, *Gathering the Sun: An Alphabet in Spanish and English*, 25
Alarcón, *Angels Ride Bikes and Other Fall Poems/Los ángeles andan en bicicleta y otros poemas de otoño*, 77

Alarcón, *From the Bellybutton of the Moon and Other Summer Poems/Del ombligo de la luna y otros poemas de verano*, 37

Alarcón, *Iguanas in the Snow and Other Winter Poems/Iguanas en la nieve y otros poemas de invierno*, 77

Alarcón, *Laughing Tomatoes and Other Spring Poems/Jitomates risueños y otros poemas de primavera*, 77

Americanos: Latino Life in the United States/La vida latina en los Estados Unidos, 79

¡Cámara! Ciudad de México: Monumentos de una nueva generación/Picture Mexico City: Landmarks of a New Generation, 40

Ehlert, *Cuckoo/Cucú*, 43

Gonzalez, *My First Book of Proverbs/Mi primer libro de dichos*, 46

Herrera, *Grandma and Me at the Flea/Los meros meros remateros*, 93

Lomas Garza, *In My Family/En mi familia*, 98

Lowell, *Los tres pequeños jabalíes/The Three Little Javelinas*, 100

Martí, *Versos sencillos/Simple Verses*, 13

Orozco, *Diez deditos/Ten Little Fingers and Other Play Rhymes and Action Songs from Latin America*, 32

Twentieth-Century Latin American Poetry: A Bilingual Anthology, 34

Vargo, *Señor Felipe's Alphabet Adventure: El alfabeto español*, 35

Winter, *Josefina*, 57

BIOGRAPHY

Altman, *Cesar Chavez*, 135

Alvarez, *Something to Declare*, 78

Aronson, *Sir Walter Ralegh and the Quest for El Dorado*, 62, 72

Baca, *A Place to Stand: The Making of a Poet*, 81

Benson, *Gloria Estefan*, 126

Boulais, *Andres Galarraga*, 139

Boulais, *Gloria Estefan*, 139

Boulais and Marvis, *Tommy Nuñez*, 139

Brill, *Journey for Peace: The Story of Rigoberta Menchú*, 23

Byers, *Jaime Escalante: Sensational Teacher*, 134

Carrillo, *Edward James Olmos*, 127

Carrillo, *Oscar de la Renta*, 127

Carroll, *Pancho Villa*, 135

Chrisp, *Christopher Columbus: Explorer of the New World*, 130

Christopher, *At the Plate with . . . Sammy Sosa*, 17

Cockcroft, *Latino Visions: Contemporary Chicano, Puerto Rican and Cuban American Artists*, 83

Cole, *Jimmy Smits*, 139

Cole, *Mariah Carey*, 139

Cole, *Mary Joe Fernandez*, 139

Collins, *Farmworker's Friend: The Story of Cesar Chavez*, 83

Cooper and Gordon, *Anthony Reynoso: Born to Rope*, 84

Crawford, *Encyclopedia of the Mexican-American War*, 42, 85

Cruz, *Frida Kahlo: Portrait of a Mexican Painter*, 134

Cruz, *José Clemente Orozco: Mexican Artist*, 134

Cruz, *Raúl Julia: Actor and Humanitarian*, 134

Cruz, *Rubén Blades: Salsa Singer and Social Activist*, 134

Davis, *Cesar Chavez: A Photo-Illustrated Biography*, 139

Davis, *Three Roads to the Alamo: The Lives and Fortunes of David Crockett, James Bowie, and William Barret Travis*, 85

DeMarco, *Ivan Rodriguez*, 137

DeMarco, *Vinny Castilla*, 137

Doak, *Francisco Vázquez de Coronado: Exploring the Southwest*, 131

Dougherty, *Sammy Sosa*, 136

Dujovne Ortiz, *Eva Perón*, 1

Encyclopedia of Latin American History and Culture, 27

Encyclopedia of Latin American Literature, 28

Fernandez, *Puerto Rico Past and Present: An Encyclopedia*, 66

Fernandez Barrios, *Blessed by Thunder: Memoir of a Cuban Girlhood*, 10

Ferriss and Sandoval, *The Fight in the Fields: Cesar Chavez and the Farmworkers Movement*, 88

Foss, *Fidel Castro*, 10

Fradin, *Maria de Sautuola: The Bulls in the Cave*, 72

Gallagher, *Alex Rodriguez*, 137

Gallagher, *Pedro Martinez*, 137

Gallagher, *Ramon Martinez*, 137

Genet, *Father Junípero Serra: Founder of California Missions*, 134

George and George, *Luis Muñoz Marín: Father of Modern Puerto Rico*, 127

Gibb, *Fidel Castro: Leader of Cuba's Revolution*, 11

Gonzales, *Cesar Chavez: Leader for Migrant Farm Workers*, 134

Gonzales, *Diego Rivera: His Art, His Life*, 134

Gonzales, *Gloria Estefan: Singer and Entertainer*, 134

Gonzales, *Richard "Pancho" Gonzalez: Tennis Champion*, 134

Goodnough, *José Martí: Cuban Patriot and Poet*, 134

Goodnough, *Pablo Casals: Cellist for the World*, 134

Goodnough, *Pablo Neruda: Nobel Prize-Winning Poet*, 135

Goodnough, *Plácido Domingo: Opera Superstar*, 135

Goodnough, *Simón Bolívar: South American Liberator*, 135

Gourse, *Gloria Estefan: Pop Sensation*, 126

Granados, *Christina Aguilera*, 139

Granados, *Enrique Iglesias: Latino Pop Star*, 139

Granados, *Sheila E.*, 139

Heinrichs, *De Soto: Hernando de Soto Explores the Southeast*, 131

Heinrichs, *Ponce de León: Juan Ponce de León Searches for the Fountain of Youth*, 131

Helly and Courgeon, *Montezuma and the Aztecs*, 47

Henderson, *A Reference Guide to Latin American History*, 29

Hill, *Ten Hispanic American Authors*, 93

Kanellos, *Hispanic Firsts: 500 Years of Extraordinary Achievement*, 95

Kimmel, *Montezuma and the Fall of the Aztecs*, 48

Kline, *Christopher Columbus*, 130

Kline, *Francisco Coronado*, 130

Kline, *Francisco Pizarro*, 130

Kline, *Francisco Vázquez de Coronado*, 130

Kline, *Hernán Cortés*, 130

Kline, *Ponce de León*, 130

Krauze, *Mexico, Biography of Power: A History of Modern Mexico, 1810-1996*, 48

Latino Encyclopedia, The, 31

Lilley, *Hernando Cortes*, 135

Ling, *José Canseco*, 127

Macht, *Roberto Alomar: An Authorized Biography*, 137

MacLean, *Sammy Sosa: Cubs Clubber*, 140

Macnow, *Alex Rodriguez*, 140

Manning, *Francisco Pizarro*, 134

Márquez, *Latin Sensations*, 126

Marrin, *Terror of the Spanish Main: Sir Henry Morgan and His Buccaneers*, 73

Marvis, *Rafael Palmeiro*, 139

Marvis, *Robert Rodriguez*, 139

Marvis, *Selena*, 139

Meadows, *Pablo Picasso*, 74

Menard, *Cheech Marin: Actor, Comedian*, 139

Menard, *Cristina Saralegui*, 139

Menard, *Jennifer Lopez: Latina Singer/Actress*, 139

Menard, *Oscar De la Hoya*, 139
Menard, *Ricky Martin*, 139
Menard, *Salma Hayek*, 139
Menard and Boulais, *Trent Dimas*, 139
Mirriam-Goldberg, *Sandra Cisneros: Latina Writer and Activist*,
    135
Morey and Dunn, *Famous Hispanic Americans*, 103
Muskat, *Bernie Williams*, 137
Muskat, *Moises Alou: An Authorized Biography*, 137
Muskat, *Sammy Sosa*, 139
Muskat, *Sammy Sosa: An Authorized Biography*, 137
Oleksy, *Hispanic-American Scientists*, 125
Parker, *Locks, Crocs, & Skeeters: The Story of the Panama Canal*,
    61
Parker, *Mariah Carey*, 126
Parker, *Ricky Martin*, 126
Pérez, *Dolores Huerta*, 127
Pérez and Weil, *Raul Julia*, 127
Roberts, *Pedro Menéndez de Avilés*, 137
Rodriguez, *Gloria Estefan*, 127
Rodriguez, *Nely Galan*, 127
Romero, *Ellen Ochoa: The First Hispanic Woman Astronaut*, 133
Romero, *Henry Cisneros: A Man of the People*, 133
Romero, *Jaime Escalante: Inspiring Educator*, 133
Romero, *Joan Baez: Folksinger for Peace*, 133
Romero, *Roberto Clemente: Baseball Hall of Famer*, 133
Romero, *Selena Perez: Queen of Tejano Music*, 133
Sanchez, *My Bloody Life: The Making of a Latin King*, 110
Santiago, *Almost a Woman*, 68
Savage, *Rebecca Lobo*, 140
Savage, *Sammy Sosa: Home Run Hero*, 18
Schiaffino, *Goya*, 74
Schwartz, *Luis Rodriguez*, 127
Shirey, *Latin American Writers*, 34
Sinclair, *Che Guevara*, 2, 14
Soto, *Jessie De La Cruz: A Profile of a United Farm Worker*, 112
St. Aubin de Terán, *The Hacienda*, 123
Stein, *The Mexican Revolution: 1910-1920*, 55
Stewart, *Alex Rodriguez: Gunning for Greatness*, 126
Stewart, *Andres Galarraga: The Big Cat*, 140
Stewart, *Ivan Rodriguez: Armed and Dangerous*, 140
Stewart, *Pedro Martinez: Pitcher Perfect*, 140

Stewart, *Ramon Martinez: Master of the Mound*, 140
Talmadge, *Christina Aguilera*, 127
Talmadge, *Enrique Iglesias*, 127
Torres, *Bobby Bonilla*, 137
Torres, *Marc Anthony: Latino Recording Artist*, 139
Torres, *Oscar De la Hoya*, 140
Torres, *Tino Martinez*, 137
Twentieth-Century Latin American Poetry: A Bilingual Anthology, 34
United States and Mexico at War. Nineteenth-Century Expansionism and Conflict, The, 56, 118
Vascallaro, *Manny Ramirez*, 137
Vázquez-Gómez, *Dictionary of Mexican Rulers, 1325-1997*, 57
Venezia, *El Greco*, 75, 133
Venezia, *Frida Kahlo*, 133
Venezia, *Rivera*, 133
Whiting, *Francisco Vásquez de Coronado*, 137
Wilson, *Shakira: Latina Pop Rock Artist/Actress*, 140
Winick, *Pedro and Me: Friendship, Loss, and What I Learned*, 121
Winter, *¡Béisbol! Latino Baseball Pioneers and Legends*, 121
Zannos, *Cesar Chavez*, 140

BIRDS—FOLKLORE
Ehlert, *Cuckoo/Cucú*, 43
Patent, *Quetzal: Sacred Bird of the Cloud Forest*, 4, 52

BIRTHDAYS
King, *Quinceañera: Celebrating Fifteen*, 96
Salcedo, *Quinceañera!: The Essential Guide to Planning the Perfect Sweet Fifteen Celebration*, 109

BIRTHDAYS—FICTION
Kleven, *Hooray, a Piñata!*, 97
Mora, *Uno, dos, tres, One, Two, Three*, 51
Ryan, *Mice and Beans*, 109
Soto, *Chato and the Party Animals*, 112
Spurr, *Mama's Birthday Surprise*, 115
Tripp, *Happy Birthday, Josefina!*, 117

BOLIVIA
Augustin, *Bolivia*, 130
Bolivia, 132

Bolivia in Pictures, 142
Hermes, *The Children of Bolivia*, 144
Klingel and Noyed, *Bolivia*, 132
Pateman, *Bolivia*, 129

BOOKS AND READING—FICTION
Mora, *Tomás and the Library Lady*, 102

BUTTERFLIES—FICTION
Joose, *Ghost Wings*, 47
Kroll, *Butterfly Boy*, 49
Swope, *Gotta Go! Gotta Go!*, 55

BUTTERFLIES—FOLKLORE
Sierra, *The Beautiful Butterfly: A Folktale from Spain*, 75

BUTTERFLIES—MEXICO
Pringle, *An Extraordinary Life: The Story of a Monarch Butterfly*, 53

CALIFORNIA
Ancona, *Barrio: José's Neighborhood*, 80
Ancona, *Harvest*, 38, 80
Fernandez Barrios, *Blessed by Thunder: Memoir of a Cuban Girlhood*, 10

CALIFORNIA—FICTION
Calhoun, *Tonio's Cat*, 82
Herrera, *Grandma and Me at the Flea/Los meros meros remateros*, 93
Jiménez, *Breaking Through*, 94
Johnston, *Uncle Rain Cloud*, 95
McGinley, *Joaquin Strikes Back*, 101
Murray, *What It Takes to Get to Vegas*, 103
Reeve, *Lolo & Red-Legs*, 106
Ryan, *Esperanza Rising*, 108
Soto, *Buried Onions*, 111
Soto, *Nerdlandia: A Play*, 113
Soto, *Petty Crimes*, 114
Spurr, *Mama's Birthday Surprise*, 115
Talbert, *Star of Luís*, 115
Velásquez, *Rina's Family Secret*, 118

CALIFORNIA—HISTORY
Collins, *Farmworker's Friend: The Story of Cesar Chavez*, 83
Ferriss and Sandoval, *The Fight in the Fields: Cesar Chavez and the Farmworkers Movement*, 88
Fraser, *A Mission for the People: The Story of La Purísima*, 88

CALIFORNIA—POETRY
Alarcón, *Angels Ride Bikes and Other Fall Poems/Los ángeles andan en bicicleta y otros poemas de otoño*, 77
Alarcón, *Iguanas in the Snow and Other Winter Poems/Iguanas en la nieve y otros poemas de invierno*, 77

CASTRO, FIDEL, 1927-
Salas and Salas, *Fidel's Cuba: A Revolution in Pictures*, 14
Staub, *Children of Cuba*, 15

CASTRO, FIDEL, 1927- —BIOGRAPHY
Foss, *Fidel Castro*, 10
Gibb, *Fidel Castro: Leader of Cuba's Revolution*, 11

CATS—FICTION
Calhoun, *Tonio's Cat*, 82
Soto, *Chato and the Party Animals*, 112
Willard, *The Tortilla Cat*, 120

CENTRAL AMERICA
(*See also* COSTA RICA, EL SALVADOR, GUATEMALA, LATIN AMERICA, PANAMA)
Bramwell, *Central and South America*, 144
Deedrick, *Maya*, 126
Franklin, *Mexico & Central America*, 126
Galvin, *The Ancient Maya*, 129
Kallen, *The Mayans*, 138
Martin, *Monkeys of Central and South America*, 141
Oxford Encyclopedia of Mesoamerican Cultures: The Civilizations of Mexico and Central America, The, 33
Patent, *Quetzal: Sacred Bird of the Cloud Forest*, 4, 52
Press, *The Maya*, 132
Sharer, *Daily Life in Maya Civilization*, 130
Viesti and Hall, *Celebrate! in Central America*, 4

CENTRAL AMERICA—SOCIAL LIFE AND CUSTOMS
Viesti and Hall, *Celebrate! in Central America*, 4

CHÁVEZ, CÉSAR, 1927-1993—BIOGRAPHY
Collins, *Farmworker's Friend: The Story of Cesar Chavez*, 83
Ferriss and Sandoval, *The Fight in the Fields: Cesar Chavez and the Farmworkers Movement*, 88

CHÁVEZ, CÉSAR, 1927-1993—POETRY
Anaya, *Elegy on the Death of César Chávez*, 79

CHICAGO (IL)—SOCIAL CONDITIONS
Sanchez, *My Bloody Life: The Making of a Latin King*, 110

CHICANO ART
Cockcroft, *Latino Visions: Contemporary Chicano, Puerto Rican and Cuban American Artists*, 83
Latin American Art in the Twentieth Century, 30

CHICANO LITERATURE
Herrera, *CrashBoomLove*, 92
Soto, *Chato and the Party Animals*, 112

CHICANO SOLDIERS—VIETNAM
Ramirez, *A Patriot after All: The Story of a Chicano Vietnam Vet*, 106

CHICANO YOUTH—DRAMA
Soto, *Nerdlandia: A Play*, 113

CHICANOS
(*See also* LATINOS, MEXICAN AMERICANS)
Castro, *Dictionary of Chicano Folklore*, 82
Gonzales, *Mexicanos: A History of Mexicans in the United States*, 90
Rosales, *Chicano!: The History of the Mexican American Civil Rights Movement*, 108

CHICANOS—FICTION
Ramos, *Blues for the Buffalo*, 106

CHILDREN
Ancona, *Cuban Kids*, 9
Hoyt-Goldsmith, *Migrant Worker: A Boy from the Rio Grande Valley*, 94
Staub, *Children of Cuba*, 15

CHILDREN—FICTION
Calhoun, *Tonio's Cat*, 82
Pomerantz, *Mangaboom*, 33
Rice, *Crazy Loco*, 107
Uribe, *Buzz, Buzz, Buzz*, 70

CHILDREN'S PLAYS
Soto, *Nerdlandia: A Play*, 113
Soto, *Novio Boy: A Play*, 113
Winther, *Plays from Hispanic Tales: One-Act, Royalty-Free Dramatizations for Young People, from Hispanic Stories and Folktales*, 35

CHILDREN'S POETRY
Ada, *Gathering the Sun: An Alphabet in Spanish and English*, 25
Alarcón, *Angels Ride Bikes and Other Fall Poems/Los ángeles andan en bicicleta y otros poemas de otoño*, 77
Alarcón, *From the Bellybutton of the Moon and Other Summer Poems/Del ombligo de la luna y otros poemas de verano*, 37
Alarcón, *Iguanas in the Snow and Other Winter Poems/Iguanas en la nieve y otros poemas de invierno*, 77
Alarcón, *Laughing Tomatoes and Other Spring Poems/Jitomates risueños y otros poemas de primavera*, 77
Love to Mamá: A Tribute to Mothers, 99
Mora, *Confetti: Poems for Children*, 101
Mora, *This Big Sky*, 102

CHILDREN'S SONGS
Orozco, *Diez deditos/Ten Little Fingers and Other Play Rhymes and Action Songs from Latin America*, 32

CHILE
Chile, 132
Chile in Pictures, 142
Klingel and Noyed, *Chile*, 132
McNair, *Chile*, 130

Pickering, *Chile: Where the Land Ends*, 131
Roraff, *Chile*, 132

CHILE—FICTION
Pitcher, *Mariana and the Merchild: A Folk Tale from Chile*, 5

CHRISTMAS
Hoyt-Goldsmith, *Las Posadas: An Hispanic Christmas Celebration*, 93
Las Christmas: Favorite Latino Authors Share Their Holiday Memories, 97
Noche Buena: Hispanic American Christmas Stories, 104

CHRISTMAS—FICTION
Bunting, *Going Home*, 39
Johnston, *The Magic Maguey*, 47
Tripp, *Josefina's Surprise: A Christmas Story*, 117

CHUMASH INDIANS (CA)
Fraser, *A Mission for the People: The Story of La Purísima*, 88

CIGUAPAS (LEGENDARY CHARACTER)
Alvarez, *The Secret Footprints*, 16

CINCO DE MAYO (MEXICAN HOLIDAY)
Urrutia and Orozco, *Cinco de Mayo: Yesterday and Today*, 56

CINCO DE MAYO, BATTLE OF, 1862
Urrutia and Orozco, *Cinco de Mayo: Yesterday and Today*, 56

CINDERELLA (FICTITIOUS CHARACTER)
Coburn, *Domitila: A Cinderella Tale from the Mexican Tradition*, 41
San Souci, *Little Gold Star: A Spanish American Cinderella Tale*, 109

CITIES AND TOWNS
Macdonald, *Inca Town*, 63
Parker, *Mexico*, 52

CIVIL RIGHTS DEMONSTRATIONS
   Rosales, *Chicano!: The History of the Mexican American Civil Rights Movement*, 108

CLOUD FORESTS
   Collard, *Monteverde: Science and Scientists in a Costa Rican Cloud Forest*, 7

COLOMBIA
   Colombia in Pictures, 142
   Fox, *A Visit to Colombia*, 142
   Jermyn, *Colombia*, 128
   Lim, *Welcome to Colombia*, 143
   Markham, *Colombia: The Gateway to South America*, 131
   Morrison, *Colombia*, 130
   Rawlins, *The Orinoco River*, 6
   Williams and Guerrieri, *Culture and Customs of Colombia*, 129

COLOMBIA—FICTION
   Jenkins, *So Loud a Silence*, 6

COMMUNITY LIFE—FICTION
   Bunting, *Going Home*, 39
   Herrera, *Grandma and Me at the Flea/Los meros meros remateros*, 93
   Reeve, *Lolo & Red-Legs*, 106

CONDUCT OF LIFE
   Castillo, *My Daughter, My Son, the Eagle, the Dove: An Aztec Chant*, 40

COOKING
   Las Christmas: Favorite Latino Authors Share Their Holiday Memories, 97
   Ward, *The Young Chef's Mexican Cookbook*, 57

COOKING—FICTION
   Geeslin, *How Nanita Learned to Make Flan*, 45
   Wing, *Jalapeño Bagels*, 120

CORN—FOLKLORE
   Gerson, *People of Corn: A Mayan Story*, 24, 45

COSTA RICA
  Collard, *Monteverde: Science and Scientists in a Costa Rican Cloud Forest*, 7
  Costa Rica in Pictures, 142
  Fisher, *Costa Rica*, 131
  Fox, *A Visit to Costa Rica*, 142
  Frank, *Costa Rica*, 128
  Garret and Frank, *Welcome to Costa Rica*, 143
  Morrison, *Costa Rica*, 130
  West, *Costa Rica*, 133, 141

COSTA RICA—FICTION
  Strauss, *When Woman Became the Sea: A Costa Rican Creation Myth*, 7

COUNTING—FICTION
  Elya, *Eight Animals on the Town*, 43
  Mora, *Uno, dos, tres, One, Two, Three*, 51
  Winter, *Josefina*, 57

COUNTRY LIFE—CELESTÚN (MEXICO)
  Parker, *Mexico*, 52

COUSINS—FICTION
  Marzollo, *Soccer Cousins*, 50

COWHANDS
  Ancona, *Charro: The Mexican Cowboy*, 38
  Cooper and Gordon, *Anthony Reynoso: Born to Rope*, 84
  Sandler, *Vaqueros: America's First Cowmen*, 110

COYOTES—FOLKLORE
  Lowell, *Los tres pequeños jabalíes/The Three Little Javelinas*, 100

CREATION—FOLKLORE
  Delacre, *Golden Tales: Myths, Legends and Folktales from Latin America*, 25
  Gerson, *People of Corn: A Mayan Story*, 24, 45
  Jaffe, *The Golden Flower: A Taino Myth from Puerto Rico*, 67
  Strauss, *When Woman Became the Sea: A Costa Rican Creation Myth*, 7

CUBA
  Ancona, *Cuban Kids*, 9
  Brubaker, *The Cuban Missile Crisis in American History*, 135
  Cramer, *Cuba*, 128
  Fox, *Cuba*, 138
  Gillis, *A Visit to Cuba*, 142
  Gow, *The Cuban Missile Crisis*, 143
  Harvey and Newhouse, *Cuba*, 11
  Haverstock, *Cuba in Pictures*, 142
  Hoff and Regler, *Uneasy Neighbors: Cuba and the United States*, 11
  Kohli, *Cuba*, 12
  Mara, *Cuba*, 128
  Missen, *Memories of Cuba*, 14
  Morrison, *Cuba*, 128, 130
  Peterson, *Cuba*, 141
  Salas and Salas, *Fidel's Cuba: A Revolution in Pictures*, 14
  Staub, *Children of Cuba*, 15, 144
  Wolf, *Cuba: After the Revolution*, 15
  Yip and Cramer, *Welcome to Cuba*, 143

CUBA—BIOGRAPHY
  Fernandez Barrios, *Blessed by Thunder: Memoir of a Cuban
      Girlhood*, 10
  Foss, *Fidel Castro*, 10
  Gibb, *Fidel Castro: Leader of Cuba's Revolution*, 11
  Sinclair, *Che Guevara*, 2, 14

CUBA—DESCRIPTION
  Harvey and Newhouse, *Cuba*, 11
  Kohli, *Cuba*, 12

CUBA—FICTION
  Ephron, *White Rose/Una rosa blanca*, 9
  García, *The Agüero Sisters*, 10
  Lamazares, *The Sugar Island*, 12
  Leiner, *Mama Does the Mambo*, 13
  Leonard, *Cuba Libre*, 13
  Martí, *Versos sencillos/Simple Verses*, 13

CUBA—HISTORY
  Ancona, *Cuban Kids*, 9

Fernandez Barrios, *Blessed by Thunder: Memoir of a Cuban Girlhood*, 10
Foss, *Fidel Castro*, 10
Gibb, *Fidel Castro: Leader of Cuba's Revolution*, 11
Hoff and Regler, *Uneasy Neighbors: Cuba and the United States*, 11
Missen, *Memories of Cuba*, 14
Sinclair, *Che Guevara*, 2, 14
Staub, *Children of Cuba*, 15

CUBA—HISTORY—1895-1898, REVOLUTION—FICTION
Ephron, *White Rose/Una rosa blanca*, 9
Leonard, *Cuba Libre*, 13

CUBA—HISTORY—1958-1959, REVOLUTION
Salas and Salas, *Fidel's Cuba: A Revolution in Pictures*, 14
Staub, *Children of Cuba*, 15

CUBA—HISTORY—1961, INVASION
Salas and Salas, *Fidel's Cuba: A Revolution in Pictures*, 14

CUBA—PICTORIAL WORKS
Harvey and Newhouse, *Cuba*, 11
Kohli, *Cuba*, 12
Missen, *Memories of Cuba*, 14
Salas and Salas, *Fidel's Cuba: A Revolution in Pictures*, 14
Staub, *Children of Cuba*, 15
Wolf, *Cuba: After the Revolution*, 15

CUBA—SOCIAL LIFE AND CUSTOMS
Ancona, *Cuban Kids*, 9
Harvey and Newhouse, *Cuba*, 11
Kohli, *Cuba*, 12
Salas and Salas, *Fidel's Cuba: A Revolution in Pictures*, 14
Staub, *Children of Cuba*, 15
Wolf, *Cuba: After the Revolution*, 15

CUBAN AMERICANS
(*See also* LATINOS)

CUBAN AMERICANS—CALIFORNIA
Fernandez Barrios, *Blessed by Thunder: Memoir of a Cuban Girlhood*, 10

CUBAN AMERICANS—ETHNIC IDENTITY—FICTION
Obejas, *Days of Awe*, 104

CUBAN AMERICANS—MIAMI (FL)—FICTION
García, *The Agüero Sisters*, 10
Lamazares, *The Sugar Island*, 12

CUBAN AMERICANS—SOCIAL LIFE AND CUSTOMS—
FICTION
Obejas, *Days of Awe*, 104

CUBAN POETRY
Martí, *Versos sencillos/Simple Verses*, 13

CULTURE CONFLICT—FICTION
Abelove, *Go and Come Back*, 62

CUMULATIVE STORIES
Ryan, *Mice and Beans*, 109

CUNA INDIANS (PANAMA)
Presilla, *Mola: Cuna Life Stories and Art*, 61

DANCE—FICTION
Leiner, *Mama Does the Mambo*, 13
Soto, *Snapshots from the Wedding*, 114
Tamar, *Alphabet City Ballet*, 68
Torres, *Liliana's Grandmothers*, 116
Tripp, *Again, Josefina!*, 117
Zamorano, *Let's Eat*, 76

DANCE—LATIN AMERICA
Stewart, *Musica!: Salsa, Rumba, Merengue and More*, 115

DATING (SOCIAL CUSTOMS)—DRAMA
Soto, *Novio Boy: A Play*, 113

DAY OF THE DEAD (MEXICAN HOLIDAY)
Amado, *Barrilete: A Kite for the Day of the Dead*, 23

DAY OF THE DEAD (MEXICAN HOLIDAY)—FICTION
Joose, *Ghost Wings*, 47
Marzollo, *Soccer Cousins*, 50

DENVER (CO)—FICTION
  Ramos, *Blues for the Buffalo*, 106

DICTATORS
  Alvarez, *Something to Declare*, 78
  Lindop, *Panama and the United States: Divided by the Canal*, 60

DICTATORS—LATIN AMERICA—FICTION
  Skármeta, *The Composition*, 34

DISEASES
  Parker, *Locks, Crocs, & Skeeters: The Story of the Panama Canal*,
    61
  Winick, *Pedro and Me: Friendship, Loss, and What I Learned*, 121

DIVORCE—FICTION
  Alvarez, *How Tía Lola Came to (Visit) Stay*, 78

DOMINICAN AMERICANS
  (*See also* LATINOS)

DOMINICAN AMERICANS—NEW YORK (NY)—FICTION
  Pérez, *Geographies of Home*, 105

DOMINICAN AMERICANS—SOCIAL LIFE AND CUSTOMS—
    FICTION
  Alvarez, *¡Yo!*, 78
  Pérez, *Geographies of Home*, 105

DOMINICAN AMERICANS—VERMONT—FICTION
  Alvarez, *How Tía Lola Came to (Visit) Stay*, 78

DOMINICAN REPUBLIC
  Brown, *Culture and Customs of the Dominican Republic*, 129
  Dubois, *Dominican Republic*, 128
  Haverstock, *Dominican Republic in Pictures*, 142
  Landau, *The Dominican Republic*, 141
  Preller, *McGwire & Sosa: A Season to Remember*, 17
  Rogers and Radcliffe, *The Dominican Republic*, 131

DOMINICAN REPUBLIC—BIOGRAPHY
  Christopher, *At the Plate with . . . Sammy Sosa*, 17

Savage, *Sammy Sosa: Home Run Hero*, 18

DOMINICAN REPUBLIC—FICTION
Alvarez, *The Secret Footprints*, 16
Appelbaum, *Cocoa Ice*, 16
Joseph, *The Color of My Words*, 17

DOMINICAN REPUBLIC—HISTORY—1950-
Alvarez, *Something to Declare*, 78

DOMINICAN REPUBLIC—SOCIAL LIFE AND CUSTOMS—
FICTION
Alvarez, *How Tía Lola Came to (Visit) Stay*, 78
Appelbaum, *Cocoa Ice*, 16

DRUG ABUSE
Baca, *A Place to Stand: The Making of a Poet*, 81
Ramirez, *A Patriot after All: The Story of a Chicano Vietnam Vet*,
106
Sanchez, *My Bloody Life: The Making of a Latin King*, 110

DRUG ABUSE—FICTION
Durán, *Don't Spit on My Corner*, 86
Herrera, *CrashBoomLove*, 92
Quiñonez, *Bodega Dreams*, 106
Ramos, *Blues for the Buffalo*, 106
Tamar, *Alphabet City Ballet*, 68
Weaver, *Rooster*, 119

EATING CUSTOMS
Johnson, *Tomatoes, Potatoes, Corn, and Beans: How the Foods of
the Americas Changed Eating around the World*, 30

EATING CUSTOMS—FICTION
Torres, *Liliana's Grandmothers*, 116
Wing, *Jalapeño Bagels*, 120

ECOLOGY
Collard, *Monteverde: Science and Scientists in a Costa Rican Cloud
Forest*, 7
Pringle, *An Extraordinary Life: The Story of a Monarch Butterfly*,
53

Tagliaferro, *Galápagos Islands: Nature's Delicate Balance at Risk*,
20

ECUADOR
Beirne, *Children of Ecuadorean Highlands*, 144
Blum, *Galápagos in 3-D*, 19
Daniels, *Ecuador*, 128
Handelsman, *Culture and Customs of Ecuador*, 129
Heller, *Galápagos Means "Tortoises,"* 19
Lourie, *Lost Treasure of the Inca*, 20
Morrison, *Ecuador*, 130
Sumwalt, *Ecuador in Pictures*, 142
Tagliaferro, *Galápagos Islands: Nature's Delicate Balance at Risk*,
20

ECUADOR—FICTION
Lewin, *Nilo and the Tortoise*, 19

EL DORADO—GEOGRAPHICAL MYTHS
Aronson, *Sir Walter Ralegh and the Quest for El Dorado*, 62, 72

EL SALVADOR
Benítez, *Bitter Grounds*, 21
Gorkin, *From Grandmother to Granddaughter: Salvadoran
    Women's Stories*, 22
Morrison, *El Salvador*, 130
Nickles, *El Salvador: The Land*, 22
Nickles, *El Salvador: The People and Culture*, 22

EL SALVADOR—DESCRIPTION
Nickles, *El Salvador: The Land*, 22

EL SALVADOR—FICTION
Alphin, *A Bear for Miguel*, 21

EL SALVADOR—HISTORY
Benítez, *Bitter Grounds*, 21
Gorkin, *From Grandmother to Granddaughter: Salvadoran
    Women's Stories*, 22
Nickles, *El Salvador: The People and Culture*, 22

EL SALVADOR—SOCIAL CONDITIONS
Benítez, *Bitter Grounds*, 21
Gorkin, *From Grandmother to Granddaughter: Salvadoran Women's Stories*, 22

EL SALVADOR—SOCIAL LIFE AND CUSTOMS
Nickles, *El Salvador: The People and Culture*, 22

EL YUNQUE (PR)—FICTION
London, *Hurricane!*, 67
Mohr, *Old Letivia and the Mountain of Sorrows*, 67

ENGLISH AS A SECOND LANGUAGE—FICTION
Elya, *Home at Last*, 86
English, *Speak English for Us, Marisol!*, 86
Figueredo, *When This World Was New*, 88
Johnston, *Uncle Rain Cloud*, 95
Rodríguez, *América Is Her Name*, 107
Welter, *I Want to Buy a Vowel: A Novel of Illegal Alienation*, 120

ENVIRONMENTAL POLICY—AMERICA
Gold, *Environments of the Western Hemisphere*, 28

ENVIRONMENTAL PROTECTION
Collard, *Monteverde: Science and Scientists in a Costa Rican Cloud Forest*, 7
Pringle, *An Extraordinary Life: The Story of a Monarch Butterfly*, 53

ETHNIC RELATIONS
Gonzalez, *Harvest of Empire: A History of Latinos in America*, 90

EXPLORATION
Aronson, *Sir Walter Ralegh and the Quest for El Dorado*, 62, 72
Marrin, *Empires Lost and Won: The Spanish Heritage in the Southwest*, 100
Tanaka, *Lost Temple of the Aztecs*, 55

FAIRY TALES
Ada, *The Three Golden Oranges*, 71
Kimmel, *The Runaway Tortilla*, 96
Pomerantz, *Mangaboom*, 33

San Souci, *Little Gold Star: A Spanish American Cinderella Tale*, 109

FAMILY LIFE
Ancona, *Barrio: José's Neighborhood*, 80
Lomas Garza, *In My Family/En mi familia*, 98

FAMILY LIFE—FICTION
Alphin, *A Bear for Miguel*, 21
Alvarez, *How Tía Lola Came to (Visit) Stay*, 78
Alvarez, *¡Yo!*, 78
Berrocal Essex, *Delia's Way*, 59
Bunting, *Going Home*, 39
Calhoun, *Tonio's Cat*, 82
Cowley, *Gracias, the Thanksgiving Turkey*, 84
Elya, *Home at Last*, 86
English, *Speak English for Us, Marisol!*, 86
García, *The Agüero Sisters*, 10
Garland, *A Line in the Sand: The Alamo Diary of Lucinda Lawrence*, 89
Jiménez, *Breaking Through*, 94
Jiménez, *The Circuit: Stories from the Life of a Migrant Child*, 94
Johnston, *The Magic Maguey*, 47
Joseph, *The Color of My Words*, 17
Kroll, *Butterfly Boy*, 49
Martinez, *Parrot in the Oven: Mi Vida*, 100
Obejas, *Days of Awe*, 104
Ortiz Cofer, *The Year of Our Revolution: New and Selected Stories and Poems*, 105
Skármeta, *The Composition*, 34
Soto, *Snapshots from the Wedding*, 114
Spurr, *Mama's Birthday Surprise*, 115
Talbert, *Star of Luís*, 115
Torres, *Liliana's Grandmothers*, 116
Weaver, *Rooster*, 119
Winter, *Josefina*, 57
Zamorano, *Let's Eat*, 76

FARM LIFE—FICTION
Olson, *Joyride*, 105

FARM PRODUCE
Ancona, *Harvest*, 38, 80

FATHER-DAUGHTER RELATIONSHIP—FICTION
Chambers, *Marisol and Magdalena: The Sound of Our Sisterhood*, 59
Geeslin, *How Nanita Learned to Make Flan*, 45
Love, *I Remember the Alamo*, 99
Newman, *Isabella: A Wish for Miguel, Peru, 1820*, 64

FATHER-SON RELATIONSHIP—FICTION
Figueredo, *When This World Was New*, 88

FATHERS—DEATH—FICTION
Leiner, *Mama Does the Mambo*, 13
Ryan, *Esperanza Rising*, 108

FEAR—FICTION
Figueredo, *When This World Was New*, 88

FESTIVALS—CENTRAL AMERICA
Viesti and Hall, *Celebrate! in Central America*, 4

FESTIVALS—GUATEMALA
Amado, *Barrilete: A Kite for the Day of the Dead*, 23

FESTIVALS—MEXICO
Ancona, *Fiesta Fireworks*, 38

FESTIVALS—MEXICO—FICTION
Yacowitz, *Pumpkin Fiesta*, 58

FESTIVALS—PERU
Jermyn, *Peru*, 63

FESTIVALS—PUERTO RICO
Foley, *Puerto Rico*, 66

FINGER PLAY
Orozco, *Diez deditos/Ten Little Fingers and Other Play Rhymes and Action Songs from Latin America*, 32

FLAN (RECIPE)
Geeslin, *How Nanita Learned to Make Flan*, 45
Las Christmas: Favorite Latino Authors Share Their Holiday Memories, 97

FLORIDA—FICTION
García, *The Agüero Sisters*, 10
Lamazares, *The Sugar Island*, 12
Weaver, *Rooster*, 119

FOLKLORE—CHILE
Pitcher, *Mariana and the Merchild: A Folk Tale from Chile*, 5

FOLKLORE—COSTA RICA
Strauss, *When Woman Became the Sea: A Costa Rican Creation Myth*, 7

FOLKLORE—DOMINICAN REPUBLIC
Alvarez, *The Secret Footprints*, 16

FOLKLORE—GUATEMALA
Gerson, *People of Corn: A Mayan Story*, 24, 45

FOLKLORE—LATIN AMERICA
González, *Señor Cat's Romance and Other Favorite Stories from Latin America*, 29
Latin American Folktales: Stories from Hispanic and Indian Traditions, 31
Winther, *Plays from Hispanic Tales: One-Act, Royalty-Free Dramatizations for Young People, from Hispanic Stories and Folktales*, 35

FOLKLORE—MEXICO
Anaya, *Maya's Children: The Story of La Llorona*, 37
Climo, *The Little Red Ant and the Great Big Crumb: A Mexican Fable*, 41
Coburn, *Domitila: A Cinderella Tale from the Mexican Tradition*, 41
Ehlert, *Cuckoo/Cucú*, 43
Gerson, *Fiesta Femenina: Celebrating Women in Mexican Folktale*, 45
Gollub, *Uncle Snake*, 46

Pohl, *The Legend of Lord Eight Deer: An Epic of Ancient Mexico*, 53

FOLKLORE—PUERTO RICO
Jaffe, *The Golden Flower: A Taino Myth from Puerto Rico*, 67
Mohr, *Old Letivia and the Mountain of Sorrows*, 67
Montes, *Juan Bobo Goes to Work: A Puerto Rican Folktale*, 68

FOLKLORE—SOUTHWESTERN STATES
Anaya, *Roadrunner's Dance*, 80
Hayes, *Juan Verdades: The Man Who Couldn't Tell a Lie*, 91
Lowell, *Los tres pequeños jabalíes/The Three Little Javelinas*, 100
San Souci, *Little Gold Star: A Spanish American Cinderella Tale*, 109

FOLKLORE—SPAIN
Ada, *Jordi's Star*, 71
Ada, *The Three Golden Oranges*, 71
Sierra, *The Beautiful Butterfly: A Folktale from Spain*, 75
Winther, *Plays from Hispanic Tales: One-Act, Royalty-Free Dramatizations for Young People, from Hispanic Stories and Folktales*, 35

FOLKLORE—UNITED STATES
González, *Señor Cat's Romance and Other Favorite Stories from Latin America*, 29
Hayes, *Juan Verdades: The Man Who Couldn't Tell a Lie*, 91
Kimmel, *The Runaway Tortilla*, 96
Lowell, *Los tres pequeños jabalíes/The Three Little Javelinas*, 100

FOOD
Johnson, *Tomatoes, Potatoes, Corn, and Beans: How the Foods of the Americas Changed Eating around the World*, 30
Las Christmas: Favorite Latino Authors Share Their Holiday Memories, 97
Ward, *The Young Chef's Mexican Cookbook*, 57

FOOD—FICTION
Appelbaum, *Cocoa Ice*, 16
Ehlert, *Market Day: A Story Told with Folk Art*, 26
Fine, *Under the Lemon Moon*, 44
Geeslin, *How Nanita Learned to Make Flan*, 45

Weaver, *Rooster*, 119
Wing, *Jalapeño Bagels*, 120
Yacowitz, *Pumpkin Fiesta*, 58
Zamorano, *Let's Eat*, 76

FORESTS AND FORESTRY
Collard, *Monteverde: Science and Scientists in a Costa Rican Cloud Forest*, 7
Gold, *Environments of the Western Hemisphere*, 28

FORGIVENESS—FICTION
Fine, *Under the Lemon Moon*, 44

FRIENDSHIP
Winick, *Pedro and Me: Friendship, Loss, and What I Learned*, 121

FRIENDSHIP—FICTION
Ada, *Jordi's Star*, 71
Chambers, *Marisol and Magdalena: The Sound of Our Sisterhood*, 59
Cowan, *My Life with the Wave*, 41
Cowley, *Gracias, the Thanksgiving Turkey*, 84
Garland, *A Line in the Sand: The Alamo Diary of Lucinda Lawrence*, 89
Laden, *When Pigasso Met Mootisse*, 73
Love, *I Remember the Alamo*, 99
Olson, *Joyride*, 105
Pomerantz, *Mangaboom*, 33
Soto, *Chato and the Party Animals*, 112
Soto, *Nerdlandia: A Play*, 113
Welter, *I Want to Buy a Vowel: A Novel of Illegal Alienation*, 120

FRONTIER AND PIONEER LIFE—FICTION
Garland, *A Line in the Sand: The Alamo Diary of Lucinda Lawrence*, 89

GALÁPAGOS ISLANDS
Blum, *Galápagos in 3-D*, 19
Tagliaferro, *Galápagos Islands: Nature's Delicate Balance at Risk*, 20

GALÁPAGOS ISLANDS—DESCRIPTION
Blum, *Galápagos in 3-D*, 19
Heller, *Galápagos Means "Tortoises,"* 19

GALÁPAGOS ISLANDS—FICTION
Lewin, *Nilo and the Tortoise*, 19

GANGS
Atkin, *Voices from the Streets: Young Former Gang Members Tell Their Stories*, 81

GANGS—FICTION
Durán, *Don't Spit on My Corner*, 86
Ewing, *Party Girl*, 87
Herrera, *CrashBoomLove*, 92
Soto, *Buried Onions*, 111

GARDENING—FICTION
Yacowitz, *Pumpkin Fiesta*, 58

GIANTS—FICTION
Pomerantz, *Mangaboom*, 33

GINGERBREAD MAN (FICTITIOUS CHARACTER)
Kimmel, *The Runaway Tortilla*, 96

GODS AND GODDESSES
Anaya, *Maya's Children: The Story of La Llorona*, 37
Fisher, *Gods and Goddesses of the Ancient Maya*, 44
Gerson, *Fiesta Femenina: Celebrating Women in Mexican Folktale*, 45
Gerson, *People of Corn: A Mayan Story*, 45
Johnston, *Uncle Rain Cloud*, 95
McDermott, *Musicians of the Sun*, 50
Patent, *Quetzal: Sacred Bird of the Cloud Forest*, 52

GOOD AND EVIL—FICTION
Mohr, *Old Letivia and the Mountain of Sorrows*, 67

GOYA, FRANCISCO DE, 1746-1828—BIOGRAPHY
Schiaffino, *Goya*, 74

GRANDFATHERS—FICTION
Marzollo, *Soccer Cousins*, 50
Reeve, *Lolo & Red-Legs*, 106

GRANDMOTHERS—DEATH—FICTION
Joose, *Ghost Wings*, 47

GRANDMOTHERS—FICTION
Chambers, *Marisol and Magdalena: The Sound of Our Sisterhood*, 59
Cordova, *Abuelita's Heart*, 84
Herrera, *Grandma and Me at the Flea/Los meros meros remateros*, 93
Jenkins, *So Loud a Silence*, 6
Ryan, *Mice and Beans*, 109
Slate, *The Secret Stars*, 111
Torres, *Liliana's Grandmothers*, 116

GRANDMOTHERS—POETRY
Love to Mamá: A Tribute to Mothers, 99

GRANDPARENT-GRANDCHILD RELATIONSHIP—FICTION
Kroll, *Butterfly Boy*, 49
Velasquez, *Grandma's Records*, 69

GREAT BRITAIN—HISTORY
Aronson, *Sir Walter Ralegh and the Quest for El Dorado*, 62, 72
Lace, *Defeat of the Spanish Armada*, 72

GREAT DEPRESSION, 1929-1939—FICTION
Ryan, *Esperanza Rising*, 108

GRECO, 1541-1614—BIOGRAPHY
Venezia, *El Greco*, 75

GUADALAJARA (MEXICO)—FICTION
Spurr, *Mama's Birthday Surprise*, 115

GUADALUPE, OUR LADY OF
Gerson, *Fiesta Femenina: Celebrating Women in Mexican Folktale*, 45
Serrano, *Our Lady of Guadalupe*, 54

GUATEMALA
Amado, *Barrilete: A Kite for the Day of the Dead*, 23
Dahl, *Guatemala*, 128
Gerson, *People of Corn: A Mayan Story*, 24, 45
Guatemala, 132
Guatemala in Pictures, 142
Hadden, *Teenage Refugees from Guatemala Speak Out*, 136
Hermes, *Children of Guatemala*, 144
Hoepker, *Return of the Maya: Guatemala—a Tale of Survival*, 24
Malone, *A Guatemalan Family*, 136
Sheehan, *Guatemala*, 129
Silverstone, *Rigoberta Menchu: Defending Human Rights in Guatemala*, 143

GUATEMALA—BIOGRAPHY
Brill, *Journey for Peace: The Story of Rigoberta Menchú*, 23

GUATEMALA—FICTION
Gage, *Pascual's Magic Pictures*, 24

GUATEMALA—HISTORY
Brill, *Journey for Peace: The Story of Rigoberta Menchú*, 23

GUATEMALA—PICTORIAL WORKS
Hoepker, *Return of the Maya: Guatemala—a Tale of Survival*, 24

GUATEMALA—SOCIAL LIFE AND CUSTOMS
Hoepker, *Return of the Maya: Guatemala—a Tale of Survival*, 24

GUATEMALANS—TEXAS—FICTION
Welter, *I Want to Buy a Vowel: A Novel of Illegal Alienation*, 120

GUERRILLA WARFARE—FICTION
Alphin, *A Bear for Miguel*, 21
Jenkins, *So Loud a Silence*, 6

GUEVARA, ERNESTO 'CHE', 1928-1967
Salas and Salas, *Fidel's Cuba: A Revolution in Pictures*, 14
Symmes, *Chasing Che: A Motorcycle Journey in Search of the Guevara Legend*, 3

GUEVARA, ERNESTO 'CHE', 1928-1967—BIOGRAPHY
Sinclair, *Che Guevara*, 2, 14

HEADS OF STATE—CUBA
Foss, *Fidel Castro*, 10
Gibb, *Fidel Castro: Leader of Cuba's Revolution*, 11
Staub, *Children of Cuba*, 15

HEADS OF STATE—MEXICO
Burr, *When the Viceroy Came*, 40
Stein, *The Mexican Revolution: 1910-1920*, 55
Vázquez-Gómez, *Dictionary of Mexican Rulers, 1325-1997*, 57

HELPING BEHAVIOR—FICTION
English, *Speak English for Us, Marisol!*, 86
Fine, *Under the Lemon Moon*, 44
Johnston, *Uncle Rain Cloud*, 95
Soto, *The Old Man and His Door*, 114
Welter, *I Want to Buy a Vowel: A Novel of Illegal Alienation*, 120

HISPANIC AMERICA—LITERARY COLLECTIONS
*Latino Reader: An American Literary Tradition from 1542 to the
Present, The*, 97
Noche Buena: Hispanic American Christmas Stories, 104
Oxford Book of Latin American Short Stories, The, 32

HISTORIC SITES
Lourie, *The Mystery of the Maya: Uncovering the Lost City of
Palenque*, 49
Macdonald, *Inca Town*, 63
Mann, *Machu Picchu*, 63

HISPANIC AMERICANS
(*See* CHICANOS, CUBAN AMERICANS, DOMINICAN
AMERICANS, LATINOS, MEXICAN AMERICANS,
PANAMANIAN AMERICANS, PUERTO RICANS)

HISTORICAL FICTION
Bridal, *The Tree of Red Stars*, 122
Eboch, *The Well of Sacrifice*, 42
Ephron, *White Rose/Una rosa blanca*, 9

Garland, *A Line in the Sand: The Alamo Diary of Lucinda Lawrence*, 89

Harrigan, *The Gates of the Alamo*, 91

Jenkins, *So Loud a Silence*, 6

Leonard, *Cuba Libre*, 13

Love, *I Remember the Alamo*, 99

Newman, *Isabella: A Wish for Miguel, Peru, 1820*, 64

Stanley, *Elena*, 54

Tripp, *Again, Josefina!*, 117

Tripp, *Changes for Josefina: A Winter Story*, 117

Tripp, *Happy Birthday, Josefina!*, 117

Tripp, *Josefina Learns a Lesson: A School Story*, 117

Tripp, *Josefina Saves the Day: A Summer Story*, 117

Tripp, *Josefina's Surprise: A Christmas Story*, 117

Tripp, *Meet Josefina: An American Girl*, 117

HOLIDAYS

Ancona, *Fiesta Fireworks*, 38

Chambers, *All Saints, All Souls, and Halloween*, 144

Chambers, *Carnival*, 144

Gnojewski, *Cinco de Mayo: Celebrating Hispanic Pride*, 132

Hoyt-Goldsmith, *Las Posadas: An Hispanic Christmas Celebration*, 93

Las Christmas: Favorite Latino Authors Share Their Holiday Memories, 97

Schaefer, *Cinco de Mayo*, 135

Vázquez, *Cinco de Mayo*, 144

HOLIDAYS—FICTION

Carlson, *Hurray for Three Kings' Day!*, 82

Cowley, *Gracias, the Thanksgiving Turkey*, 84

Marzollo, *Soccer Cousins*, 50

Slate, *The Secret Stars*, 111

HONDURAS

McGaffey, *Honduras*, 129

HUMOROUS FICTION

Cowley, *Gracias, the Thanksgiving Turkey*, 84

Laden, *When Pigasso Met Mootisse*, 73

Soto, *The Old Man and His Door*, 114

Yacowitz, *Pumpkin Fiesta*, 58

HURRICANES—FICTION
  London, *Hurricane!*, 67

IMMIGRANTS
  Ancona, *Barrio: José's Neighborhood*, 80
  Gonzales, *Mexicanos: A History of Mexicans in the United States*, 90
  Rosales, *Chicano!: The History of the Mexican American Civil Rights Movement*, 108
  Santiago, *Almost a Woman*, 68

IMMIGRANTS—FICTION
  Bunting, *Going Home*, 39
  Figueredo, *When This World Was New*, 88
  Ortiz Cofer, *The Year of Our Revolution: New and Selected Stories and Poems*, 105
  Ryan, *Esperanza Rising*, 108
  Welter, *I Want to Buy a Vowel: A Novel of Illegal Alienation*, 120

IMMIGRATION AND EMIGRATION
  Cozic, *Illegal Immigration*, 85

INCAS (SOUTH AMERICA)
  Hinds, *The Incas*, 62
  Lourie, *Lost Treasure of the Inca*, 20
  Macdonald, *Inca Town*, 63
  Mann, *Machu Picchu*, 63
  Martell, *Civilizations of Peru before 1535*, 64
  Reinhard, *Discovering the Inca Ice Maiden: My Adventures on Ampato*, 64
  Wood, *The Incas*, 65

INQUISITION
  Stewart, *Life during the Spanish Inquisition*, 75

INSECTS
  Parker, *Locks, Crocs, & Skeeters: The Story of the Panama Canal*, 61

INSECTS—FICTION
  Climo, *The Little Red Ant and the Great Big Crumb: A Mexican Fable*, 41

Uribe, *Buzz, Buzz, Buzz*, 70

JEWISH COOKING—FICTION
 Wing, *Jalapeño Bagels*, 120

JEWS—UNITED STATES—FICTION
 Talbert, *Star of Luís*, 115

JUAN BOBO (LEGENDARY CHARACTER)
 Montes, *Juan Bobo Goes to Work: A Puerto Rican Folktale*, 68

JUNGLES
 Lourie, *The Mystery of the Maya: Uncovering the Lost City of Palenque*, 49

JUNGLES—FICTION
 Abelove, *Go and Come Back*, 62
 Gage, *Pascual's Magic Pictures*, 24

KITES
 Amado, *Barrilete: A Kite for the Day of the Dead*, 23

LA LLORONA (LEGENDARY CHARACTER)
 Anaya, *Maya's Children: The Story of La Llorona*, 37

LABOR MOVEMENT
 Collins, *Farmworker's Friend: The Story of Cesar Chavez*, 83
 Ferriss and Sandoval, *The Fight in the Fields: Cesar Chavez and the Farmworkers Movement*, 88
 Soto, *Jessie De La Cruz: A Profile of a United Farm Worker*, 112

LATIN AMERICA
 (*See also* CENTRAL AMERICA *and individual countries*)
 Chin-Lee and Peña, *A Is for the Americas*, 25
 Dent, *The Legacy of the Monroe Doctrine: A Reference Guide to U.S. Involvement in Latin America and the Caribbean*, 26
 Encyclopedia of Contemporary Latin American and Caribbean Cultures, 27
 Encyclopedia of Latin American and Caribbean Art, 27
 Encyclopedia of Latin American History and Culture, 27
 Encyclopedia of Latin American Literature, 28
 Gold, *Environments of the Western Hemisphere*, 28

Gold, *Governments of the Western Hemisphere*, 28

Henderson, *A Reference Guide to Latin American History*, 29

Johnson, *Tomatoes, Potatoes, Corn, and Beans: How the Foods of the Americas Changed Eating around the World*, 30

Latin American Art in the Twentieth Century, 30

Latino Encyclopedia, The, 31

Marley, *Wars of the Americas: A Chronology of Armed Conflict in the New World, 1492 to the Present*, 31

Orozco, *Diez deditos/Ten Little Fingers and Other Play Rhymes and Action Songs from Latin America*, 32

Oxford Encyclopedia of Mesoamerican Cultures: The Civilizations of Mexico and Central America, The, 33

Shirey, *Latin American Writers*, 34

LATIN AMERICA—BIOGRAPHY

Encyclopedia of Latin American History and Culture, 27

Encyclopedia of Latin American Literature, 28

Henderson, *A Reference Guide to Latin American History*, 29

Sinclair, *Che Guevara*, 14

LATIN AMERICA—ENCYCLOPEDIAS

Encyclopedia of Contemporary Latin American and Caribbean Cultures, 27

Encyclopedia of Latin American and Caribbean Art, 27

Encyclopedia of Latin American History and Culture, 27

Encyclopedia of Latin American Literature, 28

Oxford Encyclopedia of Mesoamerican Cultures: The Civilizations of Mexico and Central America, The, 33

LATIN AMERICA—FICTION

Ada, *Gathering the Sun: An Alphabet in Spanish and English*, 25

Delacre, *Golden Tales: Myths, Legends and Folktales from Latin America*, 25

Ehlert, *Market Day: A Story Told with Folk Art*, 26

González, *Señor Cat's Romance and Other Favorite Stories from Latin America*, 29

Jade and Iron: Latin American Tales from Two Cultures, 29

Latin American Folktales: Stories from Hispanic and Indian Traditions, 31

Oxford Book of Latin American Short Stories, The, 32

Pomerantz, *Mangaboom*, 33

Skármeta, *The Composition*, 34

Torres, *Liliana's Grandmothers*, 34
Twentieth-Century Latin American Poetry: A Bilingual Anthology, 34
Winther, *Plays from Hispanic Tales: One-Act, Royalty-Free Dramatizations for Young People, from Hispanic Stories and Folktales*, 35

LATIN AMERICA—HISTORY—CHRONOLOGY
Henderson, *A Reference Guide to Latin American History*, 29
Marley, *Wars of the Americas: A Chronology of Armed Conflict in the New World, 1492 to the Present*, 31

LATIN AMERICAN LITERATURE—HISTORY AND CRITICISM
Encyclopedia of Latin American Literature, 28
Shirey, *Latin American Writers*, 34

LATIN AMERICANS—BIOGRAPHY
Shirey, *Latin American Writers*, 34
Twentieth-Century Latin American Poetry: A Bilingual Anthology, 34

LATINOS
(*See also* CHICANOS, CUBAN AMERICANS, DOMINICAN AMERICANS, MEXICAN AMERICANS, PANAMANIAN AMERICANS, PUERTO RICANS)
Bankston, *Careers in Community Service*, 136
Garcia, *Careers in Technology*, 136
Menard, *Careers in Sports*, 136
Torres, *Careers in the Music Industry*, 136
Wade, *Careers in Law and Politics*, 137
Wilson, *Careers in Entertainment*, 137
Wilson, *Careers in Publishing and Communications*, 137
Zannos, *Careers in Education*, 137
Zannos, *Careers in Science and Medicine*, 137
Zannos, *Latino Entrepreneurs*, 137

LATINOS—BIOGRAPHY
Cockcroft, *Latino Visions: Contemporary Chicano, Puerto Rican and Cuban American Artists*, 83
Hill, *Ten Hispanic American Authors*, 93
Kanellos, *Hispanic Firsts: 500 Years of Extraordinary Achievement*, 95

Latino Encyclopedia, The, 31
Morey and Dunn, *Famous Hispanic Americans*, 103
Winter, *¡Béisbol! Latino Baseball Pioneers and Legends*, 121

LATINOS—EMPLOYMENT
  Kenig, *Best Careers for Bilingual Latinos: Market Your Fluency in Spanish to Get Ahead on the Job*, 95

LATINOS—ENCYCLOPEDIAS
  Latino Encyclopedia, The, 31

LATINOS—HISTORY
  Fernández-Shaw, *The Hispanic Presence in North America: From 1492 to Today*, 87
  Gonzalez, *Harvest of Empire: A History of Latinos in America*, 90
  Nickles, *The Hispanics*, 103
  Ochoa, *The New York Public Library Amazing Hispanic American History: A Book of Answers for Kids*, 104

LATINOS—HISTORY—CHRONOLOGY
  Kanellos, *Hispanic Firsts: 500 Years of Extraordinary Achievement*, 95

LATINOS—KINGSVILLE (TX)
  Lomas Garza, *In My Family/En mi familia*, 98

LATINOS—MISCELLANEA
  Ochoa, *The New York Public Library Amazing Hispanic American History: A Book of Answers for Kids*, 104

LATINOS—PICTORIAL WORKS
  Americanos: Latino Life in the United States/La vida latina en los Estados Unidos, 79

LATINOS—POETRY
  Touching the Fire: Fifteen Poets of Today's Latino Renaissance, 116

LATINOS—SOCIAL CONDITIONS
  Americanos: Latino Life in the United States/La vida latina en los Estados Unidos, 79

LATINOS—SOCIAL LIFE AND CUSTOMS
  Americanos: Latino Life in the United States/La vida latina en los Estados Unidos, 79
  Kanellos, *Hispanic Firsts: 500 Years of Extraordinary Achievement*, 95
  King, *Quinceañera: Celebrating Fifteen*, 96
  Las Christmas: Favorite Latino Authors Share Their Holiday Memories, 97
  Lomas Garza, *In My Family/En mi familia*, 98
  Salcedo, *Quinceañera!: The Essential Guide to Planning the Perfect Sweet Fifteen Celebration*, 109

LATINOS—SOCIAL LIFE AND CUSTOMS—FICTION
  Carlson, *Hurray for Three Kings' Day!*, 82
  Cordova, *Abuelita's Heart*, 84
  English, *Speak English for Us, Marisol!*, 86

LATINOS—UNITED STATES
  Kanellos, *Hispanic Firsts: 500 Years of Extraordinary Achievement*, 95
  Latino Encyclopedia, The, 31

LEGENDS—AMERICA
  Latin American Folktales: Stories from Hispanic and Indian Traditions, 31

LEGENDS—LATIN AMERICA
  Delacre, *Golden Tales: Myths, Legends and Folktales from Latin America*, 25

LEGENDS—MEXICO
  Anaya, *Maya's Children: The Story of La Llorona*, 37
  Pohl, *The Legend of Lord Eight Deer: An Epic of Ancient Mexico*, 53

LEGENDS—PUERTO RICO
  Mohr, *Old Letivia and the Mountain of Sorrows*, 67
  Montes, *Juan Bobo Goes to Work: A Puerto Rican Folktale*, 68

LIBRARIANS—FICTION
  Mora, *Tomás and the Library Lady*, 102

LIFE CYCLES (BIOLOGY)
Pringle, *An Extraordinary Life: The Story of a Monarch Butterfly*, 53

LIFE CYCLES (BIOLOGY)—FICTION
Swope, *Gotta Go! Gotta Go!*, 55

LOS ANGELES (CA)—DRAMA
Soto, *Nerdlandia: A Play*, 113

LOS ANGELES (CA)—POETRY
Alarcón, *Angels Ride Bikes and Other Fall Poems/Los ángeles andan en bicicleta y otros poemas de otoño*, 77

MACHU PICCHU SITE (PERU)
Mann, *Machu Picchu*, 63

MAGIC—FICTION
Johnston, *The Magic Maguey*, 47
Mohr, *Old Letivia and the Mountain of Sorrows*, 67
Willard, *The Tortilla Cat*, 120

MAINE—SOCIAL LIFE AND CUSTOMS—FICTION
Appelbaum, *Cocoa Ice*, 16

MARIACHIS—FICTION
Soto, *Snapshots from the Wedding*, 114

MARKETS—FICTION
Alphin, *A Bear for Miguel*, 21
Ehlert, *Market Day: A Story Told with Folk Art*, 26
Elya, *Eight Animals on the Town*, 43
Gage, *Pascual's Magic Pictures*, 24
Herrera, *Grandma and Me at the Flea/Los meros meros remateros*, 93
Mora, *Uno, dos, tres, One, Two, Three*, 51

MARY, BLESSED VIRGIN, SAINT—FICTION
de Paola, *The Night of Las Posadas*, 85

MASKS (FACIAL)
Gollub, *Uncle Snake*, 46

MATISSE, HENRI, 1869-1954—FICTION
Laden, *When Pigasso Met Mootisse*, 73

MAY DAY (EUROPEAN HOLIDAY)—FICTION
Mora, *The Rainbow Tulip*, 101

MAYAS (CENTRAL AMERICA)
Ancona, *Mayeros: A Yucatec Maya Family*, 38
Day, *Your Travel Guide to Ancient Mayan Civilization*, 42
Ehlert, *Cuckoo/Cucú*, 43
Fisher, *Gods and Goddesses of the Ancient Maya*, 44
Gerson, *People of Corn: A Mayan Story*, 24, 45
Lourie, *The Mystery of the Maya: Uncovering the Lost City of
    Palenque*, 49

MAYAS (CENTRAL AMERICA)—FICTION
Eboch, *The Well of Sacrifice*, 42

MAYAS (CENTRAL AMERICA)—PICTORIAL WORKS
Ancona, *Mayeros: A Yucatec Maya Family*, 38

MAYAS (CENTRAL AMERICA)—SOCIAL CONDITIONS
Hoepker, *Return of the Maya: Guatemala—a Tale of Survival*, 24

McGWIRE, MARK, 1963-
Preller, *McGwire & Sosa: A Season to Remember*, 17

MENCHÚ, RIGOBERTA, 1959- —BIOGRAPHY
Brill, *Journey for Peace: The Story of Rigoberta Menchú*, 23

MENTALLY HANDICAPPED CHILDREN—FICTION
Weaver, *Rooster*, 119

MERMAIDS AND MERMEN—FOLKLORE
Pitcher, *Mariana and the Merchild: A Folk Tale from Chile*, 5

MEXICAN AMERICAN POETS
Baca, *A Place to Stand: The Making of a Poet*, 81

MEXICAN AMERICANS
(*See also* CHICANOS, LATINOS, UNITED STATES)
Collins, *Farmworker's Friend: The Story of Cesar Chavez*, 83

Ferriss and Sandoval, *The Fight in the Fields: Cesar Chavez and the Farmworkers Movement*, 88

MEXICAN AMERICANS—CALIFORNIA—FICTION
Herrera, *Grandma and Me at the Flea/Los meros meros remateros*, 93
McGinley, *Joaquin Strikes Back*, 101
Ryan, *Esperanza Rising*, 108
Soto, *Petty Crimes*, 114

MEXICAN AMERICANS—CHICAGO (IL)—FICTION
Rodríguez, *América Is Her Name*, 107

MEXICAN AMERICANS—EMPLOYMENT
Hoyt-Goldsmith, *Migrant Worker: A Boy from the Rio Grande Valley*, 94

MEXICAN AMERICANS—EMPLOYMENT—FICTION
Jiménez, *The Circuit: Stories from the Life of a Migrant Child*, 94

MEXICAN AMERICANS—FICTION
Calhoun, *Tonio's Cat*, 82
Elya, *Home at Last*, 86
Kleven, *Hooray, a Piñata!*, 97
Mora, *The Rainbow Tulip*, 101
Mora, *Tomás and the Library Lady*, 102
Soto, *If the Shoe Fits*, 112
Soto, *The Old Man and His Door*, 114

MEXICAN AMERICANS—FOLKLORE—DICTIONARIES
Castro, *Dictionary of Chicano Folklore*, 82

MEXICAN AMERICANS—FRESNO (CA)—FICTION
Soto, *Buried Onions*, 111

MEXICAN AMERICANS—HISTORY
Gonzales, *Mexicanos: A History of Mexicans in the United States*, 90
Rosales, *Chicano!: The History of the Mexican American Civil Rights Movement*, 108

MEXICAN AMERICANS—LOS ANGELES (CA)—FICTION
Johnston, *Uncle Rain Cloud*, 95
Murray, *What It Takes to Get to Vegas*, 103
Reeve, *Lolo & Red-Legs*, 106
Spurr, *Mama's Birthday Surprise*, 115
Talbert, *Star of Luís*, 115

MEXICAN AMERICANS—POETRY
Alarcón, *Laughing Tomatoes and Other Spring Poems/Jitomates
  risueños y otros poemas de primavera*, 77
Anaya, *Elegy on the Death of César Chávez*, 79

MEXICAN AMERICANS—SAN FRANCISCO (CA)
Ancona, *Barrio: José's Neighborhood*, 80

MEXICAN AMERICANS—SOCIAL LIFE AND CUSTOMS
Alarcón, *Angels Ride Bikes and Other Fall Poems/Los ángeles
  andan en bicicleta y otros poemas de otoño*, 77
Ancona, *Barrio: José's Neighborhood*, 80
Hoyt-Goldsmith, *Las Posadas: An Hispanic Christmas Celebration*,
  93
Ramirez, *A Patriot after All: The Story of a Chicano Vietnam Vet*,
  106
*Welcome to Josefina's World, 1824: Growing Up on America's
  Southwest Frontier*, 119

MEXICAN AMERICANS—SOCIAL LIFE AND CUSTOMS—
DICTIONARIES
Castro, *Dictionary of Chicano Folklore*, 82

MEXICAN AMERICANS—SOCIAL LIFE AND CUSTOMS—
FICTION
Alarcón, *Iguanas in the Snow and Other Winter Poems/Iguanas en
  la nieve y otros poemas de invierno*, 77
Martinez, *Parrot in the Oven: Mi Vida*, 100
Rice, *Crazy Loco*, 107
Ryan, *Esperanza Rising*, 108
Soto, *Nerdlandia: A Play*, 113
Soto, *Snapshots from the Wedding*, 114
Stanley, *Elena*, 54

MEXICAN AMERICANS—TEXAS
   Hoyt-Goldsmith, *Migrant Worker: A Boy from the Rio Grande Valley*, 94

MEXICAN COOKING
   Ward, *The Young Chef's Mexican Cookbook*, 57

MEXICAN COOKING—FICTION
   Geeslin, *How Nanita Learned to Make Flan*, 45
   Wing, *Jalapeño Bagels*, 120

MEXICAN FOLK ART—FICTION
   Winter, *Josefina*, 57

MEXICAN WAR, 1846-1848—ENCYCLOPEDIAS
   Crawford, *Encyclopedia of the Mexican-American War*, 42, 85

MEXICANS
   (*See* CHICANOS, LATINOS, MEXICAN AMERICANS)

MEXICANS—UNITED STATES—FICTION
   Bunting, *Going Home*, 39

MEXICO
   Alcraft, *A Visit to Mexico*, 142
   Ancona, *Charro: The Mexican Cowboy*, 38
   Ancona, *Fiesta Fireworks*, 38
   Ancona, *The Fiestas*, 142
   Ancona, *The Folk Arts*, 142
   Ancona, *The Foods*, 142
   Ancona, *Harvest*, 38, 80
   Ancona, *Mayeros: A Yucatec Maya Family*, 38
   Ancona, *The Past*, 142
   Ancona, *The People*, 142
   Barghusen, *The Aztecs: End of a Civilization*, 135
   Berendes, *Mexico*, 39, 131
   Berg, *Mexico*, 131
   Burr, *Broken Shields*, 39
   Burr, *When the Viceroy Came*, 40
   ¡Cámara! Ciudad de México: Monumentos de una nueva generación/Picture Mexico City: Landmarks of a New Generation, 40

Carey, Jr., *The Mexican War: "Mr. Polk's War,"* 125

Carrasco, *Daily Life of the Aztecs: People of the Sun and Earth,* 129

Castillo, *My Daughter, My Son, the Eagle, the Dove: An Aztec Chant,* 40

Chapman, *The Aztecs,* 129

Chrisp, *The Aztecs,* 135

Collier and Collier, *Hispanic America, Texas, and the Mexican War, 1835-1850,* 130

Cory, *Daily Life in Ancient and Modern Mexico City,* 127

Crawford, *Encyclopedia of the Mexican-American War,* 42, 85

Dahl, *Mexico,* 128

Day, *Your Travel Guide to Ancient Mayan Civilization,* 42

Encyclopedia of Mexico: History, Society & Culture, 44

Fisher, *Gods and Goddesses of the Ancient Maya,* 44

Flowers, *Cortés and the Conquest of the Aztec Empire,* 136

Franklin, *Mexico & Central America,* 126

Frost and Keegan, *The Mexican Revolution,* 143

Gerson, *Fiesta Femenina: Celebrating Women in Mexican Folktale,* 45

Gerson, *People of Corn: A Mayan Story,* 24, 45

Goldstein, *The Journey of Diego Rivera,* 46

Gonzalez, *My First Book of Proverbs/Mi primer libro de dichos,* 46

Goodwin, *Mexico,* 138

Gray, *Mexico,* 132

Green, *Mexico,* 138

Gresko, *Mexico,* 137

Hadden, *Teenage Refugees from Mexico Speak Out,* 136

Harvey, *Look What Came from Mexico,* 138

Heinrichs, *Mexico,* 141

Helly and Courgeon, *Montezuma and the Aztecs,* 47

Hewitt, *The Aztecs,* 132

Hull, *The Aztecs,* 126

Jermyn, *Mexico,* 128

Jermyn and Conboy, *Welcome to Mexico,* 143

Kalman and Lewis, *Mexico from A to Z,* 125

Kent, *Mexico: Rich in Spirit and Tradition,* 131

Kimmel, *Montezuma and the Fall of the Aztecs,* 48

Kirkwood, *The History of Mexico,* 134

Levitt, *Mexico City,* 49

Lilley, *The Conquest of Mexico,* 143

Lourie, *The Mystery of the Maya: Uncovering the Lost City of Palenque,* 49

Lourie, *Rio Grande: From the Rocky Mountains to the Gulf of Mexico*, 50

Macdonald, *The Ancient Aztecs: Secrets of a Lost Civilization to Unlock and Discover*, 50

Márquez, *Destination Veracruz*, 139

Marx, *Mexico*, 140

Mexican War of Independence, The, 143

Mexico in Pictures, 142

Nardo, *The Mexican-American War*, 143

Oppenheimer, *Bordering on Chaos: Guerrillas, Stockbrokers, Politicians and Mexico's Road to Prosperity*, 51

Oxford Encyclopedia of Mesoamerican Cultures: The Civilizations of Mexico and Central America, The, 33

Parker, *Mexico*, 52, 128

Pascoe, *Mexico and the United States: Cooperation and Conflict*, 52

Patent, *Quetzal: Sacred Bird of the Cloud Forest*, 52

Platt, *Aztecs: The Fall of the Aztec Capital*, 53, 130

Pringle, *An Extraordinary Life: The Story of a Monarch Butterfly*, 53

Rees, *The Aztecs*, 141

Staub, *The Children of Sierra Madre*, 144

Staub, *Children of Yucatán*, 144

Steele, *The Aztec News*, 54

Stein, *The Aztec Empire*, 129

Stein, *The Mexican Revolution: 1910-1920*, 55

Stein, *Mexico*, 131

Stein, *Mexico City*, 127

Streissguth, *Mexico*, 133, 141

Tanaka, *Lost Temple of the Aztecs*, 55

United States and Mexico at War. Nineteenth-Century Expansionism and Conflict, The, 56, 118

Urrea, *By the Lake of Sleeping Children: The Secret Life of the Mexican Border*, 56

Urrutia and Orozco, *Cinco de Mayo: Yesterday and Today*, 56

Vázquez-Gómez, *Dictionary of Mexican Rulers, 1325-1997*, 57

Ward, *The Young Chef's Mexican Cookbook*, 57

MEXICO—BIOGRAPHY

Crawford, *Encyclopedia of the Mexican-American War*, 42

Krauze, *Mexico, Biography of Power: A History of Modern Mexico, 1810-1996*, 48

Stein, *The Mexican Revolution: 1910-1920*, 55

Vázquez-Gómez, *Dictionary of Mexican Rulers, 1325-1997*, 57

MEXICO—BOUNDARIES
Lourie, *Rio Grande: From the Rocky Mountains to the Gulf of Mexico*, 50, 98

MEXICO—CIVILIZATION—ENCYCLOPEDIAS
Encyclopedia of Mexico: History, Society & Culture, 44

MEXICO—DESCRIPTION
Berendes, *Mexico*, 39
Levitt, *Mexico City*, 49

MEXICO—ECONOMIC POLICY
Oppenheimer, *Bordering on Chaos: Guerrillas, Stockbrokers, Politicians and Mexico's Road to Prosperity*, 51
Urrea, *By the Lake of Sleeping Children: The Secret Life of the Mexican Border*, 56

MEXICO—ENCYCLOPEDIAS
Crawford, *Encyclopedia of the Mexican-American War*, 42
Encyclopedia of Mexico: History, Society & Culture, 44

MEXICO—FICTION
Alarcón, *From the Bellybutton of the Moon and Other Summer Poems/Del ombligo de la luna y otros poemas de verano*, 37
Anaya, *Maya's Children: The Story of La Llorona*, 37
Bunting, *Going Home*, 39
Climo, *The Little Red Ant and the Great Big Crumb: A Mexican Fable*, 41
Coburn, *Domitila: A Cinderella Tale from the Mexican Tradition*, 41
Cowan, *My Life with the Wave*, 41
Eboch, *The Well of Sacrifice*, 42
Ehlert, *Cuckoo/Cucú*, 43
Elya, *Eight Animals on the Town*, 43
Fine, *Under the Lemon Moon*, 44
Geeslin, *How Nanita Learned to Make Flan*, 45
Gollub, *Uncle Snake*, 46
Johnston, *The Magic Maguey*, 47
Joose, *Ghost Wings*, 47
Kroll, *Butterfly Boy*, 49

Marzollo, *Soccer Cousins*, 50
McDermott, *Musicians of the Sun*, 50
Mora, *Uno, dos, tres, One, Two, Three*, 51
Pohl, *The Legend of Lord Eight Deer: An Epic of Ancient Mexico*, 53
Ramos, *Blues for the Buffalo*, 106
Ryan, *Mice and Beans*, 109
Serrano, *Our Lady of Guadalupe*, 54
Stanley, *Elena*, 54
Swope, *Gotta Go! Gotta Go!*, 55
Winter, *Josefina*, 57
Yacowitz, *Pumpkin Fiesta*, 58

MEXICO—HISTORY
Burr, *When the Viceroy Came*, 40
Crawford, *Encyclopedia of the Mexican-American War*, 42, 85
Krauze, *Mexico, Biography of Power: A History of Modern Mexico, 1810-1996*, 48
Oppenheimer, *Bordering on Chaos: Guerrillas, Stockbrokers, Politicians and Mexico's Road to Prosperity*, 51
Urrutia and Orozco, *Cinco de Mayo: Yesterday and Today*, 56

MEXICO—HISTORY—1519-1540, CONQUEST
Burr, *Broken Shields*, 39
Helly and Courgeon, *Montezuma and the Aztecs*, 47
Kimmel, *Montezuma and the Fall of the Aztecs*, 48
Macdonald, *The Ancient Aztecs: Secrets of a Lost Civilization to Unlock and Discover*, 50
Tanaka, *Lost Temple of the Aztecs*, 55

MEXICO—HISTORY—1910-1920, REVOLUTION
Stein, *The Mexican Revolution: 1910-1920*, 55

MEXICO—HISTORY—1910-1920, REVOLUTION—FICTION
Stanley, *Elena*, 54

MEXICO—HISTORY—CHRONOLOGY
Vázquez-Gómez, *Dictionary of Mexican Rulers, 1325-1997*, 57

MEXICO—HISTORY—ENCYCLOPEDIAS
Encyclopedia of Mexico: History, Society & Culture, 44

MEXICO—PICTORIAL WORKS
Berendes, *Mexico*, 39
¡Cámara! Ciudad de México: Monumentos de una nueva generación/Picture Mexico City: Landmarks of a New Generation, 40
Levitt, *Mexico City*, 49
Parker, *Mexico*, 52

MEXICO—POETRY
Alarcón, *From the Bellybutton of the Moon and Other Summer Poems/Del ombligo de la luna y otros poemas de verano*, 37

MEXICO—SOCIAL CONDITIONS
Urrea, *By the Lake of Sleeping Children: The Secret Life of the Mexican Border*, 56

MEXICO—SOCIAL LIFE AND CUSTOMS
Ancona, *Charro: The Mexican Cowboy*, 38
Ancona, *Mayeros: A Yucatec Maya Family*, 38
Berendes, *Mexico*, 39
Burr, *When the Viceroy Came*, 40
Parker, *Mexico*, 52

MEXICO—SOCIAL LIFE AND CUSTOMS—FICTION
Yacowitz, *Pumpkin Fiesta*, 58

MIGRANT LABOR
Ancona, *Harvest*, 38, 80
Hoyt-Goldsmith, *Migrant Worker: A Boy from the Rio Grande Valley*, 94

MIGRANT LABOR—FICTION
Bunting, *Going Home*, 39
Jiménez, *Breaking Through*, 94
Jiménez, *The Circuit: Stories from the Life of a Migrant Child*, 94
Mora, *Tomás and the Library Lady*, 102
Olson, *Joyride*, 105
Ryan, *Esperanza Rising*, 108

MIGRANT LABOR—POETRY
Ada, *Gathering the Sun: An Alphabet in Spanish and English*, 25
Anaya, *Elegy on the Death of César Chávez*, 79

MISSING PERSONS—FICTION
Ramos, *Blues for the Buffalo*, 106

MISSION LA PURÍSIMA CONCEPCIÓN (CA)
Fraser, *A Mission for the People: The Story of La Purísima*, 88

MIXTECS (MEXICO)
Pohl, *The Legend of Lord Eight Deer: An Epic of Ancient Mexico*, 53

MOCTEZUMA II, EMPEROR OF MEXICO, 1466-1520—
BIOGRAPHY
Helly and Courgeon, *Montezuma and the Aztecs*, 47
Kimmel, *Montezuma and the Fall of the Aztecs*, 48

MONEY—FICTION
Spurr, *Mama's Birthday Surprise*, 115

MONROE DOCTRINE
Dent, *The Legacy of the Monroe Doctrine: A Reference Guide to U.S. Involvement in Latin America and the Caribbean*, 26

MONTEVERDE CLOUD FOREST PRESERVE (COSTA RICA)
Collard, *Monteverde: Science and Scientists in a Costa Rican Cloud Forest*, 7

MOON—FICTION
Fine, *Under the Lemon Moon*, 44

MORGAN, SIR HENRY, 1635-1688—BIOGRAPHY
Marrin, *Terror of the Spanish Main: Sir Henry Morgan and His Buccaneers*, 73

MOTHER-DAUGHTER RELATIONSHIP—FICTION
Atkins, *Get Set! Swim!*, 81
Lamazares, *The Sugar Island*, 12
Leiner, *Mama Does the Mambo*, 13

MOTHERS—DEATH—FICTION
Willard, *The Tortilla Cat*, 120

MOTHERS—FICTION
Stanley, *Elena*, 54

MOTHERS—POETRY
Love to Mamá: A Tribute to Mothers, 99

MOTORCYCLING
Symmes, *Chasing Che: A Motorcycle Journey in Search of the Guevara Legend*, 3

MUMMIES
Reinhard, *Discovering the Inca Ice Maiden: My Adventures on Ampato*, 64

MURAL PAINTING AND DECORATION
Ancona, *Barrio: José's Neighborhood*, 80
Cockcroft, *Latino Visions: Contemporary Chicano, Puerto Rican and Cuban American Artists*, 83
Goldstein, *The Journey of Diego Rivera*, 46

MUSIC
Orozco, *Diez deditos/Ten Little Fingers and Other Play Rhymes and Action Songs from Latin America*, 32
Stewart, *Musica!: Salsa, Rumba, Merengue and More*, 115

MUSIC—FICTION
Tripp, *Again, Josefina!*, 117
Velasquez, *Grandma's Records*, 69

MUSIC—FOLKLORE
McDermott, *Musicians of the Sun*, 50

MYSTERY FICTION
Ramos, *Blues for the Buffalo*, 106

NARRATIVE POETRY
Herrera, *CrashBoomLove*, 92
Lind, *The Alamo: An Epic*, 98
Parker, *Locks, Crocs, & Skeeters: The Story of the Panama Canal*, 61

NATIONAL LIBERATION MOVEMENTS—CUBA
Foss, *Fidel Castro*, 10
Gibb, *Fidel Castro: Leader of Cuba's Revolution*, 11

NATIONAL LIBERATION MOVEMENTS—SOUTH AMERICA
Sinclair, *Che Guevara*, 2, 14

NATIONAL LIBERATION MOVEMENTS—URUGUAY—
FICTION
Bridal, *The Tree of Red Stars*, 122

NATIVE AMERICAN COSTUME—CENTRAL AMERICA
Presilla, *Mola: Cuna Life Stories and Art*, 61

NATIVE AMERICAN GAMES—MEXICO
Macdonald, *The Ancient Aztecs: Secrets of a Lost Civilization to Unlock and Discover*, 50

NATIVE AMERICANS
(*See also* AZTECS, CHUMASH INDIANS, CUNA INDIANS, INCAS, MAYAS, MIXTECS, TAÍNO INDIANS)

NATIVE AMERICANS—ANTIQUITIES
Oxford Encyclopedia of Mesoamerican Cultures: The Civilizations of Mexico and Central America, The, 33

NATIVE AMERICANS—ANTIQUITIES—MEXICO
Lourie, *The Mystery of the Maya: Uncovering the Lost City of Palenque*, 49

NATIVE AMERICANS—CALIFORNIA
Fraser, *A Mission for the People: The Story of La Purísima*, 88

NATIVE AMERICANS—CENTRAL AMERICA
Day, *Your Travel Guide to Ancient Mayan Civilization*, 42

NATIVE AMERICANS—CENTRAL AMERICA—FICTION
Eboch, *The Well of Sacrifice*, 42

NATIVE AMERICANS—CHRISTIAN MISSIONS
Fraser, *A Mission for the People: The Story of La Purísima*, 88

NATIVE AMERICANS—ECUADOR
Lourie, *Lost Treasure of the Inca*, 20

NATIVE AMERICANS—ENCYCLOPEDIAS
Oxford Encyclopedia of Mesoamerican Cultures: The Civilizations of Mexico and Central America, The, 33

NATIVE AMERICANS—FICTION
Abelove, *Go and Come Back*, 62
Eboch, *The Well of Sacrifice*, 42
Newman, *Isabella: A Wish for Miguel, Peru, 1820*, 64

NATIVE AMERICANS—FOLKLORE—CENTRAL AMERICA
Gerson, *People of Corn: A Mayan Story*, 24, 45
Patent, *Quetzal: Sacred Bird of the Cloud Forest*, 4, 52
Viesti and Hall, *Celebrate! in Central America*, 4

NATIVE AMERICANS—FOLKLORE—LATIN AMERICA
Delacre, *Golden Tales: Myths, Legends and Folktales from Latin America*, 25
Latin American Folktales: Stories from Hispanic and Indian Traditions, 31

NATIVE AMERICANS—FOLKLORE—MEXICO
Castillo, *My Daughter, My Son, the Eagle, the Dove: An Aztec Chant*, 40
Ehlert, *Cuckoo/Cucú*, 43
Gollub, *Uncle Snake*, 46
Jade and Iron: Latin American Tales from Two Cultures, 29
McDermott, *Musicians of the Sun*, 50
Patent, *Quetzal: Sacred Bird of the Cloud Forest*, 4, 52
Pohl, *The Legend of Lord Eight Deer: An Epic of Ancient Mexico*, 53
Serrano, *Our Lady of Guadalupe*, 54

NATIVE AMERICANS—FOLKLORE—SOUTH AMERICA
Jade and Iron: Latin American Tales from Two Cultures, 29

NATIVE AMERICANS—FOLKLORE—WEST INDIES
Alvarez, *The Secret Footprints*, 16
Jaffe, *The Golden Flower: A Taino Myth from Puerto Rico*, 67

NATIVE AMERICANS—GUATEMALA
  Brill, *Journey for Peace: The Story of Rigoberta Menchú*, 23

NATIVE AMERICANS—HISTORY—MEXICO
  Burr, *Broken Shields*, 39
  Helly and Courgeon, *Montezuma and the Aztecs*, 47
  Kimmel, *Montezuma and the Fall of the Aztecs*, 48
  Macdonald, *The Ancient Aztecs: Secrets of a Lost Civilization to
    Unlock and Discover*, 50
  Patent, *Quetzal: Sacred Bird of the Cloud Forest*, 4, 52
  Platt, *Aztecs: The Fall of the Aztec Capital*, 53
  Steele, *The Aztec News*, 54

NATIVE AMERICANS—HISTORY—PERU
  Martell, *Civilizations of Peru before 1535*, 64

NATIVE AMERICANS—HISTORY—SOUTH AMERICA
  Hinds, *The Incas*, 62
  Wood, *The Incas*, 65

NATIVE AMERICANS—MEXICO
  Ancona, *Mayeros: A Yucatec Maya Family*, 38
  Burr, *Broken Shields*, 39
  Day, *Your Travel Guide to Ancient Mayan Civilization*, 42
  Macdonald, *The Ancient Aztecs: Secrets of a Lost Civilization to
    Unlock and Discover*, 50
  Platt, *Aztecs: The Fall of the Aztec Capital*, 53
  Steele, *The Aztec News*, 54
  Tanaka, *Lost Temple of the Aztecs*, 55

NATIVE AMERICANS—MEXICO—FICTION
  Eboch, *The Well of Sacrifice*, 42

NATIVE AMERICANS—PANAMA
  Presilla, *Mola: Cuna Life Stories and Art*, 61

NATIVE AMERICANS—PERU
  Jermyn, *Peru*, 63

NATIVE AMERICANS—PERU—FICTION
  Newman, *Isabella: A Wish for Miguel, Peru, 1820*, 64

NATIVE AMERICANS—POLITICS AND GOVERNMENT—
SOUTH AMERICA
Gold, *Governments of the Western Hemisphere*, 28

NATIVE AMERICANS—RELIGION—CENTRAL AMERICA
Fisher, *Gods and Goddesses of the Ancient Maya*, 44

NATIVE AMERICANS—SOUTH AMERICA
Hinds, *The Incas*, 62
Macdonald, *Inca Town*, 63
Mann, *Machu Picchu*, 63
Martell, *Civilizations of Peru before 1535*, 64
Reinhard, *Discovering the Inca Ice Maiden: My Adventures on
    Ampato*, 64
Wood, *The Incas*, 65

NATIVE AMERICANS—SOUTH AMERICA—FICTION
Abelove, *Go and Come Back*, 62

NATURAL DISASTERS—FICTION
London, *Hurricane!*, 67
Mohr, *Old Letivia and the Mountain of Sorrows*, 67
Tripp, *Josefina Learns a Lesson: A School Story*, 117

NATURAL HISTORY—GALÁPAGOS ISLANDS
Blum, *Galápagos in 3-D*, 19

NATURE
Tagliaferro, *Galápagos Islands: Nature's Delicate Balance at Risk*,
    20

NATURE—FICTION
Ada, *Gathering the Sun: An Alphabet in Spanish and English*, 25
Ada, *Jordi's Star*, 71
Alarcón, *Laughing Tomatoes and Other Spring Poems/Jitomates
    risueños y otros poemas de primavera*, 77
Kroll, *Butterfly Boy*, 49
Patent, *Quetzal: Sacred Bird of the Cloud Forest*, 52

NEW YORK (NY)—FICTION
Cowley, *Gracias, the Thanksgiving Turkey*, 84
Figueredo, *When This World Was New*, 88

NEW YORK (NY)—SOCIAL LIFE AND CUSTOMS—FICTION
Abelove, *Go and Come Back*, 62

NICARAGUA
Haverstock, *Nicaragua in Pictures*, 142
Malone, *A Nicaraguan Family*, 136
Morrison, *Nicaragua*, 130
Riehecky, *Nicaragua*, 128

NORTH AMERICA—FOREIGN INFLUENCES—LATIN
AMERICA
Nickles, *The Hispanics*, 103

NURSERY RHYMES
Orozco, *Diez deditos/Ten Little Fingers and Other Play Rhymes and
Action Songs from Latin America*, 32

OCCUPATIONS
Kenig, *Best Careers for Bilingual Latinos: Market Your Fluency in
Spanish to Get Ahead on the Job*, 95

OCEAN WAVES—FICTION
Cowan, *My Life with the Wave*, 41

OCEAN—FOLKLORE
Pitcher, *Mariana and the Merchild: A Folk Tale from Chile*, 5
Strauss, *When Woman Became the Sea: A Costa Rican Creation
Myth*, 7

ORAL HISTORY
Gorkin, *From Grandmother to Granddaughter: Salvadoran
Women's Stories*, 22

PAINTERS—MEXICO
Goldstein, *The Journey of Diego Rivera*, 46

PAINTERS—MEXICO—FICTION
Winter, *Josefina*, 57

PAINTERS—SPAIN
Schiaffino, *Goya*, 74

PALENQUE SITE (MEXICO)
  Lourie, *The Mystery of the Maya: Uncovering the Lost City of Palenque*, 49

PANAMA
  Gaines, *The Panama Canal in American History*, 135
  Gold, *The Panama Canal Transfer: Controversy at the Crossroads*, 60
  Lindop, *Panama and the United States: Divided by the Canal*, 60
  Markun, *It's Panama's Canal!*, 60
  McNeese, *Panama Canal, The*, 126
  Panama in Pictures, 142
  Parker, *Locks, Crocs, & Skeeters: The Story of the Panama Canal*, 61
  Presilla, *Mola: Cuna Life Stories and Art*, 61
  Rau, *Panama*, 141
  Winkelman, *The Panama Canal*, 128

PANAMA—BIOGRAPHY
  Parker, *Locks, Crocs, & Skeeters: The Story of the Panama Canal*, 61

PANAMA—FICTION
  Berrocal Essex, *Delia's Way*, 59
  Chambers, *Marisol and Magdalena: The Sound of Our Sisterhood*, 59

PANAMA—HISTORY—1989, INVASION
  Lindop, *Panama and the United States: Divided by the Canal*, 60

PANAMA—SOCIAL LIFE AND CUSTOMS—FICTION
  Berrocal Essex, *Delia's Way*, 59
  Chambers, *Marisol and Magdalena: The Sound of Our Sisterhood*, 59

PANAMA CANAL (PANAMA)—HISTORY
  Gold, *The Panama Canal Transfer: Controversy at the Crossroads*, 60
  Lindop, *Panama and the United States: Divided by the Canal*, 60
  Markun, *It's Panama's Canal!*, 60
  Parker, *Locks, Crocs, & Skeeters: The Story of the Panama Canal*, 61

PANAMA CITY (PANAMA)—1671, DESTRUCTION
Marrin, *Terror of the Spanish Main: Sir Henry Morgan and His Buccaneers*, 73

PANAMANIAN AMERICANS—FICTION
Chambers, *Marisol and Magdalena: The Sound of Our Sisterhood*, 59

PARAGUAY
Haverstock, *Paraguay in Pictures*, 142
Jermyn, *Paraguay*, 129

PARTIES—FICTION
Kleven, *Hooray, a Piñata!*, 97
Soto, *Chato and the Party Animals*, 112
Soto, *The Old Man and His Door*, 114
Zamorano, *Let's Eat*, 76

PEER PRESSURE—FICTION
Quiñonez, *Bodega Dreams*, 106

PERÓN, EVA, 1919-1952—BIOGRAPHY
Dujovne Ortiz, *Eva Perón*, 1

PERU
Aronson, *Sir Walter Ralegh and the Quest for El Dorado*, 62, 72
Corona, *Peru*, 138
Halvorsen, *Peru*, 137
Heisey, *Peru*, 128
Hinds, *The Incas*, 62
Jermyn, *Peru*, 63, 131
King, *Peru: Lost Cities, Found Hopes*, 131
Landau, *Peru*, 141
Macdonald, *Inca Town*, 63
Mann, *Machu Picchu*, 63
Martell, *Civilizations of Peru before 1535*, 64
Morrison, *Peru*, 130
Peru, 132
Peru in Pictures, 142
Reinhard, *Discovering the Inca Ice Maiden: My Adventures on Ampato*, 64
Thoennes, *Peru*, 128

Wood, *The Incas*, 65
Yip and Heisey, *Welcome to Peru*, 143

PERU—FICTION
    Abelove, *Go and Come Back*, 62
    Newman, *Isabella: A Wish for Miguel, Peru, 1820*, 64

PERU—HISTORY—1522-1548, CONQUEST
    Martell, *Civilizations of Peru before 1535*, 64

PERU—HISTORY—FICTION
    Newman, *Isabella: A Wish for Miguel, Peru, 1820*, 64

PERU—SOCIAL LIFE AND CUSTOMS
    Jermyn, *Peru*, 63

PHOTOGRAPHY—FICTION
    Gage, *Pascual's Magic Pictures*, 24
    Vargo, *Señor Felipe's Alphabet Adventure: El alfabeto español*, 35

PICASSO, PABLO RUIZ, 1881-1973—BIOGRAPHY
    Meadows, *Pablo Picasso*, 74

PICASSO, PABLO RUIZ, 1881-1973—FICTION
    Laden, *When Pigasso Met Mootisse*, 73

PIGS—FOLKLORE
    Lowell, *Los tres pequeños jabalíes/The Three Little Javelinas*, 100

PIÑATAS—FICTION
    Kleven, *Hooray, a Piñata!*, 97
    Ryan, *Mice and Beans*, 109
    Slate, *The Secret Stars*, 111
    Soto, *Chato and the Party Animals*, 112

PIONEERS
    Davis, *Three Roads to the Alamo: The Lives and Fortunes of David
        Crockett, James Bowie, and William Barret Travis*, 85

POETRY
    Espada, *A Mayan Astronomer in Hell's Kitchen*, 87
    Martí, *Versos sencillos/Simple Verses*, 13

Twentieth-Century Latin American Poetry: A Bilingual Anthology, 34

POETRY—HISTORY AND CRITICISM
Borges, *This Craft of Verse*, 1

POETS—FICTION
Rodríguez, *América Is Her Name*, 107

POLITICAL CORRUPTION
Oppenheimer, *Bordering on Chaos: Guerrillas, Stockbrokers, Politicians and Mexico's Road to Prosperity*, 51

POLITICAL SCIENCE
Brill, *Journey for Peace: The Story of Rigoberta Menchú*, 23
Gold, *Governments of the Western Hemisphere*, 28
Harlan, *Puerto Rico: Deciding Its Future*, 66
Hoepker, *Return of the Maya: Guatemala—a Tale of Survival*, 24
Krauze, *Mexico, Biography of Power: A History of Modern Mexico, 1810-1996*, 48
Oppenheimer, *Bordering on Chaos: Guerrillas, Stockbrokers, Politicians and Mexico's Road to Prosperity*, 51
Staub, *Children of Cuba*, 15
Symmes, *Chasing Che: A Motorcycle Journey in Search of the Guevara Legend*, 3

POLITICAL SCIENCE—FICTION
Bridal, *The Tree of Red Stars*, 122
Soto, *Off and Running*, 113

POPULAR CULTURE—LATIN AMERICA
Encyclopedia of Contemporary Latin American and Caribbean Cultures, 27

POSADAS (SOCIAL CUSTOMS)
Hoyt-Goldsmith, *Las Posadas: An Hispanic Christmas Celebration*, 93

POSADAS (SOCIAL CUSTOMS)—FICTION
de Paola, *The Night of Las Posadas*, 85
Tripp, *Josefina's Surprise: A Christmas Story*, 117

POVERTY
Urrea, *By the Lake of Sleeping Children: The Secret Life of the Mexican Border*, 56

POVERTY—FICTION
Quiñonez, *Bodega Dreams*, 106

PREJUDICES—FICTION
Martinez, *Parrot in the Oven: Mi Vida*, 100
McGinley, *Joaquin Strikes Back*, 101
Olson, *Joyride*, 105
Rodríguez, *América Is Her Name*, 107
Talbert, *Star of Luís*, 115

PRINCESSES—FICTION
Ada, *The Three Golden Oranges*, 71

PROBLEM SOLVING—FICTION
Climo, *The Little Red Ant and the Great Big Crumb: A Mexican Fable*, 41

PROVERBS
Coburn, *Domitila: A Cinderella Tale from the Mexican Tradition*, 41
Gonzalez, *My First Book of Proverbs/Mi primer libro de dichos*, 46

PUERTO RICANS
(*See also* LATINOS)

PUERTO RICANS—CALIFORNIA—FICTION
Velásquez, *Rina's Family Secret*, 118

PUERTO RICANS—CHICAGO (IL)
Sanchez, *My Bloody Life: The Making of a Latin King*, 110

PUERTO RICANS—FICTION
Cowley, *Gracias, the Thanksgiving Turkey*, 84

PUERTO RICANS—NEW YORK (NY)—FICTION
Tamar, *Alphabet City Ballet*, 68
Velasquez, *Grandma's Records*, 69

PUERTO RICANS—SOCIAL LIFE AND CUSTOMS—FICTION
Ortiz Cofer, *The Year of Our Revolution: New and Selected Stories and Poems*, 105

PUERTO RICANS—UNITED STATES
Harlan, *Puerto Rico: Deciding Its Future*, 66

PUERTO RICANS—UNITED STATES—FICTION
Atkins, *Get Set! Swim!*, 81

PUERTO RICO
Davis, *Puerto Rico*, 125
Feeney, *Puerto Rico: Facts and Symbols*, 140
Fernandez, *Puerto Rico Past and Present: An Encyclopedia*, 66
Foley, *Puerto Rico*, 66, 131
Foster, *A Visit to Puerto Rico*, 142
Harlan, *Puerto Rico: Deciding Its Future*, 66
Johnston, *Puerto Rico*, 134
Landau, *Puerto Rico*, 141
Márquez, *Destination San Juan*, 139
Milivojevic, *Puerto Rico*, 133, 141
Puerto Rico, 132
Puerto Rico in Pictures, 142
Ross, *Children of Puerto Rico*, 144
Santiago, *Almost a Woman*, 68

PUERTO RICO—BIOGRAPHY
Fernandez, *Puerto Rico Past and Present: An Encyclopedia*, 66

PUERTO RICO—ENCYCLOPEDIAS
Fernandez, *Puerto Rico Past and Present: An Encyclopedia*, 66

PUERTO RICO—FICTION
Jaffe, *The Golden Flower: A Taino Myth from Puerto Rico*, 67
London, *Hurricane!*, 67
Mohr, *Old Letivia and the Mountain of Sorrows*, 67
Montes, *Juan Bobo Goes to Work: A Puerto Rican Folktale*, 68
Tamar, *Alphabet City Ballet*, 68
Velasquez, *Grandma's Records*, 69

PUERTO RICO—HISTORY
Harlan, *Puerto Rico: Deciding Its Future*, 66

PUERTO RICO—HISTORY—CHRONOLOGY
Fernandez, *Puerto Rico Past and Present: An Encyclopedia*, 66

PUERTO RICO—SOCIAL LIFE AND CUSTOMS
Foley, *Puerto Rico*, 66

PUERTO RICO—SOCIAL LIFE AND CUSTOMS—FICTION
London, *Hurricane!*, 67

PUMPKINS—FICTION
Yacowitz, *Pumpkin Fiesta*, 58

QUESTIONS AND ANSWERS
Ochoa, *The New York Public Library Amazing Hispanic American History: A Book of Answers for Kids*, 104

QUETZALCOATL (AZTEC DIETY)
Patent, *Quetzal: Sacred Bird of the Cloud Forest*, 4, 52

QUINCEAÑERA (SOCIAL CUSTOMS)
King, *Quinceañera: Celebrating Fifteen*, 96
Salcedo, *Quinceañera!: The Essential Guide to Planning the Perfect Sweet Fifteen Celebration*, 109

RALEIGH, SIR WALTER, 1554-1618—BIOGRAPHY
Aronson, *Sir Walter Ralegh and the Quest for El Dorado*, 62, 72

RANCH LIFE
Sandler, *Vaqueros: America's First Cowmen*, 110

RANCH LIFE—FICTION
Hayes, *Juan Verdades: The Man Who Couldn't Tell a Lie*, 91
Tripp, *Again, Josefina!*, 117
Tripp, *Changes for Josefina: A Winter Story*, 117
Tripp, *Happy Birthday, Josefina!*, 117
Tripp, *Josefina Learns a Lesson: A School Story*, 117
Tripp, *Josefina Saves the Day: A Summer Story*, 117
Tripp, *Josefina's Surprise: A Christmas Story*, 117
Tripp, *Meet Josefina: An American Girl*, 117

RANCH LIFE—PICTORIAL WORKS
Aira, *Argentina: The Great Estancias*, 1

REFERENCE BOOKS
  Castro, *Dictionary of Chicano Folklore*, 82
  *Encyclopedia of Contemporary Latin American and Caribbean
    Cultures*, 27
  Encyclopedia of Latin American and Caribbean Art, 27
  Encyclopedia of Latin American History and Culture, 27
  Encyclopedia of Latin American Literature, 28
  Encyclopedia of Mexico: History, Society & Culture, 44
  Fernandez, *Puerto Rico Past and Present: An Encyclopedia*, 66
  Henderson, *A Reference Guide to Latin American History*, 29
  Hill, *Ten Hispanic American Authors*, 93
  Kanellos, *Hispanic Firsts: 500 Years of Extraordinary Achievement*,
    95
  Latino Encyclopedia, The, 31
  Marley, *Wars of the Americas: A Chronology of Armed Conflict in
    the New World, 1492 to the Present*, 31
  *Oxford Encyclopedia of Mesoamerican Cultures: The Civilizations
    of Mexico and Central America, The*, 33
  *United States and Mexico at War. Nineteenth-Century Expansionism
    and Conflict, The*, 56, 118
  Vázquez-Gómez, *Dictionary of Mexican Rulers, 1325-1997*, 57

RELIGIOUS FICTION
  Ada, *Jordi's Star*, 71
  Carlson, *Hurray for Three Kings' Day!*, 82
  de Paola, *The Night of Las Posadas*, 85
  Serrano, *Our Lady of Guadalupe*, 54
  Slate, *The Secret Stars*, 111

RIO GRANDE VALLEY (TX)—FICTION
  Rice, *Crazy Loco*, 107

RIO GRANDE VALLEY (TX)—PICTORIAL WORKS
  Lourie, *Rio Grande: From the Rocky Mountains to the Gulf of
    Mexico*, 98

RIVERA, DIEGO, 1886-1957
  Goldstein, *The Journey of Diego Rivera*, 46

ROADRUNNERS—FICTION
  Anaya, *Roadrunner's Dance*, 80

232 Subject Index

SALSA (MUSIC)
Stewart, *Musica!: Salsa, Rumba, Merengue and More*, 115

SAN BLAS ISLANDS (PANAMA)
Presilla, *Mola: Cuna Life Stories and Art*, 61

SAN FRANCISCO (CA)—PICTORIAL WORKS
Ancona, *Barrio: José's Neighborhood*, 80

SAN FRANCISCO (CA)—POETRY
Alarcón, *Iguanas in the Snow and Other Winter Poems/Iguanas en la nieve y otros poemas de invierno*, 77

SANTA FE (NM)—FICTION
de Paola, *The Night of Las Posadas*, 85

SCHOOLS—FICTION
Elya, *Home at Last*, 86
Herrera, *CrashBoomLove*, 92
Jiménez, *Breaking Through*, 94
Mora, *The Rainbow Tulip*, 101
Rodríguez, *América Is Her Name*, 107
Skármeta, *The Composition*, 34
Soto, *Off and Running*, 113
Tamar, *Alphabet City Ballet*, 68
Tripp, *Josefina Learns a Lesson: A School Story*, 117
Velásquez, *Rina's Family Secret*, 118
Wing, *Jalapeño Bagels*, 120

SELF-ESTEEM—FICTION
Atkins, *Get Set! Swim!*, 81
Climo, *The Little Red Ant and the Great Big Crumb: A Mexican Fable*, 41

SHEPHERDS—FICTION
Ada, *Jordi's Star*, 71

SHOES—FICTION
Soto, *If the Shoe Fits*, 112

SHORT STORIES
    González, *Señor Cat's Romance and Other Favorite Stories from Latin America*, 29
    Herrera, *CrashBoomLove*, 92
    Jiménez, *The Circuit: Stories from the Life of a Migrant Child*, 94
    Ortiz Cofer, *The Year of Our Revolution: New and Selected Stories and Poems*, 105
    Oxford Book of Latin American Short Stories, The, 32
    Rice, *Crazy Loco*, 107
    Soto, *Petty Crimes*, 114

SIBLINGS—FICTION
    Ada, *The Three Golden Oranges*, 71
    Alvarez, *¡Yo!*, 78
    Berrocal Essex, *Delia's Way*, 59
    Bunting, *Going Home*, 39
    Carlson, *Hurray for Three Kings' Day!*, 82
    Eboch, *The Well of Sacrifice*, 42
    García, *The Agüero Sisters*, 10
    Joseph, *The Color of My Words*, 17
    Mora, *Uno, dos, tres, One, Two, Three*, 51
    Pérez, *Geographies of Home*, 105
    San Souci, *Little Gold Star: A Spanish American Cinderella Tale*, 109
    Tamar, *Alphabet City Ballet*, 68
    Tripp, *Changes for Josefina: A Winter Story*, 117
    Tripp, *Happy Birthday, Josefina!*, 117
    Tripp, *Josefina Learns a Lesson: A School Story*, 117
    Tripp, *Josefina Saves the Day: A Summer Story*, 117
    Tripp, *Josefina's Surprise: A Christmas Story*, 117
    Tripp, *Meet Josefina: An American Girl*, 117
    Zamorano, *Let's Eat*, 76

SICK—FICTION
    Willard, *The Tortilla Cat*, 120

SINGING GAMES
    Orozco, *Diez deditos/Ten Little Fingers and Other Play Rhymes and Action Songs from Latin America*, 32

SINGLE-PARENT FAMILIES—FICTION
    Willard, *The Tortilla Cat*, 120

SNAKES—FICTION
Anaya, *Roadrunner's Dance*, 80

SNAKES—FOLKLORE
Gollub, *Uncle Snake*, 46

SNOW—FICTION
Alarcón, *Iguanas in the Snow and Other Winter Poems/Iguanas en
la nieve y otros poemas de invierno*, 77
Figueredo, *When This World Was New*, 88

SOCCER—FICTION
Marzollo, *Soccer Cousins*, 50
McGinley, *Joaquin Strikes Back*, 101

SOCIAL CLASSES
Benítez, *Bitter Grounds*, 21

SOCIAL CLASSES—FICTION
Bridal, *The Tree of Red Stars*, 122

SOCIAL PROBLEMS—FICTION
Quiñonez, *Bodega Dreams*, 106

SONGBOOKS
Orozco, *Diez deditos/Ten Little Fingers and Other Play Rhymes and
Action Songs from Latin America*, 32

SOSA, SAMMY, 1968-
Preller, *McGwire & Sosa: A Season to Remember*, 17

SOSA, SAMMY, 1968- —BIOGRAPHY
Christopher, *At the Plate with . . . Sammy Sosa*, 17
Savage, *Sammy Sosa: Home Run Hero*, 18

SOUTH AMERICA
(*See also individual countries*)
Arnold, *South American Animals*, 70
Bramwell, *Central and South America*, 144
Eagen, *The Aymara of South America*, 132
Fowler, *South America*, 140
Hinds, *The Incas*, 129

Kallen, *Life in the Amazon Rain Forest*, 142

Malpass, *Daily Life in the Inca Empire*, 130

Martin, *Monkeys of Central and South America*, 141

Nishi, *The Inca Empire*, 143

O'Mara, *Rain Forests*, 139

Peterson, *South America*, 141

Rees, *The Incas*, 141

Sammis, *South America*, 138

Sayer, *The Incas*, 126

Tahan, *The Yanomami of South America*, 132

Thomson, *The Rainforest Indians*, 132

Worth, *Pizarro and the Conquest of the Incan Empire*, 136

SOUTH AMERICA—DESCRIPTION

Symmes, *Chasing Che: A Motorcycle Journey in Search of the Guevara Legend*, 3

SOUTH AMERICA—FICTION

Torres, *Liliana's Grandmothers*, 116

Uribe, *Buzz, Buzz, Buzz*, 70

SOUTHWESTERN STATES

Welcome to Josefina's World, 1824: Growing Up on America's Southwest Frontier, 119

SOUTHWESTERN STATES—FICTION

Cordova, *Abuelita's Heart*, 84

Slate, *The Secret Stars*, 111

Talbert, *Star of Luís*, 115

Tripp, *Again, Josefina!*, 117

Tripp, *Changes for Josefina: A Winter Story*, 117

Tripp, *Happy Birthday, Josefina!*, 117

Tripp, *Josefina Learns a Lesson: A School Story*, 117

Tripp, *Josefina Saves the Day: A Summer Story*, 117

Tripp, *Josefina's Surprise: A Christmas Story*, 117

Tripp, *Meet Josefina: An American Girl*, 117

SOUTHWESTERN STATES—HISTORY

Marrin, *Empires Lost and Won: The Spanish Heritage in the Southwest*, 100

Welcome to Josefina's World, 1824: Growing Up on America's Southwest Frontier, 119

SOUTHWESTERN STATES—HISTORY—FICTION
　　Tripp, *Changes for Josefina: A Winter Story*, 117
　　Tripp, *Happy Birthday, Josefina!*, 117
　　Tripp, *Josefina Learns a Lesson: A School Story*, 117
　　Tripp, *Josefina Saves the Day: A Summer Story*, 117
　　Tripp, *Josefina's Surprise: A Christmas Story*, 117
　　Tripp, *Meet Josefina: An American Girl*, 117

SOUTHWESTERN STATES—POETRY
　　Mora, *Confetti: Poems for Children*, 101
　　Mora, *This Big Sky*, 102

SOUTHWESTERN STATES—SOCIAL LIFE AND CUSTOMS
　　Hoyt-Goldsmith, *Las Posadas: An Hispanic Christmas Celebration*,
　　　　93
　　*Welcome to Josefina's World, 1824: Growing Up on America's
　　　　Southwest Frontier*, 119

SPAIN
　　Aronson, *Sir Walter Ralegh and the Quest for El Dorado*, 62, 72
　　Berendes, *Spain*, 131
　　Chicoine, *Spain: Bridge between Continents*, 131
　　Collins, *The Spanish-American War*, 128
　　Deady, *Spain*, 128
　　Grabowski, *Spain*, 138
　　Grinsted, *Spain*, 128
　　Kent, *Madrid*, 127
　　Kohen, *Spain*, 129
　　Lace, *Defeat of the Spanish Armada*, 72
　　Lior and Steele, *Spain: The Culture*, 73
　　Lior and Steele, *Spain: The Land*, 73
　　Lior and Steele, *Spain: The People*, 73
　　Mann, *Isabel, Ferdinand and Fifteenth-Century Spain*, 140
　　McKay, *Spain*, 131
　　McNeese, *Remember the Main: The Spanish-American War Begins*,
　　　　132
　　Meadows, *Pablo Picasso*, 74
　　Mesenas, *Welcome to Spain*, 143
　　Millar, *Spain in the Age of Exploration*, 74, 129
　　Patent, *Treasures of the Spanish Main*, 133
　　Pierson, *The History of Spain*, 134
　　Rogers, *Spain*, 130

Somerlott, *The Spanish-American War: "Remember the Maine!,"*
    125
Spain, 132
Stalcup, *The Inquisition*, 141
Stewart, *Life during the Spanish Inquisition*, 75, 143

SPAIN—BIOGRAPHY
    Fradin, *Maria de Sautuola: The Bulls in the Cave*, 72
    Marrin, *Terror of the Spanish Main: Sir Henry Morgan and His
        Buccaneers*, 73
    Schiaffino, *Goya*, 74
    Venezia, *El Greco*, 75

SPAIN—CHURCH HISTORY
    Stewart, *Life during the Spanish Inquisition*, 75

SPAIN—CIVILIZATION
    Lior and Steele, *Spain: The Culture*, 73

SPAIN—DESCRIPTION
    Lior and Steele, *Spain: The Land*, 73

SPAIN—FICTION
    Ada, *Jordi's Star*, 71
    Ada, *The Three Golden Oranges*, 71
    Laden, *When Pigasso Met Mootisse*, 73
    Sierra, *The Beautiful Butterfly: A Folktale from Spain*, 75
    Zamorano, *Let's Eat*, 76

SPAIN—HISTORY
    Millar, *Spain in the Age of Exploration*, 74
    Stewart, *Life during the Spanish Inquisition*, 75

SPAIN—NAVAL HISTORY
    Lace, *Defeat of the Spanish Armada*, 72

SPAIN—SOCIAL LIFE AND CUSTOMS
    Lior and Steele, *Spain: The Culture*, 73
    Lior and Steele, *Spain: The People*, 73
    Millar, *Spain in the Age of Exploration*, 74

SPAIN—SOCIAL LIFE AND CUSTOMS—FICTION
Zamorano, *Let's Eat*, 76

SPAIN—TERRITORIES AND POSSESSIONS
Burr, *When the Viceroy Came*, 40
Marrin, *Terror of the Spanish Main: Sir Henry Morgan and His Buccaneers*, 73
Millar, *Spain in the Age of Exploration*, 74

SPANISH ARMADA, 1588
Lace, *Defeat of the Spanish Armada*, 72

SPANISH LANGUAGE—ALPHABET
Chin-Lee and Peña, *A Is for the Americas*, 25
Vargo, *Señor Felipe's Alphabet Adventure: El alfabeto español*, 35

SPANISH LANGUAGE—FOREIGN WORDS AND PHRASES
Elya, *Eight Animals on the Town*, 43

SPORTS
Christopher, *At the Plate with . . . Sammy Sosa*, 17
Cooper and Gordon, *Anthony Reynoso: Born to Rope*, 84
Horenstein, *Baseball in the Barrios*, 123
Savage, *Sammy Sosa: Home Run Hero*, 18

SPORTS—FICTION
Atkins, *Get Set! Swim!*, 81
Marzollo, *Soccer Cousins*, 50
McGinley, *Joaquin Strikes Back*, 101
Murray, *What It Takes to Get to Vegas*, 103

SPORTS RECORDS
Christopher, *At the Plate with . . . Sammy Sosa*, 17
Preller, *McGwire & Sosa: A Season to Remember*, 17
Savage, *Sammy Sosa: Home Run Hero*, 18

STARS—FICTION
Ada, *Jordi's Star*, 71
Slate, *The Secret Stars*, 111

STORIES IN RHYME
Ehlert, *Market Day: A Story Told with Folk Art*, 26

Elya, *Eight Animals on the Town*, 43
Heller, *Galápagos Means "Tortoises,"* 19
Mora, *Uno, dos, tres, One, Two, Three*, 51

TAÍNO INDIANS (PR)
Alvarez, *The Secret Footprints*, 16
Jaffe, *The Golden Flower: A Taino Myth from Puerto Rico*, 67

TARANTULAS—FICTION
Reeve, *Lolo & Red-Legs*, 106

TEDDY BEARS—FICTION
Alphin, *A Bear for Miguel*, 21

TEENAGERS
Atkin, *Voices from the Streets: Young Former Gang Members Tell Their Stories*, 81

TEENAGERS—FICTION
Durán, *Don't Spit on My Corner*, 86
Ewing, *Party Girl*, 87
Herrera, *CrashBoomLove*, 92
Jiménez, *Breaking Through*, 94
McGinley, *Joaquin Strikes Back*, 101
Obejas, *Days of Awe*, 104
Olson, *Joyride*, 105
Ortiz Cofer, *The Year of Our Revolution: New and Selected Stories and Poems*, 105
Soto, *Petty Crimes*, 114
Velásquez, *Rina's Family Secret*, 118
Weaver, *Rooster*, 119

TEXAS
Lomas Garza, *In My Family/En mi familia*, 98

TEXAS—FICTION
Lind, *The Alamo: An Epic*, 98
Rice, *Crazy Loco*, 107

TEXAS—HISTORY
Davis, *Three Roads to the Alamo: The Lives and Fortunes of David Crockett, James Bowie, and William Barret Travis*, 85

Garland, *Voices of the Alamo*, 89
Santella, *The Battle of the Alamo*, 111

TEXAS—HISTORY—FICTION
Garland, *A Line in the Sand: The Alamo Diary of Lucinda Lawrence*, 89
Harrigan, *The Gates of the Alamo*, 91
Love, *I Remember the Alamo*, 99

THANKSGIVING DAY—FICTION
Cowley, *Gracias, the Thanksgiving Turkey*, 84

THEATERS—STAGE AND SCENERY
Winther, *Plays from Hispanic Tales: One-Act, Royalty-Free Dramatizations for Young People, from Hispanic Stories and Folktales*, 35

THREE KINGS (SOCIAL CUSTOMS)—FICTION
Carlson, *Hurray for Three Kings' Day!*, 82
Slate, *The Secret Stars*, 111

TORTILLAS—FOLKLORE
Kimmel, *The Runaway Tortilla*, 96

TOY AND MOVABLE BOOKS
Serrano, *Our Lady of Guadalupe*, 54

TRUTH—FOLKLORE
Hayes, *Juan Verdades: The Man Who Couldn't Tell a Lie*, 91

TURKEYS—FICTION
Cowley, *Gracias, the Thanksgiving Turkey*, 84

UNCLES—FICTION
Johnston, *Uncle Rain Cloud*, 95
Soto, *If the Shoe Fits*, 112
Spurr, *Mama's Birthday Surprise*, 115

UNITED FARM WORKERS
Collins, *Farmworker's Friend: The Story of Cesar Chavez*, 83
Ferriss and Sandoval, *The Fight in the Fields: Cesar Chavez and the Farmworkers Movement*, 88

Soto, *Jessie De La Cruz: A Profile of a United Farm Worker*, 112

UNITED STATES
  (*See also* CUBAN AMERICANS, DOMINICAN AMERICANS,
    LATINOS, MEXICAN AMERICANS, PANAMANIAN
    AMERICANS, PUERTO RICANS, SOUTHWESTERN
    STATES *and names of individual states*)
  *Americanos: Latino Life in the United States/La vida latina en los
    Estados Unidos*, 79
  Ancona, *Barrio: José's Neighborhood*, 80
  Ancona, *Harvest*, 38, 80
  Atkin, *Voices from the Streets: Young Former Gang Members Tell
    Their Stories*, 81
  Bankston, *Careers in Community Service*, 136
  Burgan, *The Alamo*, 143
  Castro, *Dictionary of Chicano Folklore*, 82
  Cockcroft, *Latino Visions: Contemporary Chicano, Puerto Rican
    and Cuban American Artists*, 83
  Cozic, *Illegal Immigration*, 85
  Crawford, *Encyclopedia of the Mexican-American War*, 42
  Fernández-Shaw, *The Hispanic Presence in North America: From
    1492 to Today*, 87
  Flanagan, *Buying a Pet from Ms. Chavez*, 138
  Flanagan, *Call Mr. Vasquez, He'll Fix It*, 138
  Flanagan, *Riding the Ferry with Captain Cruz*, 138
  Fraser, *A Mission for the People: The Story of La Purísima*, 88
  Garcia, *Careers in Technology*, 136
  Garland, *Voices of the Alamo*, 89
  Gonzales, *Mexicanos: A History of Mexicans in the United States*,
    90
  Gonzalez, *Harvest of Empire: A History of Latinos in America*, 90
  González-Pando, *The Cuban Americans*, 138
  Green, *The Mission Trails in American History*, 136
  Heinrichs, *California Missions*, 143
  Henkes, *Latin American Women Artists of the United States: The
    Works of 33 Twentieth-Century Women*, 92
  Hill, *Ten Hispanic American Authors*, 93
  Hoyt-Goldsmith, *Las Posadas: An Hispanic Christmas Celebration*,
    93
  Hoyt-Goldsmith, *Migrant Worker: A Boy from the Rio Grande
    Valley*, 94

Kanellos, *Hispanic Firsts: 500 Years of Extraordinary Achievement*, 95

Kenig, *Best Careers for Bilingual Latinos: Market Your Fluency in Spanish to Get Ahead on the Job*, 95

King, *Quinceañera: Celebrating Fifteen*, 96

Lace, *The Alamo*, 143

Las Christmas: Favorite Latino Authors Share Their Holiday Memories, 97

Latino Reader: An American Literary Tradition from 1542 to the Present, The, 97

Lomas Garza, *In My Family/En mi familia*, 98

Lourie, *Rio Grande: From the Rocky Mountains to the Gulf of Mexico*, 98

Marrin, *Empires Lost and Won: The Spanish Heritage in the Southwest*, 100

Menard, *Careers in Sports*, 136

Morey and Dunn, *Famous Hispanic Americans*, 103

Nickles, *The Hispanics*, 103

Ochoa, *The New York Public Library Amazing Hispanic American History: A Book of Answers for Kids*, 104

Perl, *North across the Border: The Story of Mexican Americans*, 133

Ramirez, *A Patriot after All: The Story of a Chicano Vietnam Vet*, 106

Rosales, *Chicano!: The History of the Mexican American Civil Rights Movement*, 108

Salcedo, *Quinceañera!: The Essential Guide to Planning the Perfect Sweet Fifteen Celebration*, 109

Sandler, *Vaqueros: America's First Cowmen*, 110

Santella, *The Battle of the Alamo*, 111, 128

Sorrels, *The Alamo in American History*, 136

Stein, *In the Spanish West*, 135

Stewart, *Musica!: Salsa, Rumba, Merengue and More*, 115

Torres, *Careers in the Music Industry*, 136

Torres-Saillant and Hernández, *The Dominican Americans*, 138

United States and Mexico at War. Nineteenth-Century Expansionism and Conflict, The, 56, 118

Wade, *Careers in Law and Politics*, 137

Welcome to Josefina's World, 1824: Growing Up on America's Southwest Frontier, 119

Wilson, *Careers in Entertainment*, 137

Wilson, *Careers in Publishing and Communications*, 137

Winter, *¡Béisbol! Latino Baseball Pioneers and Legends*, 121
Young, *A Personal Tour of La Purísima*, 135
Zannos, *Careers in Education*, 137
Zannos, *Careers in Science and Medicine*, 137
Zannos, *Latino Entrepreneurs*, 137

UNITED STATES—BIOGRAPHY
Alvarez, *Something to Declare*, 78
Baca, *A Place to Stand: The Making of a Poet,* 81
Collins, *Farmworker's Friend: The Story of Cesar Chavez*, 83
Cooper and Gordon, *Anthony Reynoso: Born to Rope*, 84
Crawford, *Encyclopedia of the Mexican-American War*, 85
Davis, *Three Roads to the Alamo: The Lives and Fortunes of David Crockett, James Bowie, and William Barret Travis*, 85
Ferriss and Sandoval, *The Fight in the Fields: Cesar Chavez and the Farmworkers Movement*, 88
Sanchez, *My Bloody Life: The Making of a Latin King*, 110
Soto, *Jessie De La Cruz: A Profile of a United Farm Worker*, 112
Winick, *Pedro and Me: Friendship, Loss, and What I Learned*, 121

UNITED STATES—BOUNDARIES
Lourie, *Rio Grande: From the Rocky Mountains to the Gulf of Mexico*, 98
Urrea, *By the Lake of Sleeping Children: The Secret Life of the Mexican Border*, 56

UNITED STATES—CIVILIZATION—FOREIGN INFLUENCES
Fernández-Shaw, *The Hispanic Presence in North America: From 1492 to Today*, 87
Gonzales, *Mexicanos: A History of Mexicans in the United States*, 90
Marrin, *Empires Lost and Won: The Spanish Heritage in the Southwest*, 100
Nickles, *The Hispanics*, 103
Rosales, *Chicano!: The History of the Mexican American Civil Rights Movement*, 108

UNITED STATES—DESCRIPTION
Lourie, *Rio Grande: From the Rocky Mountains to the Gulf of Mexico*, 98

UNITED STATES—FICTION

Alarcón, *Angels Ride Bikes and Other Fall Poems/Los ángeles andan en bicicleta y otros poemas de otoño*, 77

Alarcón, *Iguanas in the Snow and Other Winter Poems/Iguanas en la nieve y otros poemas de invierno*, 77

Alarcón, *Laughing Tomatoes and Other Spring Poems/Jitomates risueños y otros poemas de primavera*, 77

Alvarez, *How Tía Lola Came to (Visit) Stay*, 78

Alvarez, *¡Yo!*, 78

Anaya, *Elegy on the Death of César Chávez*, 79

Anaya, *Roadrunner's Dance*, 80

Atkins, *Get Set! Swim!*, 81

Calhoun, *Tonio's Cat*, 82

Carlson, *Hurray for Three Kings' Day!*, 82

Cordova, *Abuelita's Heart*, 84

Cowley, *Gracias, the Thanksgiving Turkey*, 84

de Paola, *The Night of Las Posadas*, 85

Durán, *Don't Spit on My Corner*, 86

Elya, *Home at Last*, 86

English, *Speak English for Us, Marisol!*, 86

Espada, *A Mayan Astronomer in Hell's Kitchen*, 87

Ewing, *Party Girl*, 87

Figueredo, *When This World Was New*, 88

Garland, *A Line in the Sand: The Alamo Diary of Lucinda Lawrence*, 89

Harrigan, *The Gates of the Alamo*, 91

Hayes, *Juan Verdades: The Man Who Couldn't Tell a Lie*, 91

Herrera, *CrashBoomLove*, 92

Herrera, *Grandma and Me at the Flea/Los meros meros remateros*, 93

Jiménez, *Breaking Through*, 94

Jiménez, *The Circuit: Stories from the Life of a Migrant Child*, 94

Johnston, *Uncle Rain Cloud*, 95

Kimmel, *The Runaway Tortilla*, 96

Kleven, *Hooray, a Piñata!*, 97

Lind, *The Alamo: An Epic*, 98

Love, *I Remember the Alamo*, 99

Love to Mamá: A Tribute to Mothers, 99

Lowell, *Los tres pequeños jabalíes/The Three Little Javelinas*, 100

Martinez, *Parrot in the Oven: Mi Vida*, 100

McGinley, *Joaquin Strikes Back*, 101

Mora, *Confetti: Poems for Children*, 101

Mora, *The Rainbow Tulip*, 101
Mora, *This Big Sky*, 102
Mora, *Tomás and the Library Lady*, 102
Murray, *What It Takes to Get to Vegas*, 103
Noche Buena: Hispanic American Christmas Stories, 104
Obejas, *Days of Awe*, 104
Olson, *Joyride*, 105
Ortiz Cofer, *The Year of Our Revolution: New and Selected Stories and Poems*, 105
Pérez, *Geographies of Home*, 105
Quiñonez, *Bodega Dreams*, 106
Ramos, *Blues for the Buffalo*, 106
Reeve, *Lolo & Red-Legs*, 106
Rice, *Crazy Loco*, 107
Rodríguez, *América Is Her Name*, 107
Ryan, *Esperanza Rising*, 108
Ryan, *Mice and Beans*, 109
San Souci, *Little Gold Star: A Spanish American Cinderella Tale*, 109
Slate, *The Secret Stars*, 111
Soto, *Buried Onions*, 111
Soto, *Chato and the Party Animals*, 112
Soto, *If the Shoe Fits*, 112
Soto, *Nerdlandia: A Play*, 113
Soto, *Novio Boy: A Play*, 113
Soto, *Off and Running*, 113
Soto, *The Old Man and His Door*, 114
Soto, *Petty Crimes*, 114
Soto, *Snapshots from the Wedding*, 114
Spurr, *Mama's Birthday Surprise*, 115
Talbert, *Star of Luís*, 115
Torres, *Liliana's Grandmothers*, 116
Touching the Fire: Fifteen Poets of Today's Latino Renaissance, 116
Tripp, *Again, Josefina!*, 117
Tripp, *Changes for Josefina: A Winter Story*, 117
Tripp, *Happy Birthday, Josefina!*, 117
Tripp, *Josefina Learns a Lesson: A School Story*, 117
Tripp, *Josefina Saves the Day: A Summer Story*, 117
Tripp, *Josefina's Surprise: A Christmas Story*, 117
Tripp, *Meet Josefina: An American Girl*, 117
Vargo, *Señor Felipe's Alphabet Adventure: El alfabeto español*, 35

Velásquez, *Rina's Family Secret*, 118
Weaver, *Rooster*, 119
Welter, *I Want to Buy a Vowel: A Novel of Illegal Alienation*, 120
Willard, *The Tortilla Cat*, 120
Wing, *Jalapeño Bagels*, 120

UNITED STATES—FOREIGN RELATIONS—CARIBBEAN
Dent, *The Legacy of the Monroe Doctrine: A Reference Guide to
U.S. Involvement in Latin America and the Caribbean*, 26

UNITED STATES—FOREIGN RELATIONS—CUBA
Hoff and Regler, *Uneasy Neighbors: Cuba and the United States*, 11

UNITED STATES—FOREIGN RELATIONS—LATIN AMERICA
Dent, *The Legacy of the Monroe Doctrine: A Reference Guide to
U.S. Involvement in Latin America and the Caribbean*, 26

UNITED STATES—FOREIGN RELATIONS—MEXICO
Cozic, *Illegal Immigration*, 85
Oppenheimer, *Bordering on Chaos: Guerrillas, Stockbrokers,
Politicians and Mexico's Road to Prosperity*, 51
Pascoe, *Mexico and the United States: Cooperation and Conflict*, 52
*United States and Mexico at War. Nineteenth-Century Expansionism
and Conflict, The*, 56, 118
Urrea, *By the Lake of Sleeping Children: The Secret Life of the
Mexican Border*, 56

UNITED STATES—FOREIGN RELATIONS—PANAMA
Gold, *The Panama Canal Transfer: Controversy at the Crossroads*,
60
Lindop, *Panama and the United States: Divided by the Canal*, 60
Markun, *It's Panama's Canal!*, 60

UNITED STATES—FOREIGN RELATIONS—PUERTO RICO
Harlan, *Puerto Rico: Deciding Its Future*, 66

UNITED STATES—TERRITORIAL EXPANSION
*United States and Mexico at War. Nineteenth-Century Expansionism
and Conflict, The*, 56, 118

URUGUAY
Jermyn, *Uruguay*, 129

Uruguay in Pictures, 142

URUGUAY—HISTORY—FICTION
Bridal, *The Tree of Red Stars*, 122

URUGUAY—SOCIAL LIFE AND CUSTOMS—FICTION
Bridal, *The Tree of Red Stars*, 122

VEGETABLES—HISTORY
Johnson, *Tomatoes, Potatoes, Corn, and Beans: How the Foods of the Americas Changed Eating around the World*, 30

VENEZUELA
Heinrichs, *Venezuela*, 141
Horenstein, *Baseball in the Barrios*, 123
Jones, *Venezuela*, 133, 141
Rawlins, *The Orinoco River*, 123
Venezuela in Pictures, 142

VENEZUELA—BIOGRAPHY
St. Aubin de Terán, *The Hacienda*, 123

VENEZUELA—SOCIAL LIFE AND CUSTOMS
Horenstein, *Baseball in the Barrios*, 123
St. Aubin de Terán, *The Hacienda*, 123

VIETNAM WAR, 1961-1975
Ramirez, *A Patriot after All: The Story of a Chicano Vietnam Vet*, 106

VIOLENCE
Sanchez, *My Bloody Life: The Making of a Latin King*, 110

VIOLENCE—FICTION
Ewing, *Party Girl*, 87
Pérez, *Geographies of Home*, 105
Soto, *Buried Onions*, 111
Velásquez, *Rina's Family Secret*, 118

VOCATIONAL GUIDANCE
Kenig, *Best Careers for Bilingual Latinos: Market Your Fluency in Spanish to Get Ahead on the Job*, 95

WATERWAYS
   Lourie, *Rio Grande: From the Rocky Mountains to the Gulf of
      Mexico*, 98
   Rawlins, *The Orinoco River*, 6, 123

WEDDINGS—FICTION
   Soto, *Snapshots from the Wedding*, 114

WOMEN—EL SALVADOR
   Benítez, *Bitter Grounds*, 21
   Gorkin, *From Grandmother to Granddaughter: Salvadoran
      Women's Stories*, 22

WOMEN—PANAMA
   Presilla, *Mola: Cuna Life Stories and Art*, 61

WOMEN—POLITICAL ACTIVITY
   Brill, *Journey for Peace: The Story of Rigoberta Menchú*, 23
   Dujovne Ortiz, *Eva Perón*, 1

WOMEN ARTISTS
   Henkes, *Latin American Women Artists of the United States: The
      Works of 33 Twentieth-Century Women*, 92

WOMEN IN LITERATURE
   Gerson, *Fiesta Femenina: Celebrating Women in Mexican Folktale*,
      45

ZOOLOGY
   Arnold, *South American Animals*, 70
   Tagliaferro, *Galápagos Islands: Nature's Delicate Balance at Risk*,
      20

Suggested Grade Level Index

As I stated in the introduction, it is very difficult to assign a grade level to any book. And even though I have done so for the convenience of some teachers or students, please use the grade level only as a tentative guideline.

For the Young
GRADES PRESCHOOL-1
  Yacowitz, *Pumpkin Fiesta*, 58

GRADES PRESCHOOL-2
  Cowley, *Gracias, the Thanksgiving Turkey*, 84
  Ehlert, *Cuckoo/Cucú*, 43
  Ehlert, *Market Day: A Story Told with Folk Art*, 26
  Kleven, *Hooray, a Piñata!*, 97
  Mora, *Uno, dos, tres, One, Two, Three*, 51
  Ryan, *Mice and Beans*, 109
  Soto, *The Old Man and His Door*, 114
  Torres, *Liliana's Grandmothers*, 34, 116
  Uribe, *Buzz, Buzz, Buzz*, 70
  Wing, *Jalapeño Bagels*, 120
  Zamorano, *Let's Eat*, 76

GRADES PRESCHOOL-3
  Anaya, *Roadrunner's Dance*, 80
  Carlson, *Hurray for Three Kings' Day!*, 82
  English, *Speak English for Us, Marisol!*, 86
  Johnston, *Uncle Rain Cloud*, 95
  Montes, *Juan Bobo Goes to Work: A Puerto Rican Folktale*, 68
  Orozco, *Diez deditos/Ten Little Fingers and Other Play Rhymes and Action Songs from Latin America*, 32
  Winter, *Josefina*, 5

GRADES K-2

Flanagan, *Buying a Pet from Ms. Chavez*, 138
Flanagan, *Call Mr. Vasquez, He'll Fix It*, 138
Flanagan, *Riding the Ferry with Captain Cruz*, 138
Kimmel, *The Runaway Tortilla*, 96
Laden, *When Pigasso Met Mootisse*, 73
Slate, *The Secret Stars*, 111
Swope, *Gotta Go! Gotta Go!*, 55
Vargo, *Señor Felipe's Alphabet Adventure: El alfabeto español*, 35

GRADES K-3

Ada, *Jordi's Star*, 71
Alarcón, *Laughing Tomatoes and Other Spring Poems/Jitomates risueños y otros poemas de primavera*, 77
Ancona, *Fiesta Fireworks*, 38
Bunting, *Going Home*, 39
Climo, *The Little Red Ant and the Great Big Crumb: A Mexican Fable*, 41
Cordova, *Abuelita's Heart*, 84
Figueredo, *When This World Was New*, 88
Gage, *Pascual's Magic Pictures*, 24
Geeslin, *How Nanita Learned to Make Flan*, 45
Jaffe, *The Golden Flower: A Taino Myth from Puerto Rico*, 67
Johnston, *The Magic Maguey*, 47
Joose, *Ghost Wings*, 47
Leiner, *Mama Does the Mambo*, 13
London, *Hurricane!*, 67
Mora, *The Rainbow Tulip*, 101
Pomerantz, *Mangaboom*, 33
Sierra, *The Beautiful Butterfly: A Folktale from Spain*, 75
Soto, *Chato and the Party Animals*, 112
Soto, *If the Shoe Fits*, 112
Soto, *Snapshots from the Wedding*, 114
Strauss, *When Woman Became the Sea: A Costa Rican Creation Myth*, 7
Velasquez, *Grandma's Records*, 69

GRADES K-4

Alarcón, *From the Bellybutton of the Moon and Other Summer Poems/Del ombligo de la luna y otros poemas de verano*, 37
Cowan, *My Life with the Wave*, 41
de Paola, *The Night of Las Posadas*, 85

Kroll, *Butterfly Boy*, 49
McDermott, *Musicians of the Sun*, 50

GRADES 1-3
Alarcón, *Angels Ride Bikes and Other Fall Poems/Los ángeles andan en bicicleta y otros poemas de otoño*, 77
Alarcón, *Iguanas in the Snow and Other Winter Poems/Iguanas en la nieve y otros poemas de invierno*, 77
Atkins, *Get Set! Swim!*, 81
Berendes, *Mexico*, 39
Elya, *Eight Animals on the Town*, 43
Fowler, *South America*, 140
González, *Señor Cat's Romance and Other Favorite Stories from Latin America*, 29
Marx, *Mexico*, 140
Mohr, *Old Letivia and the Mountain of Sorrows*, 67
Mora, *Confetti: Poems for Children*, 101

GRADES 1-4
Alphin, *A Bear for Miguel*, 21
Alvarez, *The Secret Footprints*, 16
Gnojewski, *Cinco de Mayo: Celebrating Hispanic Pride*, 132
Pitcher, *Mariana and the Merchild: A Folk Tale from Chile*, 5

GRADES 2-3
Amado, *Barrilete: A Kite for the Day of the Dead*, 23

GRADES 2-4
Ada, *Gathering the Sun: An Alphabet in Spanish and English*, 25
Ada, *The Three Golden Oranges*, 71
Alcraft, *A Visit to Mexico*, 142
Arnold, *South American Animals*, 70
Burr, *When the Viceroy Came*, 40
Calhoun, *Tonio's Cat*, 82
Chapman, *The Aztecs*, 129
Cooper and Gordon, *Anthony Reynoso: Born to Rope*, 84
Dahl, *Guatemala*, 128
Dahl, *Mexico*, 128
Davis, *Cesar Chavez: A Photo-Illustrated Biography*, 139
Deady, *Spain*, 128
Deedrick, *Maya*, 126
Dell'Oro, *Argentina*, 141

Dubois, *Argentina*, 128
Dubois, *Dominican Republic*, 128
Elya, *Home at Last*, 86
Feeney, *Puerto Rico: Facts and Symbols*, 140
Fine, *Under the Lemon Moon*, 44
Foster, *A Visit to Puerto Rico*, 142
Fox, *A Visit to Colombia*, 142
Fox, *A Visit to Costa Rica*, 142
Garret and Frank, *Welcome to Costa Rica*, 143
Gerson, *People of Corn: A Mayan Story*, 24, 45
Gillis, *A Visit to Cuba*, 142
Harvey, *Look What Came from Mexico*, 138
Jermyn and Conboy, *Welcome to Mexico*, 143
Jones, *Venezuela*, 141
Kline, *Christopher Columbus*, 130
Kline, *Francisco Coronado*, 130
Kline, *Francisco Pizarro*, 130
Kline, *Francisco Vázquez de Coronado*, 130
Kline, *Hernán Cortés*, 130
Kline, *Ponce de León*, 130
Lim, *Welcome to Colombia*, 143
Lowell, *Los tres pequeños jabalíes/The Three Little Javelinas*, 100
Mara, *Cuba*, 128
Marzollo, *Soccer Cousins*, 50
Mesenas, *Welcome to Spain*, 143
Mesenas and Frank, *Welcome to Argentina*, 143
Milivojevic, *Puerto Rico*, 141
Mora, *Tomás and the Library Lady*, 102
O'Mara, *Rain Forests*, 139
Riehecky, *Nicaragua*, 128
Rodríguez, *América Is Her Name*, 107
Romero, *Ellen Ochoa: The First Hispanic Woman Astronaut*, 133
Romero, *Henry Cisneros: A Man of the People*, 133
Romero, *Jaime Escalante: Inspiring Educator*, 133
Romero, *Joan Baez: Folksinger for Peace*, 133
Romero, *Roberto Clemente: Baseball Hall of Famer*, 133
Romero, *Selena Perez: Queen of Tejano Music*, 133
San Souci, *Little Gold Star: A Spanish American Cinderella Tale*, 109
Streissguth, *Mexico*, 141
Thoennes, *Peru*, 128
Urrutia and Orozco, *Cinco de Mayo: Yesterday and Today*, 56

West, *Costa Rica*, 141
Yip and Cramer, *Welcome to Cuba*, 143
Yip and Heisey, *Welcome to Peru*, 143

GRADES 2-5
Anaya, *Maya's Children: The Story of La Llorona*, 37
Appelbaum, *Cocoa Ice*, 16
Berendes, *Mexico*, 131
Berendes, *Spain*, 131
Hayes, *Juan Verdades: The Man Who Couldn't Tell a Lie*, 91
Herrera, *Grandma and Me at the Flea/Los meros meros remateros*, 93
Hewitt, *The Aztecs*, 132
Love to Mamá: A Tribute to Mothers, 99
Thomson, *The Rainforest Indians*, 132

GRADES 3-4
Spurr, *Mama's Birthday Surprise*, 115

For the Middle Grades
GRADES 3-5
Ancona, *Cuban Kids*, 9
Ancona, *The Fiestas*, 142
Ancona, *The Folk Arts*, 142
Ancona, *The Foods*, 142
Ancona, *The Past*, 142
Ancona, *The People*, 142
Beirne, *Children of Ecuadorean Highlands*, 144
Berg, *Mexico*, 131
Bolivia, 132
Brill, *Journey for Peace: The Story of Rigoberta Menchú*, 23
Burgan, *Argentina*, 141
Chambers, *All Saints, All Souls, and Halloween*, 144
Chambers, *Carnival*, 144
Chile, 132
Chin-Lee and Peña, *A Is for the Americas*, 25
Coburn, *Domitila: A Cinderella Tale from the Mexican Tradition*, 41
Collins, *Farmworker's Friend: The Story of Cesar Chavez*, 83
Dougherty, *Sammy Sosa*, 136
Fisher, *Costa Rica*, 131
Foley, *Puerto Rico*, 66, 131

Fradin, *Maria de Sautuola: The Bulls in the Cave*, 72
Furlong, *Argentina*, 131
George and George, *Luis Muñoz Marín: Father of Modern Puerto Rico*, 127
Gollub, *Uncle Snake*, 46
Gray, *Mexico*, 132
Gresko, *Mexico*, 137
Guatemala, 132
Halvorsen, *Peru*, 137
Heinrichs, *Mexico*, 141
Heinrichs, *Venezuela*, 141
Heller, *Galápagos Means "Tortoises,"* 19
Hermes, *The Children of Bolivia*, 144
Hermes, *Children of Guatemala*, 144
Jermyn, *Peru*, 63, 131
Johnston, *Puerto Rico*, 134
Kalman and Lewis, *Mexico from A to Z*, 125
Kent, *Buenos Aires*, 127
Kent, *Madrid*, 127
Kimmel, *Montezuma and the Fall of the Aztecs*, 48
Klingel and Noyed, *Bolivia*, 132
Klingel and Noyed, *Chile*, 132
Landau, *The Dominican Republic*, 141
Landau, *Peru*, 141
Landau, *Puerto Rico*, 141
Lior and Steele, *Spain: The Culture*, 73
Lior and Steele, *Spain: The Land*, 73
Lior and Steele, *Spain: The People*, 73
MacLean, *Sammy Sosa: Cubs Clubber*, 140
Mann, *Machu Picchu*, 63
Manning, *Francisco Pizarro*, 134
Martin, *Monkeys of Central and South America*, 141
McKay, *Spain*, 131
Mora, *This Big Sky*, 102
Nickles, *Argentina: The Culture*, 2
Nickles, *Argentina: The Land*, 2
Nickles, *Argentina: The People*, 2
Nickles, *El Salvador: The Land*, 22
Nickles, *El Salvador: The People and Culture*, 22
Parker, *Locks, Crocs, & Skeeters: The Story of the Panama Canal*, 61
Peru, 132

Peterson, *Cuba*, 141
Peterson, *South America*, 141
Press, *The Maya*, 132
Puerto Rico, 132
Rau, *Panama*, 141
Roraff, *Chile*, 132
Ross, *Children of Puerto Rico*, 144
Skármeta, *The Composition*, 34
Spain, 132
Stanley, *Elena*, 54
Staub, *Children of Cuba*, 144
Staub, *The Children of Sierra Madre*, 144
Staub, *Children of Yucatán*, 144
Stein, *Mexico City*, 127
Stewart, *Andres Galarraga: The Big Cat*, 140
Stewart, *Ivan Rodriguez: Armed and Dangerous*, 140
Stewart, *Pedro Martinez: Pitcher Perfect*, 140
Stewart, *Ramon Martinez: Master of the Mound*, 140
Tripp, *Again, Josefina!*, 117
Tripp, *Changes for Josefina: A Winter Story*, 117
Tripp, *Happy Birthday, Josefina!*, 117
Tripp, *Josefina Learns a Lesson: A School Story*, 117
Tripp, *Josefina Saves the Day: A Summer Story*, 117
Tripp, *Josefina's Surprise: A Christmas Story*, 117
Tripp, *Meet Josefina: An American Girl*, 117
Vázquez, *Cinco de Mayo*, 144
Viesti and Hall, *Celebrate! in Central America*, 4
Willard, *The Tortilla Cat*, 120

GRADES 3-6
Ancona, *Barrio: José's Neighborhood*, 80
Burgan, *The Alamo*, 143
Burr, *Broken Shields*, 39
Collins, *The Spanish-American War*, 128
Cory, *Daily Life in Ancient and Modern Mexico City*, 127
Franklin, *Mexico & Central America*, 126
Garland, *Voices of the Alamo*, 89
Heinrichs, *California Missions*, 143
Horenstein, *Baseball in the Barrios*, 123
Jade and Iron: Latin American Tales from Two Cultures, 29
Newman, *Isabella: A Wish for Miguel, Peru, 1820*, 64
Presilla, *Mola: Cuna Life Stories and Art*, 61

Rees, *The Aztecs*, 141
Rees, *The Incas*, 141
Santella, *The Battle of the Alamo*, 111, 128
Serrano, *Our Lady of Guadalupe*, 54
Staub, *Children of Cuba*, 15
Venezia, *El Greco*, 75, 133
Venezia, *Frida Kahlo*, 133
Venezia, *Rivera*, 133
Winkelman, *The Panama Canal*, 128
Young, *A Personal Tour of La Purísima*, 135

GRADES 3-7
Gonzalez, *My First Book of Proverbs/Mi primer libro de dichos*, 46
Pringle, *An Extraordinary Life: The Story of a Monarch Butterfly*, 53

GRADES 3-8
Boulais, *Andres Galarraga*, 139
Boulais, *Gloria Estefan*, 139
Boulais and Marvis, *Tommy Nuñez*, 139
Cole, *Jimmy Smits*, 139
Cole, *Mariah Carey*, 139
Cole, *Mary Joe Fernandez*, 139
Granados, *Christina Aguilera*, 139
Granados, *Enrique Iglesias: Latino Pop Star*, 139
Granados, *Sheila E.*, 139
Marvis, *Rafael Palmeiro*, 139
Marvis, *Robert Rodriguez*, 139
Marvis, *Selena*, 139
Menard, *Cheech Marin: Actor, Comedian*, 139
Menard, *Cristina Saralegui*, 139
Menard, *Jennifer Lopez: Latina Singer/Actress*, 139
Menard, *Oscar De la Hoya*, 139
Menard, *Ricky Martin*, 139
Menard, *Salma Hayek*, 139
Menard and Boulais, *Trent Dimas*, 139
Muskat, *Sammy Sosa*, 139
Torres, *Marc Anthony: Latino Recording Artist*, 139
Wilson, *Shakira: Latina Pop Rock Artist/Actress*, 140
Zannos, *Cesar Chavez*, 140

GRADES 4-6
  Ancona, *Mayeros: A Yucatec Maya Family*, 38
  Chrisp, *The Aztecs*, 135
  Dell'Oro, *Argentina*, 133
  Doak, *Francisco Vázquez de Coronado: Exploring the Southwest*, 131
  Gibb, *Fidel Castro: Leader of Cuba's Revolution*, 11
  Heinrichs, *De Soto: Hernando de Soto Explores the Southeast*, 131
  Heinrichs, *Ponce de León: Juan Ponce de León Searches for the Fountain of Youth*, 131
  Hoyt-Goldsmith, *Las Posadas: An Hispanic Christmas Celebration*, 93
  Jones, *Venezuela*, 133
  Lewin, *Nilo and the Tortoise*, 19
  Lourie, *Rio Grande: From the Rocky Mountains to the Gulf of Mexico*, 50, 98
  Milivojevic, *Puerto Rico*, 133
  Morrison, *Cuba*, 128
  Parker, *Mexico*, 52, 128
  Reeve, *Lolo & Red-Legs*, 106
  Soto, *Off and Running*, 113
  Stewart, *Alex Rodriguez: Gunning for Greatness*, 126
  Streissguth, *Mexico*, 133
  Welcome to Josefina's World, 1824: Growing Up on America's Southwest Frontier, 119
  West, *Costa Rica*, 133
  Wolf, *Cuba: After the Revolution*, 15

GRADES 4-7
  Alvarez, *How Tía Lola Came to (Visit) Stay*, 78
  Anaya, *Elegy on the Death of César Chávez*, 79
  Ancona, *Charro: The Mexican Cowboy*, 38
  Ancona, *Harvest*, 38, 80
  Bramwell, *Central and South America*, 144
  Bramwell, *North America and the Caribbean*, 144
  Carrillo, *Edward James Olmos*, 127
  Carrillo, *Oscar de la Renta*, 127
  Chicoine, *Spain: Bridge between Continents*, 131
  Christopher, *At the Plate with . . . Sammy Sosa*, 17
  Cramer, *Cuba*, 128
  Dalal, *Argentina*, 138
  Daniels, *Ecuador*, 128

Davis, *Puerto Rico*, 125

Day, *Your Travel Guide to Ancient Mayan Civilization*, 42

Eagen, *The Aymara of South America*, 132

Fisher, *Gods and Goddesses of the Ancient Maya*, 44

Frank, *Argentina*, 128

Frank, *Costa Rica*, 128

Green, *Mexico*, 138

Grinsted, *Spain*, 128

Heisey, *Peru*, 128

Hoyt-Goldsmith, *Migrant Worker: A Boy from the Rio Grande Valley*, 94

Jermyn, *Colombia*, 128

Jermyn, *Mexico*, 128

Kent, *Mexico: Rich in Spirit and Tradition*, 131

King, *Peru: Lost Cities, Found Hopes*, 131

Ling, *José Canseco*, 127

Lourie, *The Mystery of the Maya: Uncovering the Lost City of Palenque*, 49

Love, *I Remember the Alamo*, 99

Macdonald, *The Ancient Aztecs: Secrets of a Lost Civilization to Unlock and Discover*, 50

Macdonald, *Inca Town*, 63

Malone, *A Guatemalan Family*, 136

Malone, *A Nicaraguan Family*, 136

Markham, *Colombia: The Gateway to South America*, 131

Pérez, *Dolores Huerta*, 127

Pérez and Weil, *Raul Julia*, 127

Pickering, *Chile: Where the Land Ends*, 131

Preller, *McGwire & Sosa: A Season to Remember*, 17

Rawlins, *The Orinoco River*, 6, 123

Rodriguez, *Gloria Estefan*, 127

Rodriguez, *Nely Galan*, 127

Savage, *Sammy Sosa: Home Run Hero*, 18

Schwartz, *Luis Rodriguez*, 127

Steele, *The Aztec News*, 54

Tahan, *The Yanomami of South America*, 132

Tanaka, *Lost Temple of the Aztecs*, 55

Ward, *The Young Chef's Mexican Cookbook*, 57

GRADES 4-8

Chrisp, *Christopher Columbus: Explorer of the New World*, 130

Delacre, *Golden Tales: Myths, Legends and Folktales from Latin America*, 25

DeMarco, *Ivan Rodriguez*, 137

DeMarco, *Vinny Castilla*, 137

Fraser, *A Mission for the People: The Story of La Purísima*, 88

Gallagher, *Alex Rodriguez*, 137

Gallagher, *Pedro Martinez*, 137

Gallagher, *Ramon Martinez*, 137

Gerson, *Fiesta Femenina: Celebrating Women in Mexican Folktale*, 45

Macht, *Roberto Alomar: An Authorized Biography*, 137

Muskat, *Bernie Williams*, 137

Muskat, *Moises Alou: An Authorized Biography*, 137

Muskat, *Sammy Sosa: An Authorized Biography*, 137

Platt, *Aztecs: The Fall of the Aztec Capital*, 53, 130

Torres, *Bobby Bonilla*, 137

Torres, *Tino Martinez*, 137

Vascallaro, *Manny Ramirez*, 137

Winther, *Plays from Hispanic Tales: One-Act, Royalty-Free Dramatizations for Young People, from Hispanic Stories and Folktales*, 35

GRADES 4-9

Parker, *Mariah Carey*, 126

Parker, *Ricky Martin*, 126

Talmadge, *Christina Aguilera*, 127

Talmadge, *Enrique Iglesias*, 127

GRADES 5-7

Meadows, *Pablo Picasso*, 74

Nickles, *The Hispanics*, 103

Patent, *Treasures of the Spanish Main*, 133

Sammis, *South America*, 138

Soto, *Petty Crimes*, 114

Stein, *In the Spanish West*, 135

GRADES 5-8

Bankston, *Careers in Community Service*, 136

Benson, *Gloria Estefan*, 126

Blum, *Galápagos in 3-D*, 19

Eboch, *The Well of Sacrifice*, 42

Garcia, *Careers in Technology*, 136

Garland, *A Line in the Sand: The Alamo Diary of Lucinda Lawrence*, 89

Hadden, *Teenage Refugees from Guatemala Speak Out*, 136

Hadden, *Teenage Refugees from Mexico Speak Out*, 136

Joseph, *The Color of My Words*, 17

Lourie, *Lost Treasure of the Inca*, 20

Macnow, *Alex Rodriguez*, 140

Márquez, *Destination San Juan*, 139

Márquez, *Destination Veracruz*, 139

Márquez, *Latin Sensations*, 126

Martell, *Civilizations of Peru before 1535*, 64

McNeese, *Panama Canal, The*, 126

McNeese, *Remember the Main: The Spanish-American War Begins*, 132

Menard, *Careers in Sports*, 136

Patent, *Quetzal: Sacred Bird of the Cloud Forest*, 4, 52

Pohl, *The Legend of Lord Eight Deer: An Epic of Ancient Mexico*, 53

Roberts, *Pedro Menéndez de Avilés*, 137

Savage, *Rebecca Lobo*, 140

Silverstone, *Rigoberta Menchu: Defending Human Rights in Guatemala*, 143

Tagliaferro, *Galápagos Islands: Nature's Delicate Balance at Risk*, 20

Tamar, *Alphabet City Ballet*, 68

Torres, *Careers in the Music Industry*, 136

Torres, *Oscar De la Hoya*, 140

Wade, *Careers in Law and Politics*, 137

Whiting, *Francisco Vásquez de Coronado*, 137

Wilson, *Careers in Entertainment*, 137

Wilson, *Careers in Publishing and Communications*, 137

Winter, *¡Béisbol! Latino Baseball Pioneers and Legends*, 121

Zannos, *Careers in Education*, 137

Zannos, *Careers in Science and Medicine*, 137

Zannos, *Latino Entrepreneurs*, 137

GRADES 5-9

Argentina in Pictures, 142

Augustin, *Bolivia*, 130

Bolivia in Pictures, 142

Chile in Pictures, 142

Colombia in Pictures, 142

Costa Rica in Pictures, 142
Guatemala in Pictures, 142
Haverstock, *Cuba in Pictures*, 142
Haverstock, *Dominican Republic in Pictures*, 142
Haverstock, *Nicaragua in Pictures*, 142
Haverstock, *Paraguay in Pictures*, 142
Hintz, *Argentina*, 130
Hull, *The Aztecs*, 126
McNair, *Chile*, 130
Mexico in Pictures, 142
Morrison, *Colombia*, 130
Morrison, *Costa Rica*, 130
Morrison, *Cuba*, 130
Morrison, *Ecuador*, 130
Morrison, *El Salvador*, 130
Morrison, *Nicaragua*, 130
Morrison, *Peru*, 130
Panama in Pictures, 142
Perl, *North across the Border: The Story of Mexican Americans*, 133
Peru in Pictures, 142
Puerto Rico in Pictures, 142
Rogers, *Spain*, 130
Rogers and Radcliffe, *The Dominican Republic*, 131
Sayer, *The Incas*, 126
Stein, *Mexico*, 131
Sumwalt, *Ecuador in Pictures*, 142
Talbert, *Star of Luís*, 115
Uruguay in Pictures, 142
Venezuela in Pictures, 142

GRADES 5-10
Schiaffino, *Goya*, 74

For Older Readers
GRADES 6-9
Barghusen, *The Aztecs: End of a Civilization*, 135
Brubaker, *The Cuban Missile Crisis in American History*, 135
Byers, *Jaime Escalante: Sensational Teacher*, 134
Carey, Jr., *The Mexican War: "Mr. Polk's War,"* 125
Chambers, *Marisol and Magdalena: The Sound of Our Sisterhood*, 59

Collard, *Monteverde: Science and Scientists in a Costa Rican Cloud Forest*, 7

Collier and Collier, *Hispanic America, Texas, and the Mexican War, 1835-1850*, 130

Cruz, *Frida Kahlo: Portrait of a Mexican Painter*, 134

Cruz, *José Clemente Orozco: Mexican Artist*, 134

Cruz, *Raúl Julia: Actor and Humanitarian*, 134

Cruz, *Rubén Blades: Salsa Singer and Social Activist*, 134

Ewing, *Party Girl*, 87

Flowers, *Cortés and the Conquest of the Aztec Empire*, 136

Gaines, *The Panama Canal in American History*, 135

Galvin, *The Ancient Maya*, 129

Genet, *Father Junípero Serra: Founder of California Missions*, 134

Gold, *Environments of the Western Hemisphere*, 28

Gold, *Governments of the Western Hemisphere*, 28

Gonzales, *Cesar Chavez: Leader for Migrant Farm Workers*, 134

Gonzales, *Diego Rivera: His Art, His Life*, 134

Gonzales, *Gloria Estefan: Singer and Entertainer*, 134

Gonzales, *Richard "Pancho" Gonzalez: Tennis Champion*, 134

Goodnough, *José Martí: Cuban Patriot and Poet*, 134

Goodnough, *Pablo Casals: Cellist for the World*, 134

Goodnough, *Pablo Neruda: Nobel Prize-Winning Poet*, 135

Goodnough, *Plácido Domingo: Opera Superstar*, 135

Goodnough, *Simón Bolívar: South American Liberator*, 135

Green, *The Mission Trails in American History*, 136

Hill, *Ten Hispanic American Authors*, 93

Hinds, *The Incas*, 62, 129

King, *Quinceañera: Celebrating Fifteen*, 96

Lindop, *Panama and the United States: Divided by the Canal*, 60

Mann, *Isabel, Ferdinand and Fifteenth-Century Spain*, 140

Markun, *It's Panama's Canal!*, 60

Millar, *Spain in the Age of Exploration*, 74, 129

Mirriam-Goldberg, *Sandra Cisneros: Latina Writer and Activist*, 135

Ryan, *Esperanza Rising*, 108

Sandler, *Vaqueros: America's First Cowmen*, 110

Somerlott, *The Spanish-American War: "Remember the Maine!,"* 125

Sorrels, *The Alamo in American History*, 136

Soto, *Novio Boy: A Play*, 113

Stein, *The Aztec Empire*, 129

Stein, *The Mexican Revolution: 1910-1920*, 55

Wood, *The Incas*, 65
Worth, *Pizarro and the Conquest of the Incan Empire*, 136

GRADES 6-10
  Jenkins, *So Loud a Silence*, 6
  Jermyn, *Paraguay*, 129
  Jermyn, *Uruguay*, 129
  Kohen, *Spain*, 129
  McGaffey, *Honduras*, 129
  Pateman, *Bolivia*, 129
  Sheehan, *Guatemala*, 129

GRADES 6-12
  ¡Cámara! Ciudad de México: Monumentos de una nueva generación/Picture Mexico City: Landmarks of a New Generation, 40
  Ochoa, *The New York Public Library Amazing Hispanic American History: A Book of Answers for Kids*, 104
  Reinhard, *Discovering the Inca Ice Maiden: My Adventures on Ampato*, 64

GRADES 7-9
  Altman, *Cesar Chavez*, 135
  Carroll, *Pancho Villa*, 135
  Lilley, *Hernando Cortes*, 135

GRADES 7-10
  Aronson, *Sir Walter Ralegh and the Quest for El Dorado*, 62, 72
  Gold, *The Panama Canal Transfer: Controversy at the Crossroads*, 60
  Harlan, *Puerto Rico: Deciding Its Future*, 66
  Johnson, *Tomatoes, Potatoes, Corn, and Beans: How the Foods of the Americas Changed Eating around the World*, 30
  Kallen, *The Mayans*, 138
  Martinez, *Parrot in the Oven: Mi Vida*, 100
  McGinley, *Joaquin Strikes Back*, 101
  Morey and Dunn, *Famous Hispanic Americans*, 103
  Rice, *Crazy Loco*, 107

GRADES 7-12
  Atkin, *Voices from the Streets: Young Former Gang Members Tell Their Stories*, 81

Frost and Keegan, *The Mexican Revolution*, 143
Goldstein, *The Journey of Diego Rivera*, 46
Gow, *The Cuban Missile Crisis*, 143
Helly and Courgeon, *Montezuma and the Aztecs*, 47
Jiménez, *Breaking Through*, 94
Jiménez, *The Circuit: Stories from the Life of a Migrant Child*, 94
Kallen, *Life in the Amazon Rain Forest*, 142
Lace, *The Alamo*, 143
Lace, *Defeat of the Spanish Armada*, 72
Lilley, *The Conquest of Mexico*, 143
Marrin, *Empires Lost and Won: The Spanish Heritage in the Southwest*, 100
Mexican War of Independence, The, 143
Nardo, *The Mexican-American War*, 143
Nishi, *The Inca Empire*, 143
Oleksy, *Hispanic-American Scientists*, 125
Pascoe, *Mexico and the United States: Cooperation and Conflict*, 52
Soto, *Jessie De La Cruz: A Profile of a United Farm Worker*, 112
Stewart, *Life during the Spanish Inquisition*, 75, 143
Weaver, *Rooster*, 119

GRADES 8-12
Abelove, *Go and Come Back*, 62
Cockcroft, *Latino Visions: Contemporary Chicano, Puerto Rican and Cuban American Artists*, 83
Corona, *Peru*, 138
Fox, *Cuba*, 138
Goodwin, *Mexico*, 138
Grabowski, *Spain*, 138
Marrin, *Terror of the Spanish Main: Sir Henry Morgan and His Buccaneers*, 73
Olson, *Joyride*, 105
Shirey, *Latin American Writers*, 34
Soto, *Buried Onions*, 111
Soto, *Nerdlandia: A Play*, 113
Velásquez, *Rina's Family Secret*, 118
Winick, *Pedro and Me: Friendship, Loss, and What I Learned*, 121

GRADES 9-12
Cozic, *Illegal Immigration*, 85
Durán, *Don't Spit on My Corner*, 86
Herrera, *CrashBoomLove*, 92

Hoff and Regler, *Uneasy Neighbors: Cuba and the United States*, 11

Ortiz Cofer, *The Year of Our Revolution: New and Selected Stories and Poems*, 105

Welter, *I Want to Buy a Vowel: A Novel of Illegal Alienation*, 120

GRADES 7-ADULT

Castillo, *My Daughter, My Son, the Eagle, the Dove: An Aztec Chant*, 40

GRADES 8-ADULT

Americanos: Latino Life in the United States/La vida latina en los Estados Unidos, 79

Fernandez, *Puerto Rico Past and Present: An Encyclopedia*, 66

Kanellos, *Hispanic Firsts: 500 Years of Extraordinary Achievement*, 95

Kohli, *Cuba*, 12

Missen, *Memories of Cuba*, 14

Oxford Book of Latin American Short Stories, The, 32

Salcedo, *Quinceañera!: The Essential Guide to Planning the Perfect Sweet Fifteen Celebration*, 109

GRADES 9-ADULT

Aira, *Argentina: The Great Estancias*, 1

Alvarez, *Something to Declare*, 78

Alvarez, *¡Yo!*, 78

Baca, *A Place to Stand: The Making of a Poet*, 81

Benítez, *Bitter Grounds*, 21

Berrocal Essex, *Delia's Way*, 59

Borges, *This Craft of Verse*, 1

Bridal, *The Tree of Red Stars*, 122

Brown, *Culture and Customs of the Dominican Republic*, 129

Carrasco, *Daily Life of the Aztecs: People of the Sun and Earth*, 129

Castro, *Dictionary of Chicano Folklore*, 82

Crawford, *Encyclopedia of the Mexican-American War*, 42, 85

Davis, *Three Roads to the Alamo: The Lives and Fortunes of David Crockett, James Bowie, and William Barret Travis*, 85

Dent, *The Legacy of the Monroe Doctrine: A Reference Guide to U.S. Involvement in Latin America and the Caribbean*, 26

Encyclopedia of Contemporary Latin American and Caribbean Cultures, 27

Encyclopedia of Latin American and Caribbean Art, 27

Encyclopedia of Latin American History and Culture, 27

Encyclopedia of Latin American Literature, 28

Encyclopedia of Mexico: History, Society & Culture, 44

Ephron, *White Rose/Una rosa blanca*, 9

Espada, *A Mayan Astronomer in Hell's Kitchen*, 87

Fernandez Barrios, *Blessed by Thunder: Memoir of a Cuban Girlhood*, 10

Fernández-Shaw, *The Hispanic Presence in North America: From 1492 to Today*, 87

Ferriss and Sandoval, *The Fight in the Fields: Cesar Chavez and the Farmworkers Movement*, 88

Foss, *Fidel Castro*, 10

Foster, *Culture and Customs of Argentina*, 129

García, *The Agüero Sisters*, 10

Gonzales, *Mexicanos: A History of Mexicans in the United States*, 90

González-Pando, *The Cuban Americans*, 138

Gorkin, *From Grandmother to Granddaughter: Salvadoran Women's Stories*, 22

Gourse, *Gloria Estefan: Pop Sensation*, 126

Handelsman, *Culture and Customs of Ecuador*, 129

Harrigan, *The Gates of the Alamo*, 91

Harvey and Newhouse, *Cuba*, 11

Henderson, *A Reference Guide to Latin American History*, 29

Henkes, *Latin American Women Artists of the United States: The Works of 33 Twentieth-Century Women*, 92

Hoepker, *Return of the Maya: Guatemala—a Tale of Survival*, 24

Kenig, *Best Careers for Bilingual Latinos: Market Your Fluency in Spanish to Get Ahead on the Job*, 95

Kirkwood, *The History of Mexico*, 134

Krauze, *Mexico, Biography of Power: A History of Modern Mexico, 1810-1996*, 48

Lamazares, *The Sugar Island*, 12

Las Christmas: Favorite Latino Authors Share Their Holiday Memories, 97

Latin American Art in the Twentieth Century, 30

Latin American Folktales: Stories from Hispanic and Indian Traditions, 31

Latino Encyclopedia, The, 31

Latino Reader: An American Literary Tradition from 1542 to the Present, The, 97

Leonard, *Cuba Libre*, 13

Levitt, *Mexico City*, 49

Lind, *The Alamo: An Epic*, 98
Malpass, *Daily Life in the Inca Empire*, 130
Marley, *Wars of the Americas: A Chronology of Armed Conflict in the New World, 1492 to the Present*, 31
Martí, *Versos sencillos/Simple Verses*, 13
Murray, *What It Takes to Get to Vegas*, 103
Noche Buena: Hispanic American Christmas Stories, 104
Obejas, *Days of Awe*, 104
Oxford Encyclopedia of Mesoamerican Cultures: The Civilizations of Mexico and Central America, The, 33
Pérez, *Geographies of Home*, 105
Pierson, *The History of Spain*, 134
Ramirez, *A Patriot after All: The Story of a Chicano Vietnam Vet*, 106
Ramos, *Blues for the Buffalo*, 106
Salas and Salas, *Fidel's Cuba: A Revolution in Pictures*, 14
Sanchez, *My Bloody Life: The Making of a Latin King*, 110
Santiago, *Almost a Woman*, 68
Sharer, *Daily Life in Maya Civilization*, 130
Sinclair, *Che Guevara*, 2, 14
St. Aubin de Terán, *The Hacienda*, 123
Symmes, *Chasing Che: A Motorcycle Journey in Search of the Guevara Legend*, 3
Torres-Saillant and Hernández, *The Dominican Americans*, 138
Touching the Fire: Fifteen Poets of Today's Latino Renaissance, 116
Twentieth-Century Latin American Poetry: A Bilingual Anthology, 34
United States and Mexico at War. Nineteenth-Century Expansionism and Conflict, The, 56, 118
Urrea, *By the Lake of Sleeping Children: The Secret Life of the Mexican Border*, 56
Vázquez-Gómez, *Dictionary of Mexican Rulers, 1325-1997*, 57
Williams and Guerrieri, *Culture and Customs of Colombia*, 129

GRADES 10-ADULT
Dujovne Ortiz, *Eva Perón*, 1
Gonzalez, *Harvest of Empire: A History of Latinos in America*, 90
Oppenheimer, *Bordering on Chaos: Guerrillas, Stockbrokers, Politicians and Mexico's Road to Prosperity*, 51
Quiñonez, *Bodega Dreams*, 106

Rosales, *Chicano!: The History of the Mexican American Civil Rights Movement*, 108
Stalcup, *The Inquisition*, 141
Stewart, *Musica!: Salsa, Rumba, Merengue and More*, 115

About the Author

Dr. Isabel Schon was born in Mexico City. She came to the United States in 1972, where she obtained her doctorate in philosophy from the University of Colorado in 1974.

She has received several national and international awards, including the 1992 U.S. Role Model in Education Award presented by the U.S.-México Foundation; the 1992 Denali Press Award from the Reference and Adult Services Division of the American Library Association for "achievement in creating reference works that are outstanding in quality and significance and provide information specifically about ethnic and minority groups in the U.S."; the 1987 Women's National Book Award, as "one of seventy women who have made a difference in the world of books"; the American Library Association's 1986 Grolier Foundation Award for "unique and invaluable contributions to the stimulation and guidance of reading by children and young people"; and the 1979 Herbert W. Putnam Honor Award presented by the American Library Association "to study the effects of books on students' perceptions of Mexican American people."

She is the author of twenty-three books and more than four hundred research and literary articles in the areas of bilingual/multicultural education and literature for Latino children and adolescents.

Dr. Schon has been a consultant on bilingual/bicultural educational materials to schools, libraries, and ministries of education in Mexico, Colombia, Guatemala, Argentina, Venezuela, Chile, Spain, Italy, Ecuador, and the United States.

Currently, she is a member of the founding faculty and is the founding director of the Barahona Center for the Study of Books in Spanish for Children and Adolescents at California State University San Marcos.